POLITICAL MANAGEMENT IN PRACTICE

All organisations manage people, and politics is no different. Campaigns, parties, and government all need to manage people and resources to try to get things done. Of course, the extent to which politics is managed effectively is debatable. Recently public awareness of problematic HR in parliaments and government has grown as media reports of problems emerge. Such problematic practice is not surprising given that orientation and training of political practitioners by parties and parliament is hindered by a lack of academic research.

This comprehensive volume lays out and builds upon core theoretical foundations in the field of political management, offering a wide range of in-depth empirical research with multiple authors and chapters from different disciplinary perspectives and countries. With authors from political management programmes, political marketing, management, political psychology, and public administration, the book seeks not just to survey a topic or existing literature, but to stimulate research in the area.

This book will be highly useful for graduate students, researchers, and professionals in a variety of areas including political management, political marketing, applied politics, political science, management, political psychology, and public administration.

Jennifer Lees-Marshment is Professor of Political Marketing and Management at the University of Dundee. She is a research-led but practice-oriented cross-disciplinary academic focused on researching political marketing, political management, political leadership, and public participation. She has interviewed over 350 political practitioners including government ministers and staffers/advisers to prime ministers and presidents and is author/editor of 18 books.

POLITICAL MANAGEMENT IN PRACTICE

Lessons from around the Globe

Edited by Jennifer Lees-Marshment

Routledge
Taylor & Francis Group

LONDON AND NEW YORK

Designed cover image: DESKCUBE/Getty Images

First published 2024
by Routledge
4 Park Square, Milton Park, Abingdon, Oxon OX14 4RN

and by Routledge
605 Third Avenue, New York, NY 10158

Routledge is an imprint of the Taylor & Francis Group, an informa business

British Library Cataloguing-in-Publication Data
A catalogue record for this book is available from the British Library

Library of Congress Cataloging-in-Publication Data
Names: Lees-Marshment, Jennifer, editor.
Title: Political management in practice : lessons from around the globe / Edited by Jennifer Lees-Marshment.
Description: Abingdon, Oxon ; New York, NY : Routledge, 2024. | Includes bibliographical references and index.
Identifiers: LCCN 2023052458 (print) | LCCN 2023052459 (ebook) | ISBN 9781032197517 (hardback) | ISBN 9781032197524 (paperback) | ISBN 9781003260677 (ebook)
Subjects: LCSH: Political leadership. | Political parties--Management. | Campaign management. | Marketing--Political aspects. | Executive departments--Personnel management.
Classification: LCC JC330.3 .P6446 2024 (print) | LCC JC330.3 (ebook) | DDC 324.2/2--dc23/eng/20240214
LC record available at https://lccn.loc.gov/2023052458
LC ebook record available at https://lccn.loc.gov/2023052459

ISBN: 978-1-032-19751-7 (hbk)
ISBN: 978-1-032-19752-4 (pbk)
ISBN: 978-1-003-26067-7 (ebk)

DOI: 10.4324/9781003260677

Typeset in Sabon
by KnowledgeWorks Global Ltd.

CONTENTS

FIGURES, TABLES, AND BOX

Figures

Tables

Box

CONTRIBUTORS

Jennifer Lees-Marshment is Professor of Political Marketing and Management at the University of Dundee. She is a research-led but practice-oriented cross-disciplinary academician focused on researching political marketing, political management, political leadership, and public participation. She has interviewed over 350 political practitioners including government ministers and staffers/advisers to prime ministers and presidents and is author/editor of 18 books.

Max Stafford's research focuses upon the environments that surround political leaders and leadership. This covers everything from how they interact with advisers through to the agency that they use in relation to their institutional constraints. He has focused upon this with regard to both national and local leaders. His PhD (2020) explored the leadership capital of mayors in New York, London, and Amsterdam between 2000 and 2016. More recently, he has been exploring the role, influence, history, and significance of the Downing Street Chief of Staff (with a focus from 1997 through to the present day). He has taught at several universities and is currently a Visiting Research Fellow of the Mile End Institute (QMUL) and a Teaching Fellow with the University of Southampton. He previously worked with two former cabinet ministers. He's married to Linn and plays snooker (badly) when he gets a chance.

Dr Jean S. Encinas-Franco is a full-time Professor of political science at the University of the Philippines Diliman. She worked for 15 years at the Senate of the Philippines, the country's Upper House. Her work on gender, politics, and migration has appeared in various local and international peer-reviewed journals. She has also written policy reports on gender and development issues for various international organizations such as the UN Women and UNDP. In 2022, she received an honourable mention award from the International Studies Association Feminist Theory and Global South Section in the category of Feminist from the Global South Award.

Brandon P. De Luna is the senior media and stakeholder relations Manager of FleishmanHillard's Manila office. He received his BA Political Science degree from the University of the Philippines Diliman. He is currently pursuing his MA Communication degree programme in the same university.

His research interests are political marketing and management, character assassination and reputation management, strategic communications, and crisis communications. At present, Brandon is engaged in exploring how responding to character attacks by the incumbent administration are utilized as political branding of opposition candidates in developing democracies.

Apart from being a graduate student and a full-time public relations practitioner, Brandon is also a part-time instructor at the Holy Angel University where he teaches behavioural communication and social change, and purposeful communication.

Simon Vodrey holds a PhD and a master's degree in Communication from Carleton University's School of Journalism and Communication in Ottawa, Canada, where he also teaches. He researches and writes about political marketing, political communication, and journalism and media history.

Dr Ashley Weinberg is a Chartered Occupational Psychologist and Senior Lecturer in Psychology at Salford University, specialising in organisational and job-related factors contributing to employee well-being. He has published four books on mental health in the workplace and a number of influential reports. These include *Psychology at Work: Improving Productivity and Well-Being in the Workplace* launched by the British Psychological Society in Parliament (2017) and *Modernising Parliament: Supporting the Well-Being of MPs' Staff* (2021 and 2023) with the MPs' Staff Wellness Working Group. These resulted in an invitation to give evidence before the Westminster Parliament Speaker's Conference on the employment conditions of Members' staff. As inaugural Chair of the British Psychological Society Political Psychology Section and editor of *The Psychology of Politicians* and *Psychology of Democracy: Of the People, by the People, for the People* (both published with Cambridge University Press), he is keen to promote the efficacy of democracy.

Estelle Warhurst is an Office Manager in the House of Commons and an Executive Committee Member for the Parliamentary Wellness Working Group.

Thomas Fairweather is an Office Manager in the House of Commons and an Executive Committee Member for the Parliamentary Wellness Working Group.

Karl Magnus Johansson was formerly Professor and is now Affiliate Professor of Political Science at Södertörn University, Stockholm, Sweden. An ongoing area of research for him is government communication. His field of work centres on the intersection of political leadership, institutions and communications in central government in Sweden and elsewhere, including the role of media advisers. His monograph *The Prime Minister–Media Nexus: Centralization Logic and Application* was published in 2022 by Palgrave Macmillan.

Anita Ferguson spent ten years advising, and working alongside, political leaders in New Zealand in both government and opposition. She holds an MBA (2016) from the Victoria Business School and a BA (2002) from Victoria University of Wellington. More recently she has embarked on an international career supporting senior executives to engage with politicians and other external audiences in the UK, Africa, and the Middle East. She currently lives in Abu Dhabi.

Michael Macaulay is Professor of Public Administration at the School of Government, Te Herenga Waka, Victoria University of Wellington (NZ) and has held visiting professor posts in the UK and South Africa. Michael has worked with numerous international government agencies and NGOs including the United Nations Office on Drugs and Crime (UNODC), the Council of Europe, and Transparency International. Within New Zealand, he has co-authored evaluations on NZ Police and the State Services Commission; and worked regularly with Public Service Commission, Serious Fraud Office, and numerous other agencies on anti-corruption, workplace misconduct, and whistleblowing. He is a member of numerous editorial boards and is currently Regional Editor for *Public Management Review*.

Brian M. Conley is Professor in the Political Science and Legal Studies Department at Suffolk University in Boston. His principal research and teaching interests are in the areas of political parties, US electoral politics, political marketing, and communication. His research and writing have appeared in the *Studies in American Political Development*, *American Review of Politics*, the *Journal of American Studies*, and *Political Science Quarterly* as well as in numerous political anthologies on US politics. He has also edited, written, and co-authored several books, most recently *The Rise of the Republican Right: From Goldwater to Reagan* (Routledge, 2019), and with Jennifer Lees-Marshment, *Political Marketing: Principles and Applications*, 3rd edition (Routledge, 2019). He received his PhD in Political Science from the New School for Social Research in New York City.

Pippa Catterall is Professor of History and Policy at the University of Westminster and co-editor of *National Identities*. She has written extensively on modern British political and constitutional history and practice and her current research focuses on British prime ministers and public policy strategy in the twentieth century.

Dr Caroline Fisher is Associate Professor of Communication in the Faculty of Arts and Design at the University of Canberra. She is a core member of the News and Media Research Centre and co-author of the *Digital News Report: Australia*. Her research and teaching focuses on political and strategic communication, journalism studies, and trends in news media consumption and attitudes. Prior to academia Caroline worked as a journalist for the ABC and as a ministerial media adviser.

John Connolly is Professor of Public Policy and Associate Dean for Research in the Glasgow School of Business for Society, Glasgow Caledonian University. Professor Connolly researches and publishes in the areas of public policy and administration, crisis management, and public health. He advises civil servants in the Cabinet Office (UK Government) on evaluation research strategy as a member of the government's Evaluation and Trial Panel. He is also currently a co-investigator on an interdisciplinary research study funded by the Natural Environment Research Council that aims to research and raise awareness of antimicrobial resistance within the environment. John serves on various editorial boards and is Chief Editorial Adviser for Routledge Open Research.

Robert Pyper is Emeritus Professor of Government and Public Policy at the University of the West of Scotland. His books, book chapters, and journal articles span the fields of government, public policy, and public management, and include national and international analyses of civil service policy and management, public services reform and modernisation, and systems of accountability.

Dr André Turcotte is Associate Professor at Carleton University's School of Journalism and Communication. His work focuses on research methods, political communication, and public opinion research.

Dr Vincent Raynauld is Associate Professor in the Department of Communication Studies at Emerson College and Affiliate Professor in the Département de lettres et communication sociale at the Université du Québec à Trois-Rivières. His areas of research interest and publication include political communication and campaigning, protest politics, social media, political marketing, e-politics, identity politics, and journalism.

Anna Shavit holds a PhD in Political Science and is an assistant professor at the Department of Marketing Communication and PR at Charles University in Prague. Her research areas are political marketing (focusing on relations to political parties, citizen participation, and democratic process), government communication (covering mainly the Czech environment), and election campaigns (professionalization of campaigns, role of political consultants, etc.). She also works as a campaign strategist and has extensive experience with many campaigns in the Czech Republic and Slovakia.

Marcela Konrádová holds a PhD in political science and works as Assistant Professor in the Department of Marketing Communication and PR at Charles University in Prague. Her research fields combine political and government communication, political marketing, personalization of politics and its consequences, and electoral campaigns.

Marcela has participated in several internships and trainee programs for organisations such as KohoVolit.eu or Demagog.cz; she was also an external collaborator of the Institute of Political Marketing and Campaigns.cz. She contributed to the preparation of the movement ANO 2011 or Slovak movement Sloboda a Solidarita election campaigns. On analytical positions, Marcela has worked on international projects in Germany, Serbia, Bulgaria, and other countries. She also worked as a Spokesperson at the Prague 8 City District Office.

Petra Koudelková holds a PhD in management and economy of small- and medium-sized enterprises. She is the Head of Department of Marketing Communication and PR at Faculty of Social Sciences, Charles University. Her fields of study comprise corporate social responsibility and sustainability approach of companies, above all SMEs and marketing and institutional communication and business (and marketing) strategy.

Petra participated in several projects and is the author of many research articles and two monographs.

Hamid Reza Tafaghodi is co-founder of the Political Marketing and Management Innovation Centre associated with the Vice-Presidency for Science and Technology of Iran. He holds a PhD degree in Strategic Management and also is a strategy consultant in various private and public sectors. His research interests are focused on ecosystem management and implementing it in different fields of management, especially political management.

Soroush Sayari is a Research and Teaching Assistant at the College of Management at the University of Tehran and also Co-founder of the Political Marketing and Management Innovation Center in Iran. He obtained a master's degree in Marketing Management and a master's degree in Middle

Eastern Studies and, currently, is a PhD candidate of Marketing Management at the University of Tehran. He has published numerous books and papers on diverse facets of political marketing. His theses in master's degrees and in PhD are revolved around electioneering and political marketing in Iran. His principal research interest is focused on the intersection between management and politics particularly branding, communication, campaigning, and relationship management.

Wojciech Cwalina is Professor and Head of the Department of Social Psychology at the Maria Curie-Sklodowska University in Lublin, Poland. His research interests include political marketing, social psychology, media psychology, and environmental marketing. He is member of the editorial board of the *Journal of Political Marketing* and *Annals of Psychology*. He is the author or co-author of five books, including *A Cross-Cultural Theory of Voter Behavior* (Haworth Press/Routledge, 2007/2011) and *Political Marketing: Theoretical and Strategic Foundations* (M.E. Sharpe/Routledge, 2011/2015), and numerous articles (e.g. in *Media Psychology, Journal of Political Marketing, European Journal of Marketing, Journal of Communication Management, Journal of Environmental Psychology,* and *Social Psychology*) and book chapters.

Maria Naureen Shahid has recently completed her PhD from National University of Science & Technology (NUST) Business School, Islamabad, Pakistan. During her PhD, she published and presented papers on image and positioning of political co-brands, as well as on the influence of online cross-cutting exposure on political engagement and social anxiety. She prefers a mixed-method approach because it allows researchers to conceptually and analytically integrate/triangulate qualitative research and quantitative data. Her research interests include political marketing, CPA and its impact on consumer behaviour and the environment, CSR, and the role of AI and digital marketing in politics and consumer behaviour.

Milena Drzewiecka, PhD in Psychology, is a Psychologist and Journalist. She holds two master's degrees: one in Psychology and the other in Journalism and Social Communication. She is an Associate Lecturer at SWPS University, Poland, teaching in political marketing, media psychology, and the application of social psychology in business and politics. Her research interests include leadership, image creation, and political branding. Apart from academic activity, she has nearly 20 years of international experience in the media business. She used to work as a TV political news reporter and parliamentary correspondent in Poland and she has been working as a TV producer for German media. She is the author of the first postgraduate studies in image psychology in business and public life: Professional Image at SWPS University in Warsaw, Poland.

Mark Bennister is Associate Professor in the Department of Politics at the University of Lincoln in the School of Social and Political Sciences. Mark is Director of the *Lincoln Policy Hub* and the *Lincoln Parliamentary Research Centre* (ParliLinc). Mark's research expertise focuses on political leadership, prime ministerial power and leadership, governance, and committees in parliament. He is the author of *Prime Ministers in Power: Political Leadership in Britain and Australia* (Palgrave, 2012) and (with Worthy and 't Hart) *The Leadership Capital Index: New Perspectives on Political Leadership* (Oxford, 2017). He was a House of Commons Academic Fellow (2016–2019), researching the Prime Minister's appearances before the Liaison Committee. Mark has published on accountability in parliament, political leadership, comparative prime ministerial power, and political oratory. Mark was previously an Executive Officer at the Australian High Commission in London and a parliamentary researcher.

Todd Belt received a PhD from the University of Southern California in 2003. He is Professor and Director of the Political Management Master's Program in the Graduate School of Political Management at The George Washington University. Belt is the co-author of four books, has published over a dozen chapters in edited scholarly books and over two dozen articles appearing in academic journals. He was awarded the John W. Kluge Fellowship in Digital Studies at the Library of Congress and has held visiting positions at Wellesley College and Kyungpook University in Daegu, South Korea. He is the recipient of two teaching awards.

ACKNOWLEDGEMENTS

This book was produced over a long period beginning with a call for papers in November 2021, with a multi-stage process that included an online global workshop in 2022, with the final chapters submitted towards the end of 2023.

My thanks go not only to the individual authors who produced excellent work, but also to colleagues who came together from a range of fields and across the world to form an advisory board:

- Professor Emmanuelle Avril, Sorbonne Nouvelle University in Paris, France
- Professor Todd Belt, George Washington University, US Belt, Todd
- Associate Professor Mark Bennister, University of Lincoln, UK
- Associate Professor Caroline Fisher, University of Canberra, Australia
- Associate Professor André Turcotte, Carleton University, Canada
- Dr Kobby Mensah, University of Ghana Business School, Ghana
- Dr Ashley Weinberg, University of Salford, UK

The advisory board reviewed and provided advice on chapter proposals and presentations at the workshop. Their contributions undoubtedly strengthened the quality of the chapters as well as helped to identify broad themes that emerged from them.

I would also like to thank Dr Edward Elder who helped to organise the online workshop for his efforts and skill in meeting the challenges of timetabling participants from multiple continents and time zones. It helped to connect people and inject energy into the research and writing process, and provided a model for what is possible for future events in political management.

1

INTRODUCTION

Jennifer Lees-Marshment

Political management

Political management is all about how things get done in politics – whether it is in a campaign, party, political office or parliament, both campaigning for power and actually using it once elected. It involves campaigns, parties, political offices and a range of practitioners including politicians, ministers, party staff, political staff and advisers, volunteers and consultants.

Academically, it remains an emerging field with much work to be done to create and establish the conceptual parameters. In essence, it involves applying concepts from business management to the world of politics and government, just as its cousin political marketing applies business marketing concepts to politics. Helped by the first handbook (Johnson 2009), given substantial and crucial exposure by the two schools and programmes of political management at George Washington University in the US and Carleton University in Canada and a boost by a foundational framework (Lees-Marshment 2020), there is now a growing group of scholars interested in this important area. However, just as with political marketing when it first emerged, much work is to be done to ensure that research claiming to be political management is, actually, about management – and not just campaigns.

Similarly, in practice, there is much to improve. Despite the best efforts of dedicated professionals, the constant change of political practitioners in charge following elections removes the usual time business organisations have to learn, develop and improve professional practices. As the chapters in this book show, there is a dearth of understanding, expertise and resources devoted to managing political organisations and the people within them. Yet, practitioners do try to improve their craft, and part of the role of academic research is to capture

DOI: 10.4324/9781003260677-1

their wisdom learnt on the ground, add the objective lens that researchers can bring, and disseminate clear and usable recommendations to those who come new to the important roles in campaigns, parties and government.

But also, as the chapters in this book also illuminate, whilst management concepts and tools are of value in the political arena, they do not always transfer easily. The political environment has unusual characteristics which mean management has to be adapted. But that does not prevent the core principles from being of value. It's just complex. Political management is a very people-oriented business and lots of the activity takes place behind closed doors of power. Yet, as recent research is beginning to show, core concepts can be adapted to suit the realities of political practice – see, for example, Lees-Marshment (2024) which offers multiple best practice recommendations for managing political advisers.

This book

This book is the first edited book to apply management concepts to politics including human resource management (HRM), organisation, leadership, implementation of plans, strategy and vision. It discusses topics such as performance management, role definition, skills, training, control, power, influence, co-ordination and wellbeing in the political workplace.

It is broad in scope, discussing a range of political practitioners – prime ministers, politicians, political advisers, party figures/staff and volunteers – and their work and management in a range of political organisations – campaigns, political parties, offices of the members of the parliament (MPs), prime ministerial offices, communication and all types of political advisers.

It is also global, covering political management in the UK, US, Canada, Australia, Sweden, New Zealand, the Philippines, Germany, Czech Republic, Switzerland, Poland, Georgia, Pakistan and Iran with some chapters offering the first research on political management in that country.

It utilises rich new empirical data, going behind the scenes to collect data from practitioners carrying out these roles including political advisers, staffers, politicians, party's top management officials and volunteers, former presidents, ministers and senior political consultants. It uses interviews, surveys, participant observation and public opinion data as well as analysis of politician and party policies and statements. It is also topical – for example, the behaviour and wellbeing of political staff been in the news and subject of reviews in UK, Australia and New Zealand as have protests and crisis.

It explores practice not just theory where every core chapter includes recommendations for practitioners.

As the chapters demonstrate, there is clearly a need for political management – both more research and improved practice. Nevertheless, they also show that standard HRM practices do not easily transfer to politics in practice. Yet, at the same time, the core principles of managing people effectively remain crucial to both effectiveness and wellbeing, whether it is a campaign, party, political office or government.

Chapter structure

Chapter 2 reports on the state of HRM of political advisers in Prime Minister's Offices. This chapter explores the state of HRM for political advisers working in the highest political offices in UK, Canada, Australia and New Zealand. It draws on interviews with advisers and staffers who worked under PMs Boris Johnson, Justin Trudeau, Scott Morrison and Jacinda Ardern as well as public servants working towards reform in the management processes around them. It highlights not only the lack of effective HR but also positive practices that have emerged on an ad hoc basis or developed more recently through reform. It also presents the case for better management for political advisers, making clear why it is needed for the individuals, parties, government and democracy as a whole.

In Chapter 3, Max Stafford focuses on the role of the Chief of Staff to the UK Prime Minister exploring how they manage other special advisers and what that tells us about human resources and management in politics. The chapter discusses the extent to which the Chief of Staff performs a range of management activities including identifying staffing needs, recruiting appropriately, training and developing, motivating and encouraging excellence. Chiefs can have considerable input into the designing of staffing structures and job parameters, but there are weaknesses in their HR practices.

In Chapter 4, Jean S. Encinas-Franco and Brandon P. De Luna explore the management of volunteers through a case study of political campaign volunteers in the 2022 Leni Robredo campaign in the Philippines. The chapter discusses volunteer motivations, training, recruitment and mobilisation as well as how indigenous origins of volunteerism in the Philippines were transferred into the campaign arena. It raises the challenge of unifying messaging and controlling performance amongst untrained volunteers.

In Chapter 5, Simon Vodrey explores the problematic workplace conditions facing political staffers in Canada and the US. The chapter argues that political management can be characterised by a style of management that is dictated by an environment demonstrating great career instability, little institutional knowledge/memory due to high staff turnover and little money to be made. It explores to what extent political management can be characterised by a style of management where there is great career instability and little institutional knowledge/memory due to high staff turnover and whether financial insecurity permeates the practice of political management. It also highlights the impact of this on skill development amongst political management practitioners and institutional knowledge sharing.

In Chapter 6, Ashley Weinberg, Estelle Warhurst and Thomas Fairweather focus on the mental health and wellbeing of MPs' staff using results of a surveys of MPs' staff commissioned by the MPs' Staff Wellness Working Group. The chapter explores how MPs' staff feel about their job, sources of pressure (stressors) faced by MPs' staff and the daily working experiences of MPs' staff. It finds that MPs' staff are highly motivated and committed to serving the public but face problematic working conditions such as job insecurity, lack of career progression and modest renumeration in the face of public hostility and threats of violence. Their vital role in the functioning of democracy means that more needs to be done to ensure their wellbeing.

In Chapter 7, Karl Magnus Johansson offers real-life examples of what media advisers to prime ministers do using a case study in Sweden. The chapter explores the nature of their role and what they do during an average work day and how that links to the contexts and goals of prime ministers and their office. It highlights the importance of clarifying the nature of that role and ensuring those who undertake it have the capacity to carry out the duties required. Also, it raises the need to reflect on the broader implications of communication staff for government and democracy.

In Chapter 8, Anita Ferguson and Michael Macaulay report research into formal performance management within parliamentary political parties and how this compares with corporate approaches and theoretical best practice. Using interviews with MPs and 19 in-depth interviews conducted with MPs and senior staff from both the New Zealand Labour and New Zealand National political parties, the chapter highlights previously limited performance management. The lack of available rewards for good performance or sanctions for poor performance was a strong theme in the interviews and MPs' struggling felt isolated. The chapter suggests how performance management could work better even in an intensely political environment.

In Chapter 9, Brian M. Conley examines how to effectively co-ordinate implementing of an overall vision in federated and devolved political organisations and systems. The chapter discusses the political management challenges that have confronted both the Democratic and Republican Parties, as they sought in the last three midterm elections to organise around a common set of national policy priorities. The chapter assesses the degree of message co-ordination between the national parties and the campaigns of incumbent Democratic and Republican US Senators who sought re-election in the 2014, 2018 and 2022 midterm elections. It raises the challenges involved in implementing political plans in practice and the hurdles to crafting a coherent, unifying national party vision.

In Chapter 10, Pippa Catterall examines strategy and British Prime Ministers, focusing on how it is conceived, shaped and co-ordinated across the various bodies delivering public policy and administration and whether policy promises are effectively co-ordinated to enact some overall strategic architecture that encompasses means and processes of delivery, planning about where and how to allocate key resources and the goals all this is intended to achieve. The chapter shows that strategy is an element in the framework for decision making and choosing between policy options but whilst it is desirable in theory it is difficult in practice. Political leaders in government range from those who are more reactive, short-term, incremental and risk-averse to those who think in strategic terms but in very different ways. Across the globe, long-term planning is increasingly required to tackle existential crises like the climate emergency.

In Chapter 11, Caroline Fisher explores political media management, control and trust by prime ministers. It contributes a case study of Australian Prime Minister Scott Morrison's communication control and the implications for a controlling leadership style on election results as well as noting too much control also caused issues for Australian Labor PM Kevin Rudd and Canadian Conservative PM Stephen Harper. The chapter therefore suggests the need to avoid being over controlling, in terms of both the implications for democracy and reputation.

In Chapter 12, John Connolly and Robert Pyper examine the skills and political management strategies political leaders need for negotiating global crises at a national level. The chapter highlights the challenges and complexities of crisis management. The chapter provides an overview of the main tasks, tensions and challenges for political leaders in times of crisis which are key to political management. It covers three case studies: (1) New Zealand Prime Minister Jacinda Ardern's management of the COVID-19 pandemic, (2) German Chancellor Angela Merkel's management of the 2015 EU refugee crisis and (3) Prime Minister Theresa May's management of the 2018 Salisbury poisonings in UK.

In Chapter 13, André Turcotte and Vincent Raynauld focus on the Freedom Convoy movement in Canada in 2022. The chapter shows that leaders need to ensure that all activities run smoothly and whoever is the top of the organisation appears competent and professional. But in politics, maintaining control – even if you are the president or prime minister – is not so easy. This chapter discusses the importance of having appropriate organisational systems of market intelligence to inform decision making in a rapidly changing situation where public opinion is highly volatile.

In Chapter 14, Anna Shavit, Marcela Konrádová and Petra Koudelková focus on how parties are "managed" and go within party organisations to explore how those practitioners involved in party management see political leadership and develop strategic visions and goals. The chapter also explores political parties' approaches to diversifying power and exerting influence. The focus is on four political parties in the Czech Republic. It highlights how party managers engage in ongoing management activities to maintain organisational long-term health instead of just focusing on winning individual elections, as they have to adapt to a constantly changing environment. It involves "invisible" party management – and complex range of activities.

In Chapter 15, Hamid Reza Tafaghodi and Soroush Sayari explore the importance of ensuring effective organisation and processes in politics, arguing that an ecosystem viewpoint towards political organising can bring about a transformation in Iran's political organisations. The chapter uses 35 in-depth interviews with Iranian high-level political practitioners and officials such as former presidents, ministers, senior political consultants to supreme leader, parliament members and top political managers in Iran. It highlights how organisational layers including human capital, strategic leadership, environmental monitoring as well as promotion of values can have a direct impact on the effectiveness of the organisation and the realisation of its goals.

In Chapter 16, Wojciech Cwalina, Maria Naureen Shahid and Milena Drzewiecka explore what skills political leaders need to be received positively by voters. The chapter seeks to identify a profile of ideal political leadership style by studying leaders in nations with varying levels of democratic maturity – Switzerland, Poland, Georgia and Pakistan. It notes that leadership will never be an exact science. But neither should it be a complete mystery to those who practise it, and leaders who achieve the highest results don't rely just on one type of leadership. The optimum performance and effective positioning are created by leaders who have mastered any or all four or more leadership styles, particularly the *authoritative*, *democratic*, *affiliative* and *coaching* styles.

Finally, Chapter 17, written by myself and colleagues who were on the advisory board for this book and gave feedback on chapter proposals – Mark Bennister, Todd Belt, Caroline Fisher, André Turcotte and Ashley Weinberg – summarises the lessons for researchers and practitioners.

References

Johnson, Dennis W. (ed.). (2009). *Routledge Handbook of Political Management*. Routledge, Abingdon, Oxon.

Lees-Marshment, J. (2020) *Political Management: The Dance of Government and Politics*. Routledge, Abingdon, Oxon.

Lees-Marshment, J. (2024) *The Human Resource Management of Political Staffers: Insights from Prime Ministers' Advisers and Reformers*. Routledge, Abingdon, Oxon.

2

THE STATE OF HUMAN RESOURCE MANAGEMENT OF POLITICAL ADVISERS IN PRIME MINISTER'S OFFICES

Jennifer Lees-Marshment

Introduction

This chapter explores the state of human resource management of political advisers or staffer working in government in the UK, Canada, Australia and New Zealand. It draws on interviews with advisers who worked under political leaders Boris Johnson, Justin Trudeau, Scott Morrison and Jacinda Ardern who shared their experiences of working in the office of the Prime Minister but also for ministers and MPs. Historically, the HR architecture around political staffers has been substantially limited, with advisers starting roles with no orientation or training, receiving little constructive feedback on performance, while being subject to poor working conditions including zero job security, extreme working hours and little if any work-life balance. Such limited infrastructure has been subject to scrutiny in all four countries in the last decade, with media reports of bullying and harassment as well as parliamentary reviews and investigations identifying the lack of suitable management in what is an unusual workplace. The analysis in this chapter highlights how there has previously been a lack of effective HR, but also how positive practices occurred on an ad hoc basis or were developed more recently through reform.

Key literature

Human resource management is a key area of political management. The management of political staffers or advisers is related to both HRM within management or business studies and public administration within political science. HRM in particular encompasses the behaviour of people involved in parties, campaigns and governments. It includes how volunteers, candidates,

DOI: 10.4324/9781003260677-2

staff, party leaders and ministers are recruited and appointed to their role; oriented, trained and developed for it; and supported and motivated to perform to a high level.

This chapter focuses on political staffers or advisers who are paid for by tax payers and work in government for elected politicians – prime ministers, ministers, party leaders, MPs, Lords and Senators. They are partisan or political, not neutral or a-political like public/civil servants. In practice, they are called a range of titles including political staffer, political adviser, special adviser or SpAds, exempt staff, MOP(s) Act employees, personal staff, electorate staff and parliamentary staff.

As Maley (2010) argued, the work of partisan advisers "is vital to modern political management." They are there to enable politicians to do their job, especially those who are government ministers or the Prime Minister. There has been a significant growth in political staff employed in governments worldwide in response to the development of 24/7 media, a more consumerist public, more complex electoral and party systems requiring greater parliamentary negotiation and more complex policy making that requires action between different government departments.

There is a limited amount of research on political staffers that discusses aspects of human resource management. Indeed, this is a gap that several chapters in this edited book will go a long way to fill. But prior to the publication of this book, there was of course research on political staffers generally, such as comparative analysis by Eichbaum and Shaw (2010, 2011) and Esselment et al. (2014); and country studies – Connaughton's (2010) classification of Irish ministerial advisers; Maley's (2011) work on staffers in Australia; Rhodes and Tiernan's (2014) work on Australian Chiefs of Staff, Craft's (2013, 2016) work on partisan policy advisers in Canada; Aucoin's (2010) research also on Canada and Wilson's (2015, 2020) research on Canadian ministerial policy staff and staff in MPs offices; and Eichbaum and Shaw (2007) on New Zealand; as well as work by Kumar (2001a, 2001b) on political staffers in the US White House. But such research, while absolutely valuable in its' own right, does not take an HRM perspective.

There is however work on HR and politicians which is excellent but small in number. This includes job analysis of candidates for MPs by organizational psychologist Jo Silvester with the UK Conservative and Liberal Parties (Silvester and Dykes 2007; Silvester 2012) and Weinberg's (2015) work on politicians and political psychology.

And there is pioneering research that explores both HR in politics, and advisers which is very valuable but limited in number also. Yong and Hazell (2014) edited work uses extensive data from surveying and interviewing special advisers in the UK from 1979-2015 and noted the job insecurity advisers face, and raise issues with the lack of typical HR processes, and concludes that special advisers to be seen as a new profession with improved recruitment, supervision, induction and training and transparency. Weinberg, who pioneered work on organisational psychology and politicians recently extended that to staffers, surveying them about their well-being. This found that half of MPs staff showed clinical levels of mental distress from their work and felt under-resourced to deal with their growing workload (Weinberg 2022; see also the chapter in this volume). Lees-Marshment (2024) offers a comprehensive discussion of HRM and political advisers. This chapter builds on this work but utilises the data differently by critically reviewing the state of practice against a broader theory of HR in politics (Lees-Marshment 2020).

Methodology

The core data source for this chapter is interviews with advisers and staffers who worked under political leaders Boris Johnson, Justin Trudeau, Scott Morrison and Jacinda Ardern, as well as public servants working towards reform in the management processes and programmes they work under. Political staffers shared their experiences of working in the office of the Prime Minister but also for ministers and MPs, providing a comprehensive overview of what it is like to be an adviser in government. 337 potential participants were invited to participate in the research, of which 85 agreed to be interviewed, representing a 25% average response rate.

Data was initially coded using the computer-assisted qualitative data analysis software NVivo, and then it was re-assessed manually against broad-based principles in the theory of HR in politics – see Table 2.1. Thus, the focus was on identifying staffing needs; recruitment and selection; orientation, training and development; and understanding and motivating staff.

Research findings

Principle 1: identify staffing needs to create accurate job descriptions and selection criteria

In the political workplace, job analysis of political staffer roles is rarely carried out and staffing needs are even more rarely assessed. Job descriptions are lacking, or too generic and out of date. Often advisers get into their posts with little sense of what they will actually involve and have to try to figure out their role and responsibilities over time using trial and error.

Interviewees commented that "you don't really have a job description"; or "what I found as a hiring manager is that the JDs that go with these roles are often terribly out of date." There is "no sort of rule book about how to be the Chief Press Secretary" and "there's no 'here is a list of your responsibilities' or 'here is exactly what you want to do' so you're not always overly clear as to what you're really supposed to do." They therefore felt like they were "jumping off the deep end without any kind of indication of what my job even involved."

TABLE 2.1 Theory of political HR

Principle 1: Identify staffing needs
Research and analyse staffing needs and jobs to create accurate job descriptions and selection criteria
1a Systematically research, understand and predict future staffing requirements.
1b Conduct a job analysis to create and update job descriptions and selection criteria outlining the competencies necessary for the position

Principle 2: Recruit and select appropriately
Recruit and select staff and volunteers who meet the competencies and political loyalties the jobs require

2a Be proactive about the recruitment of prospective employees, candidates, members and volunteers including identifying the potential benefits to offer them
2b Use professional selection for party leaders, leadership and committee positions, candidates, volunteers for parties, campaigns or government programs
2c Seek political staff who will help maintain control, bring fresh energy and ideas, understanding of external stakeholders and thus help achieve organisational priority goals
2d Understand and draw on the political management benefits of non-partisan staff such as civil servants, career staff, and bureaucrats
2e Create cultures and practices that encourage diverse recruitment and thus organisational effectiveness

Principle 3: Orientate, train and develop
Orientate, train and develop politicians, staff and volunteers

3a Ensure there are effective orientation programmes to help staff, politicians and volunteers understand the organisation, its' goals, their role and performance expectations
3b Offer training, professional development and mentoring to improve and extend their skills

Principle 4: Understand and motivate individuals and teams
Understand individual and team motivations and develop an effective work environment that nurtures highly committed, engaged and satisfied staff and excellence

4a Understand what motivates politicians, staff, volunteers and donors including values, working conditions, roles and benefits
4b Offer opportunities to make a difference and recognise their contribution
4c Facilitate organisational commitment, satisfaction and positive morale
4d Shape and reinforce positive behaviour

Source: Adapted from Lees-Marshment (2020).

Yet there are also some positive recent innovations in this space. Public servants working in legislatures and related government departments have expanded their guidance to politicians, and advise them to set out clearer expectations right from the start of the process with clearer job adverts. As one noted, "the key thing to me is being open and upfront about what the role is, and that requires a well-written job description and an advert that isn't misleading." Similarly, practitioners involved in a new Office of Staff support for political staffers in Australia noted how it's really important to make "the expectations of what you need to be available to do in a sitting week" clear "because it's not achievable for everybody. It really isn't." They also undertook a job analysis exercise to professionalise job descriptions for political advisers, where they interviewed advisers about what the role involved.

Principle 2: recruit and select staff and volunteers who meet the competencies and political loyalties the jobs require

Political adviser jobs are rarely advertised openly, not least because there is pressure to staff up quickly after an election or selected of a new leader.

Interviewees recalled "there was a lot of machinating around whether someone was from one political faction or another and who it would upset, which is dire when you think about running a nation" and that "there's a huge number of people who come from the established route who are just dire" so "the whole recruitment process is basically broken." It sometimes operates more like a feudal system where staffers are selected without proper interviews or skills tests.

Typically, political advisers are recruited through party and campaign networks, and thus through word of mouth or shoulder tapping rather than professional selection. A public servant noted "we've had MPs who have met somebody at drinks reception and what's-app'd them offering them a job." The lack of professional practice was confirmed by adviser accounts, such as:

- "In my case I was sat next to another special advisor at a wedding and we talked about policy for an hour and the next day I had an e-mail saying we have a job for you."
- "My personal story was of course I'll come and help Boris and Number 10, but I can't earn any less money that I'm on now, but apart from that I'm fine. And then none of that happened…I had to actually send my CV to Dom Cummings, having already accepted the job. I was already sat in Downing Street, negotiating my wage…The whole thing was bonkers….you wouldn't expect that in a normal workplace let alone the highest office."

While ad hoc recruitment is sometimes successful, by bringing in those who had already proven themselves to be loyal and able to work under pressure on campaigns and transfer those attributes to government, it does not always work as the best way to ensure people doing the jobs actually have the required skills. This can set offices up for failure and toxicity when the required work does not get done, or done well.

Senior staffers involved in recruitment have therefore learnt to instigate more appropriate selection processes, such as asking for a writing sample, spending time talking to them informally and recruiting from internship programmes. To improve the diversity of staff they also work hard to broaden the pool of applicants, raising the visibility of these jobs. As one Chief of Staff commented, it is about "growing the awareness of what these jobs are and that they are exciting and interesting jobs, and that there's a place for people, even if you don't know anyone that has worked there."

The Canadian Liberals under Justin Trudeau and Australian Labor under Anthony Albanese both created open application processes and attempted to use more professionalised selection processes. In the Australian case, after being elected in 2022 the Labor Party set up a centralised public expression of interest process asking applicants for their CV and details including name, age, where they lived, diversity criteria and asked people what job they wanted to do, area they wanted to work in, and politician they wanted to work for if they had one in mind. They received 4,000 expressions of interest around the country for around 400 jobs, which "created a really rich data set" of "qualified people" that those hiring advisers could choose from. A full-time team worked to triage those expressions of interest to match expressions of interest with the openings and needs in each office. They were then able to monitor and encourage greater gender diversity in staffing.

This improved the appointment of suitable staff, but also enriched the diversity by opening up the process. As one Australian practitioner observed, "we want our cohort that is serving the parliamentarians for the nation to reflect the nation. So it's only in an open recruitment process that you can really do that." It's important for the individuals but also the effectiveness of government: "as we all know, if you have more diversity of thought around the decision-making table you get better outcomes. By broadening the spectrum of people who can do political staffing and also investing in them to have a long term career in staffing." Gender is an important consideration – as another senior staffer commented, "I was pretty committed to gender parity which requires intention in terms of how you do recruitment, and in terms of how you build a candidate shortlist. I found it did not require you to have intention by the end step, but it did require intention in a lot of the early steps." But diversity in many different forms is also important, as these two advisers reflected:

- "Government is best when it's diverse; not only male/female or non-binary or racially, but also geographically, and all of the various professional nuances that could be in the mix as well. If you build a government around good people, you almost never go wrong."
- "Diversity in the sense of everything – it's linguistic, it's racial, it's lived experience. It's people who may have had more difficulties in their life, such

as they lived in community housing, and really had a different perspective. You're not going to check off every box, but it's about being conscious and really trying to make sure, depending on what the file is, that you have the right team that can really add value."

Principle 3: orientate, train and develop politicians, staff and volunteers

Principles of effective orientation and training and development are rarely followed officially and consistently. The public service has historically been uncomfortable with getting involved in this for fear of crossing the line of neutrality into partisan territory. And, naturally, those previously in charge are most likely another party beaten in an election or another Prime Minister ousted by internal factions and are not going to hang around to provide advice. As one staffer recalled "when I came in my predecessor had been booted out in shame essentially. And so you walk into an empty desk."

In reality staffers are often thrown into the deep end. Orientation is very rare, and often limited to basic administrative HR, or varies in quality depending on the office. Staffers described the start of their roles as being like drinking from a fire hose where they have to learn formal and informal behaviours, strategies and tactics at high speed without any clear instruction or direction. As interviewees from all four countries commented:

- "If you come in as an outsider without the previous knowledge of 'these are the inner machinations of the party in the system' there is essentially no orientation. Nothing." (Australia)
- "There's really lousy, if any, onboarding. It's really poor. There was no real orientation. There was no training. There was IT; they told me how to log on. That's it. The rest was figure it out." (Canada)
- "It was very baptism by fire. I've had roles since then in other areas where I've seen what actual on-boarding looks like, and it just was non-existent." (New Zealand)
- "There is no support, the on-ramp is incredibly long. A couple of us all agreed upon leaving that we sort of had a 9 month on-ramp which is you being thrown into the mix." (UK)

The same goes for ongoing training, which has generally been inadequate. It means that "individuals who for political reasons find themselves in the orbit of the Prime Minister or his or her senior ministers are rushed into the process of policy making in government without a great deal of training." This is because "there's no centralized training for young political staffers to even understand that they're both trying to deliver our mandate and deliver votes." Consequently, "people are not trained on the most basic things from sexual harassment to what is legal and illegal to do in an office, what is a crime, what is ethical and unethical. None of that happens. Yet McDonald's would spend three weeks training you on how to deep fry a nugget."

Given that training tends to be left to individual offices, and time is so pressured, managers either have to devote resources to creating their own training, or do not even attempt to because they don't feel they have the time. One manager recalled "there is not a lot of systemic material available to do this. So in my own case I have probably created more informal training modules than you can imagine."

Managers draw on more piecemeal ways of on-boarding staff, such as laying out expectations, the nature of the role, introducing them to key people, and letting them shadow themselves and others in order to learn the job through observation. Whilst it takes time, as one argued "there's no point just having the person sitting there for the first month, not knowing what they're doing." Another reflected "that's something that I spent some time on. I realized that needed to be done for people who were coming in fresh." Similarly, the head of a policy unit said "many special advisers are thrown in at the deep end and whilst resourcefulness is a key quality in the job, it makes sense to impart some collective wisdom so they don't waste valuable time in their first few months." Creating and maintaining a culture where it is acceptable to ask questions is also important as it's hard for existing staffers to know exactly what new colleagues do and do not know or need to know, so making it safe for them to raise anything they are unsure of creates a positive and supportive environment to learn as they go.

Another way to orientate new staff is to provide succinct written information such as a staff handbook or office manual that covers the different jobs, expectations, common acronyms, and shares tips of the trade. As one interviewee recalled:

> One of our staffers in correspondence took it upon herself to write up a manual, because there wasn't one before, and that was an office that had a lot of turnover because it had a lot of relatively junior roles, and people would often only stay there about a year or two years on average…This staffer took it upon themselves to write out job descriptions and what the jobs involved and tips of the trades and all that, which was very helpful for people who came after them. But not all departments would have that, and not all offices would have that.

In practice, more experienced staff also informally advise and mentor new advisers. In a few places such as the Canadian Prime Minister Justin Trudeau's government, formal mentoring schemes have been created to facilitate peer connections and learning. But even informal support and relationships are very valuable – albeit ad hoc and not universal. More experienced peers can share experiences, including tips of the trade for particular jobs but also broader professional coping skills to deal with the pressures and downsides of working in Prime Minister's offices.

Senior staffers spoke of being "there as somebody who can give advice to people and to bounce ideas off" and "you develop such good relationships in other offices so you can say to younger staff, 'oh speak to this person or that person, they'll know what to do'" or that "when people that I knew became SpAds, and were new, I would often try and have a chat with them to explain the things I wish people had told me when I started."

Chiefs of Staff or Team Directors noted that they "had some people who were like middle managers who were responsible for taking some of the more and junior staff under their wings, talking to them about the expectations of the job" and that "the advisors in the Prime Minister's office also had a role of mentoring and looking after younger advisors across the building." Junior advisers strongly expressed how they benefitted from informal mentoring from more experienced peers:

- "The senior communications person in my team became a good friend of mine and was very helpful."
- "I'm fortunate to work with people who have been around since 2015 when Justin Trudeau first got elected, and they've just got a wealth of knowledge underneath them, and all of them have been very willing to share that and to be open about their experiences."
- "The benefit that you get if you join the Government half way through is that there's people who have lived a lot of that, and can assist you."
- "Here in government I learned from people who had done my job, or my direct report. So when I was a comms advisor I would learn from my Dcoms [Director of Communications] and when I was in advance I learned a lot from the Director of Tour who went around on tour with me until I got my legs under me and I could do it myself."
- "You were constantly learning from other very senior people who had worked as staffers for quite some time."

Principle 4: understand and motivate individuals and teams

Just as with orientation and training, the performance management aspects of HRM come down to the individual senior staffers in charge of a particular team on a day-to-day basis. There is typically a lack of overarching and official programmes designed to support political advisers. This partly reflects the complex and disjointed line management that advisers face, which officially and in practice includes politicians, other staffers, and public/civil servants in government departments and parliament. Added to this is the lack of training for managers and high-paced nature of political offices.

This means there is often a lack of meaningful and regular feedback. Formal performance reviews and KPIs are rare. Positive feedback is also uncommon; staffers often hear more about problems or issues not within their control or get unspecific negative comments. Staffers say there is not the time, or which fire's burning the brightest takes priority rather than sitting down to review colleague's performances. This was reported by staffers in all four countries:

- "Over 5–6 years I don't think I saw a single performance evaluation." (Australia)
- "At PMO there were never any standardized professional development meetings or review meetings performance assessments." (Canada)
- "In terms of performance reviews and things like that, we didn't really have any. I don't think I had a single performance review when I was there for three years." (New Zealand)
- "In my case I had no meaningful line management at all, which rather suited me because I was happy to get on and do stuff, but it wouldn't have suited everyone." (UK)

Unlike the public service, there are very few mandated performance programmes in government. Additionally, those involved in managing staffers are often untrained and inexperienced. Political staff often end up in positions of authority over others at a very young age because they are a good political adviser to a politician. As they themselves concede, they often lack management experience or management training.

Nevertheless, positive practices have been developed by managers in some offices as they learn over time or draw on their experiences outside politics to build and support effective teams. Political managers talked of the importance of the leadership group trying to "foster a collegial environment" and set "a tone of respect, courtesy and politeness." Building a strong team culture and sense of camaraderie where people feel included is vital. They try to share information as much as possible and "when you can't tell them something, tell them why" is really vital. That way advisers feel included rather than excluded.

It is also worth spending time with staff building a positive sense of shared purpose to create a strong team spirit. It helps to create a safe and supportive environment where staff can they and innovate and raise issues and ideas. Responding positively to mistakes – which always happen – is also important:

- "It's just really really important that people are made to feel they have the freedom to try things and get some things wrong. I'm not talking about party gate and breaking the law and stuff obviously. But I'm talking about sometimes you put in an idea that just doesn't work. But you've got to feel like you're in an environment where you can do that. Otherwise you won't get big wins."

- "Showing people it's okay to make mistakes goes a long way too. We're all human, and you wouldn't be human if you didn't make multiple mistakes. I make them every day. And so highlighting your own mistakes some-times, in a self-deprecating way, conveys it is normal, it's fine."
- "You have to have a supportive leadership for sure that allows people to make mistakes and doesn't make them feel like they're screw ups when they do but that it's natural. Everybody makes mistakes."
- "In teams with an office that size there needs to be the ability and space for discussing how we think we're tracking and an environment or a closed space where you can speak freely. Where you can say "that speech was all right, but I don't think we hit the mark.""

Some political managers also spoke of acting like a coach of a team, where everyone is seen and supported to be working alongside each other to get the win. As one senior staffer commented:

Mentoring is critical and a sense of belonging, just like a sports team... The most successful political teams I've been part of – whether it's on a two-week campaign, or a sixty campaign, or over four years in a ministry or over two plus years in the Prime Minister's office – the only successful teams had been the one where that that bond is created.

Regular, constructive and positive feedback is really important to staffers. So rather than only engage when something goes wrong, there should be continual dialogue. Otherwise staff cannot know what to improve, or indeed what is working and should be maintained. As one adviser explained:

Direct feedback is really really important. That doesn't mean that that the feedback is always critical, sometimes the feedback can be positive. And when it's critical it should be constructively critical rather than needlessly cutting or negative. But it's really important for that feedback to happen.

Often feedback will be given real time, in response to draft work or just after an event. But more reflective, annual sit downs also create more of a dialogue and chance to discuss both past and future behaviour. As one Chief of Staff noted, "we are actually trying to normalize them. I'm scheduling a performance chat with every staff member across my office at the end of this year. It's our first year in government, we've come to the end of the year, we've got through the sitting calendar, let's have a debrief."

Time also needs to be taken to note and show appreciation for high-level performance – "when people do a little bit above and beyond, you need to make sure to take the time for that too." It reinforces positive behaviours and encourages staff to keep aiming high. One junior staffer observed that in the prime minister's office they were "getting a little bit better at being more open about positive feedback and knowing when things go right, and that definitely makes a difference. You learn just as much from what goes right as you do from what goes wrong."

Lastly, understanding what motivates staff – making a difference – and reminding them of the progress they are all making is vital to maintaining motivation. Staffers involved in running teams spoke of the importance of keeping colleagues going through high pressured and sometimes dark situations. The most effective way to do this is to set a clear sense of mission and help them see the difference their work is making towards achieving that goal. Enabling staff to get out on the road with the Prime Minister to see how policy is being received and impacting people on the ground, attending key events or speeches, and being reminded of the value of the work are all effective ways to maintain morale. Thus political staffers argued:

- "A political office should be considered as very much as a cooperative type workplace, where everyone, regardless of rank and background, is working together in common cause, common purpose, and that should be clearly stated from the outset."
- "One of the most important things is even if they can't get face time with the Prime Minister that even the junior people in the office can see that they are connected to a project in a fairly proximate way."
- "It definitely helps going out on the road and seeing the Prime Minister interact with everyday Canadians and the way that they respond to him. You see the way that they react to him, and how much of a difference our government has made for the lives of so many people, and that is a huge thing."
- "If we have ruthless focus on an understanding of what we are there to achieve, then we know that we'll be delivering against something that is more important. We're going to be highly motivated and incentivized by a particular political agenda and set of policies."
- "There is an overarching point where people want to feel that their work is of value in terms of the work in the bigger sense. That isn't party political, but the point of being here is to make a difference in people's lives, and for the environment."

Recommendations for research

Clearly the management of political staffers and advisers is an area that needs more work to be up to standard. Solid job analysis, professional recruitment and selection and orientation and training is commonly lacking. But there are also positive practices and ongoing developments being brought in by individual political advisers and public/civil servants that have and will significantly improve how advisers are supported both as individuals and to enhance the performance of political offices.

This and other chapters in this edited book demonstrate the value of applying HR concepts to politics. Research in political management needs to be geared to the specific political environment, rather than just transplanting or extending public service or business concepts to the political arena. It needs adaptive cross-disciplinary conceptualization to produce appropriate frameworks that will be positively meaningful to the practitioners carrying out these roles. But now that we have academic research that visualises how HRM can work in the political workplace, future research can assess the most recent practices against these principles to both record the progress made towards higher standards and stimulate further reform and innovation.

Recommendations for practice

The main advice for practitioners is to follow the key principles of the theory of political HR. Specifically:

1 Prioritise and resource fit for purpose HRM for political staffers and advisers, with a dedicated and expert team composed of political staffers, public servants and HR experts.
2 Create accurate job descriptions that reflect the reality of adviser's roles.
3 Adopt professional processes to recruit and select people who actually have the competencies the jobs require – see Box 2.1.
4 Engage in ongoing talent management, right from pre-government staffing planning through to on-boarding, skills and upwards development of current staffers and supporting advisers exit from politics.

BOX 2.1 CORE PRINCIPLES OF AN EFFECTIVE RECRUITMENT AND SELECTION PROCESS FOR POLITICAL ADVISERS

- Involve different practitioners in the recruitment and selection process including the politicians, political staffers, and staff with HR expertise from the civil/public service.
- Integrate awareness of the multi-faceted capabilities required in political staffing jobs into all aspects of the recruitment and selection process, including loyalty, commitment, fit and capacity to cope.
- Conduct job analysis to ensure role and job descriptions reflect the realities of the job.
- Ensure job adverts are upfront about the extensive demands as well as distinctive terms and conditions.

- Engage in pre-election staffing planning to identify potential applicants
- Invite applications from the usual routes such as existing staffers, former staffers, campaign volunteers, party offices, unions and think tanks, but avoid assuming they have the capacity to do these jobs
- Be open to those who have worked outside politics and their potential to bring relevant transferrable skills to do these jobs, such as events and project management
- Run open and professional selection processes, especially at the start of a new government, to ensure selection of staff who have the capabilities these roles require, including seeking professional commitment and loyalty as opposed to assuming this comes, and only comes, from partisanship.

5 Develop bespoke and useful training that orientates and develops political advisers over time, delivered by a mix of practitioners including the civil/public service, outside experts, former and current senior staffers and parties – see Table 2.2.

6 Encourage excellence through training senior staffers and politicians involved in managing advisers on how to give effective and constructive feedback.

TABLE 2.2 Suggested content for an ongoing training programme for political advisers

Category	Further details	Potential providers
Generic skills	Respectful workplaces, unconscious bias, languages, budgeting, time management, project management, mediation, negotiation.	• Civil/public service • External professional trainers
Political but non-partisan processes and policies	Foundational information about government and parliamentary processes, committees, cabinet processes, codes of conduct.	• Civil/public service
Bespoke skills and behavioural training for political adviser jobs	Including specific skills such as video editing, writing a news release, being a case worker, as well as conduct in meetings, at events and how best to work with the public service	• External professional trainers • Former/current staffers • Political parties
Coping skills with the challenges of the job	On managing the specific challenges of the job of a political adviser, such as political prioritisation and building resilience	• Former/current staffers • Political parties
Partisan material	Issues, policies and strategies specific to a particular party	• Former/current staffers • Political parties

Lastly, it is important to note that there needs to be better management for political advisers for the individuals concerned, the politicians they serve, and democracy as a whole. Improved human resource management of political staffers will improve their effectiveness and retention, and in turn, the functioning of political offices. Politicians will then be better supported and able to be more strategic in their decision-making. This will significantly strengthen government and democracy.

Recommendations for reading

Eichbaum, Chris and Richard Shaw (2007). "Minding the minister? Ministerial advisers in New Zealand government." *Kōtuitui: New Zealand Journal of Social Sciences Online* 2(2): 95–113

Lees-Marshment, J (2024). *The Human Resource Management of Political Staffers: Insights from Prime Ministers' Advisers and Reformers.* Routledge. Abingdon, Oxon

Maley, Maria (2010). 'Australia,' Chapter 3 in Eichbaum, C. and R. Shaw (eds). *Partisan Appointees and Public Servants: An International Analysis of the Role of the Political Adviser.* Edward Elgar, Cheltenham, UK

Wilson, R. Paul. (2015). "Research note: A profile of ministerial policy staff in the Government of Canada." *Canadian Journal of Political Science* 48 (2): 455–471

Yong, B and R Hazell (Eds) (2014). *Special Advisers: Who They Are, What They Do and Why They Matter*, The Constitution Unit. Hart Publishing. Oxford, Oxfordshire

References

Aucoin, Peter (2010). "Canada" Chapter 2 in Eichbaum, C. and R. Shaw (eds). *Partisan Appointees and Public Servants: an International Analysis of the Role of the Political Adviser.* Edward Elgar, Cheltenham, UK

Connaughton, B. (2010). "'Glorified gofers, policy experts or good generalists': A classification of the roles of the Irish ministerial adviser." *Irish Political Studies* 25(3): 347–369.

Craft, Jonathan (2013). "Appointed political staffs and the diversification of policy advisory sources: Theory and evidence from Canada." *Policy and Society* 32(3): 211–223.

Craft, Jonathan (2016). *Backrooms and Beyond: Partisan Advisors and the Politics of Policy Work in Canada*, University of Toronto Press, Toronto, Ontario.

Eichbaum, Chris and Richard Shaw (2007). "Minding the minister? Ministerial advisers in New Zealand government." *Kōtuitui: New Zealand Journal of Social Sciences Online* 2(2): 95–113.

Eichbaum, C. and R. Shaw (2011). "Political staff in executive government: Conceptualising and mapping roles within the core executive." *Australian Journal of Political Science* 46(4): 583–600.

Eichbaum, C. and R. Shaw (eds). (2010). *Partisan Appointees and Public Servants: An International Analysis of the Role of the Political Adviser*, Edward Elgar, Cheltenham, UK

Esselment, A. L., J Lees-Marshment and A. Marland (2014). "The nature of political advising to prime ministers in Australia, Canada, New Zealand and the UK." *Commonwealth & Comparative Politics* 52(3): 358–375.

Kumar, M. J. (2001a). "The office of communications." *Presidential Studies Quarterly* **31**(4): 609–634.

Kumar, M. J. (2001b). "The office of the press secretary." *Presidential Studies Quarterly* 31(2): 296–322.

Lees-Marshment, J (2020). *Political Management: The Dance of Government and Politics*, Routledge, Abingdon, Oxon.

Lees-Marshment, J (2024). *The Human Resource Management of Political Staffers: Insights from Prime Ministers' Advisers and Reformers*, Routledge, Abingdon, Oxon.

Maley, M. (2011). "Strategic links in a cut-throat world: Rethinking the role and relationships of Australian ministerial staff." *Public Administration* 89(4): 1469–1488.

Maley, M (2010). 'Australia', Chapter 3 in Eichbaum, C. and R. Shaw (eds). *Partisan Appointees and Public Servants: An International Analysis of the Role of the Political Adviser*. Edward Elgar Cheltenham, UK

Rhodes, RAW and Anne Tiernan. 2014. *Lessons in Governing: A Profile of Prime Ministers' Chiefs of Staff*. Melbourne University Press, Melbourne, Victoria.

Silvester, J. and C. Dykes (2007). "Selecting political candidates: A longitudinal study of assessment centre performance and political success in the 2005 UK General Election." *Journal of Occupational & Organizational Psychology* 80(1): 11–25.

Silvester, Jo (2012). 'Recruiting politicians: Designing competency-based selection for UK parliamentary candidates', Chapter 2 in Weinberg, A. (ed). *The Psychology of Politicians*. Cambridge University Press, Cambridgeshire.

Weinberg, A (2015). "A longitudinal study of the impact of changes in the job and the expenses scandal on UK national politicians' experiences of work, stress and the home–work interface." *Parliamentary Affairs* 68(2): 248–271.

Weinberg, Ashley (2022). "Half of UK MPs' staff have clinical levels of psychological distress, study finds." *The Guardian Newspaper*. https://www.theguardian.com/politics/2022/may/23/half-uk-mps-staff-clinical-levels-psychological-distress-study

Wilson, R. Paul (2015). "Research note: A profile of ministerial policy staff in the Government of Canada." *Canadian Journal of Political Science* 48(2): 455–471.

Wilson, R. Paul (2020). "The work of Canadian political staffers in parliamentary caucus research offices." *Canadian Public Administration* 63 (3): 498–521. https://onlinelibrary.wiley.com/doi/abs/10.1111/capa.12380

Yong, B and R Hazell (Eds) (2014). *Special Advisers: Who They Are, What They Do and Why They Matter*, The Constitution Unit. Hart Publishing. Oxford, Oxfordshire.

3

THE UK PRIME MINISTER'S CHIEF OF STAFF'S MANAGEMENT OF SPECIAL ADVISERS

Max Stafford

Introduction

This chapter explores the role of the UK's Downing Street Chief of Staff, and seeks to address the following research question: "What operational leadership functions does the Downing Street Chief-of-Staff fulfil and how can observation of these contribute to understandings of political human resources and management?" The focus on human resources (HR) helps us to both narrow the focus to a particular aspect of chiefs' work and, as importantly, to explore the utility of political management theory when applied empirically to a case study that it has never been analysed before.

Key literature

The current literature concerning the role of the Downing Street Chief of Staff can, at best, be described as sparse. This is despite the existence of works on American and Australian counterparts (Rhodes and Tiernan, 2014; Whipple, 2017). The closest we come to a genuine engagement with the role, its purpose and evolution since 1997, is those accounts that have been written by former chiefs and their deputies. These vary from memoirs (Fall, 2020; Barwell, 2021) through to reflections contained within works on party politics or government affairs (Powell, 2010; Timothy, 2020). However, these remain few in number and do not form a theorised account of the role itself and how its functions may be used (though we can, of course, surmise this from authors' recollections).

DOI: 10.4324/9781003260677-3

In an attempt to capture the general responsibilities of the job, Alex Thomas (2022) of The Institute for Government recently summarised the role's preoccupations as being:

- 'Being the prime minister's most senior political adviser;
- Managing other political advisers;
- Working closely with the prime minister's principal private secretary;
- Working with the wider team of private secretaries to try to get the government machine to do what the prime minister wants;
- The gatekeeper role: sitting outside the prime minister's office and controlling who gets in and who doesn't;
- Seeing what the prime minister sees, and accompanying them to meetings; and
- Brokering deals with other ministers' advisers.'

All of these aspects are reflected in the work published by former Chiefs and Deputy Chiefs. For instance, the gatekeeper role alluded to matches to Kate Fall's (Deputy Chief of Staff, 2010–2016) description of how she controlled access to the prime minister (so that their time was protected for them to focus on their priorities) (Fall, 2020: 2). This reflects Weller's reflection (2018:90–92) that one of the key resources to manage for a prime minister (PM) and their staff is their time.

Thomas has also given an account of personnel-focused duties (Thomas, 2020). He has written that, '...as the prime minister's most important political courtier...', a chief must oversee the work and conduct of political staff across Downing Street's communications, policy, political, and parliamentary liaison functions (Thomas, 2020). In short, chiefs are involved in both recruiting staff who have the competencies and political loyalties required and, also, organising how they carry out these tasks. This covers the Human Resources (HR) aspects that Jennifer Lees-Marshment has described (Lees-Marshment, 2021: 215).

Methodology

Lees-Marshment's (2021) work on political management has been adopted as the theoretical framework used for analysing chiefs' leadership functions and HR role. This has been selected due to her work having: previously identified the lack of consideration of the Downing Street Chief of Staff as a political manager; established clear and concise criteria for assessing political HR (see below) and; having previously been used to assess counterpart chiefs (in Australia, New Zealand and Canada) in similar settings (prime ministerial offices). Her work '...lays out the conceptual architecture...' for an examination such as this and does so in a way that can be translated

TABLE 3.1 Key areas of political HR

1   Identify staffing needs
2   Recruit appropriately
3   Train and develop
4   Learn how people work
5   Motivate
6   Encourage excellence

Source: Adapted from Lees-Marshment (2021: 114).

from similar-systems (Westminster model settings) into the British context (Lees-Marshment, 2021: 1). In light of this, HR is understood to comprise those areas referred to in Table 3.1: Key Areas of Political HR. Operational leadership functions in relation to HR are understood to be those that Lees-Marshment (2021: 119) identified for chiefs-of-staff in political offices. These were: design the structure and roles within the office; recruit and line-manage staff; delineate and oversee responsibilities; delegate tasks and work areas and; set the office's tone. Thus, the analysis has been structured into a focus on each of the six areas set out in Table 3.1, with a concluding assessment of whether chiefs appear to possess an operational leadership role. Conclusions used to identify further scope for both practice and future research. Thus, the research has focused upon whether Downing Street Chiefs of Staff *have* displayed these competencies.

Data for assessing this has been gathered from various documentary re-sources. These include: memoirs and biographies, secondary literature (including work written by other authors upon the operational aspects and history of the Prime Minister's office during this period), and journalistic content. These data sources are used to collate historical evidence which, in turn, informs wider observations about the Chief's role in HR.

Research findings

The Downing Street Chief of Staff

The Downing Street Chief of Staff role has, since 1997, been occupied by fifteen people (see Table 3.2). It has either been done by someone formally possessing the title "Downing Street Chief of Staff" or, during the periods October 2008 – May 2010 and July 2019 – December 2020, by a person designated as *de facto* chief. Different chiefs have fulfilled different functions. Those with backgrounds as officials (for instance, Jeremy Heywood) have often been more preoccupied with the day-to-day operations of Downing Street whilst others (such as Nick Timothy and Fiona Hill) have pursued the position with greater focus on overall political strategy (whilst also often trying to fulfil the operational role).

TABLE 3.2 Downing Street chiefs of staff 1997–2023

Name	PM	Dates
Jonathan Powell	Tony Blair	1997–2007
Tom Scholar*	Gordon Brown	2007–2008
Stephen Carter*	Gordon Brown	2008
Jeremy Heywood*	Gordon Brown	2008–2010
Ed Llewellyn	David Cameron	2010–2016
Nick Timothy and Fiona Hill	Theresa May	2016–2017
Gavin Barwell	Theresa May	2017–2019
Dominic Cummings*	Boris Johnson	2019–2020
Eddie Lister**	Boris Johnson	2020–2021
Dan Rosenfield	Boris Johnson	2021–2022
Stephen Barclay	Boris Johnson	2022
Simone Finn**	Boris Johnson	2022
Mark Fullbrook	Liz Truss	2022
Liam Booth-Smith	Rishi Sunak	2022–present

* *De facto* (e.g. Carter essentially undertook the role whilst Director of Strategy).
**Acting.

Identify staffing needs

Various chiefs since 1997 have been brought in part way through a prime minister's tenure precisely with the mandate to restructure personnel and re-place staff members. Whilst the latter of these is discussed in Section Two, we must first assess how far chiefs control staffing structures. As Lees-Marshment (2021: 51) has written, being clear on what your staffing needs are is vital to delivering government priorities.

The case study of Gordon Brown's Downing Street operation (2007–2010) demonstrates the need for having a chief in the first place. Brown initially tried to combine the role with that of Principal Private Secretary (PPS) (Davis and Rentoul, 2019: 129–130). The PPS is a senior civil servant within the PM's private office, traditionally taking the lead on co-ordinating administration and connections with other civil servants across Whitehall (Seldon et al., 2021:165–166). However, Brown came to feel that such a set up was not working for him. The PPS's (Tom Scholar) lack of prior familiarity with the inner workings of Downing Street (not to mention his statutory inability to engage with partisan activities, as prohibited by the Civil Service Code) meant that Brown lacked a chief who could fulfil all that he needed them to (Heywood, 2021: 209–211). Consequently, he employed Stephen Carter as *de facto* Chief (he was Director of Strategy) whilst also engaging Jeremy Heywood (a former PPS) as a senior Downing Street civil servant who knew Brown's preferred working patterns and was brought in to create cohesion across the staffing structure (Garnett, 2021: 114). When Carter left (in October 2008, failing to bond with some of Brown's other staff), Heywood continued in his own *de facto* Chief role, whilst political functions were increasingly filled by those such as Peter Mandelson (another senior minister) and Balls (Riddell, 2019: 148).

Jonathan Powell and Tony Blair also had early experience of trying to reform staffing in relation to a perceived need for operational changes. They expanded the political advisor cadre in Downing Street (with the number of special advisors reaching 84 by 2005), in order to enhance their influence over policy direction, seeking what Cockerell described as ensuring that '...Whitehall danced to Number 10's tune.' (Cockerell, 2011). The Cabinet Secretary, Robin Butler, appears to have been wary of this move, with Blair describing him as cautious regarding changes (such as partisan functionaries leading the private office) (Blair, 2010: 17). Powell has offered a similar assessment of Butler but recalled the Cabinet Secretary suggesting, in 1997, that the Chief should also occupy the position of PPS (a memory substantiated by the wife of the late Heywood, then a rising civil servant) (Heywood, 2021: 63–64). Powell saw no need for this, so refused, though the new PPS (John Holmes) would in future report to him (Heywood, 2021: 75). Blick (2004: 283) has suggested that it was actually Blair and Powell who suggested merging the posts and that Butler was resistant to this, seeking to maintain Civil Service independence for the role. Whomever you believe, this early skirmish regarding staffing established both the perceived seniority of the Chief (being set alongside the PM's senior civil servant) and, as importantly, that the role had institutional input into personnel structures. Lees-Marshment (2021: 140) included the case study as an example of how the role began to become entrenched into the political management of Downing Street, with them taking control of the press, policy and political (party relations and strategy) aspects of the PM's office. They could also direct officials.

A more recent staffing innovation has been Barwell's introduction of personnel covering legislative affairs. A former government whip and minister, Barwell recognised the need to have greater links between Number 10's political operation and the House of Commons' legislative managers (Barwell, 2020). In 2017, he persuaded the PM (Theresa May) to recruit a Director of Legislative Affairs. Nikki da Costa (a former special advisor) was recruited (Barwell, 2020). In 2018, da Costa would resign due to tensions with how much information Barwell and others allowed the Legislative Affairs Unit to see of the then-forthcoming agreement with the European Union (EU) regarding the United Kingdom's exit from the bloc (Seldon and Newell, 2020: 489–490). However, Legislative Affairs role has continued and, in part, become a legacy of recent innovation of a chief responding to perceived staffing needs.

Dominic Cummings' time as a *de facto*, rather than official, holder of this office provides insight into the influence that chiefs can have over the identification of staffing requirements. Cummings had long held the view that the Civil Service was inefficient and not run appropriately. In part, this stemmed from his time as a special advisor at the Department for Education (2011–2014) and his belief that the Civil Service had, either through conspiracy or incompetence, sought to disrupt the then-Education Secretary's reforms (Bennett, 2019: 248). He seemed to take the same desire to overhaul the Civil Service and its priorities with him into Downing Street. In 2021, he told an interviewer that being able to lead on this had been a condition for him accepting the role (BBC, 2021: 16). Others have recorded how he also ensured that all government special advisors were also ultimately accountable to him (ensuring that he was able to implement his view of staffing needs beyond Downing Street, too) (Payne, 2022: 6). This was made clearest when Cummings effectively forced out Sajid Javid (Chancellor of the Exchequer, 2019–2020) from government, having demanded that Downing Street would control his special advisor appointments (Gimson, 2022: 279). Finally, this determination of staffing needs was, perhaps, best exemplified by his December 2019 'blog in which he called for '…"misfits and weirdos"…' to join the Civil Service (alluding to the need for scientists and data specialists) (Gimson, 2022: 320). To Cummings, these were gaps in the skills set available across government. It demonstrated his influence as Chief that he was given licence by the PM (when previous chiefs had not established a public presence in discussing such issues) to make this appeal in this manner.

Recruit appropriately

Cummings' tenure provides us with further evidence of how chiefs approach their role – this time with how they recruit. As Chief, he sought influence the recruitment of both civil servants and special advisers. In 2020, having obtained Johnson's agreement to reform of the Civil Service, including those leading departments or working closely with the PM, the Chief targeted the Cabinet Secretary (Mark Sedwill) for replacement. The Cabinet Secretary leads the Civil Service and is the most senior non-partisan adviser to PMs (charged, amongst other duties, with facilitating Cabinet and ensuring that wider government machinery delivers on their priorities) (Brown, 2019: 38). The Chief expressed dissatisfaction with Sedwill on the grounds that he felt that he embodied the Civil Service ethos that Cummings had spent so much time criticising (Garnett, 2021: 247). Cummings played a central role in replacing Sedwill, eventually recruiting Simon Case (a former PPS who had never led a government department) (Payne, 2022: 33).

However, whilst Cummings' individual motivations and personality may have been a factor, including a chief in considerations around recruiting to this most senior of Civil Service roles was merely part of an emerging historical pattern. Powell was closely involved in Blair's ongoing searches for a Cabinet Secretary who could help him deliver policies, especially with regards to public service reform (Davis and Rentoul, 2019: 66; 165–167). Likewise, Timothy and Hill were also part of early discussions with May about whether to replace Jeremy Heywood as Cabinet Secretary (though they eventually came to trust his determination to implement the PM's agenda) (McDonald, 2022: 106). Thus, we can see that it is now accepted as appropriate that a chief will play a role in senior Civil Service recruitment processes, by virtue of being close to the PM (who is constitutionally required to decide upon hirings).

Cummings' example offers us chance to make a counter observation. Having control of the staffing process does not mean that a chief always has full control of recruitment. Allegra Stratton's appointment as Downing Street Press Secretary is instructive, here. Cummings, along with Lee Cain (Downing Street Director of Communications, 2019–2020), had, by 2020, alighted on the idea of introducing televised press briefings (akin to those used in the modern White House) and, thus, sought to recruit a Press Secretary to lead them (Ashcroft, 2022: 217). Having held a series of interviews, they informed the PM that they wished to appoint, journalist, Ellie Price (Payne, 2022: 28). Stratton (one of three shortlisted) was appointed, instead. Reportedly, it was Carrie Johnson (the PM's wife and a former media special adviser) making private representations in favour of Stratton that led to her appointment (Payne, 2022: 28). It is difficult to substantiate this evidence, based as it is on second-hand reporting of anonymised briefings. However, it does suggest that an influential chief who has identified staffing needs and initiated a recruitment process could find their efforts thwarted by informal sources of power that they will find it harder to control.

Sometimes chiefs inherit existing staff. This is the case when one chief succeeds another part way through a PM's tenure (see Table 3.2). This then leaves incoming chiefs with decisions to make about whether or not to retain these staff. When Barwell arrived (following the 2017 General Election), he needed to ensure that he implemented considerable cultural change in the building[1]. Some of this was facilitated by the pre-election creation of vacancies in key posts such as the Director of Communications (previously held by Katie Perrior) and the above-mentioned introduction of a Legislative Affairs Unit (Ross and McTague, 2017: 39). He also identified a need for providing a sense of stabilisation, given that the departure of his predecessors (Timothy and Hill) had created a sense of crisis regarding perceptions of the PM's internal operation (Richards, 2019: 375). Thus, he asked the existing Deputy Chief, Joanna "JoJo" Penn, to stay (Barwell, 2021: 23). He has since stated that he believed her continuation in the role to have been essential in creating a conduit who could facilitate his introduction to staff who remained and he made clear that she was to be regarded as speaking for him when he was absent (Seldon and Newell, 2020: 259). So, chiefs must be as aware of the need to identify who to retain as to select whom they wish to dismiss.

Train and develop

This is one of the most under-written areas regarding how Downing Street chiefs undertake political management responsibilities. There is simply not much existing evidence (primary or secondary) and, as discussed later, it is an area ripe for academic research. To that end, it exemplifies the point made earlier regarding how much there is to investigate about the role and how it is conducted.

There is some evidence, however, regarding how chiefs have sought to develop staff skills and promote other advisors up the internal hierarchy. Powell was instrumental in arranging training sessions for shadow cabinet ministers ahead of the 1997 General Election (Riddell, 2019: 46–47). This, of course, does not cover how the Chief *manages* others' training (given that they are not ministers' line-managers). However, it does give a sense of how a leader (Blair) sought to rely upon an aide's (Powell) organisational abilities in establishing processes for addressing perceived deficiencies in a wider team (even if, as Riddell attests, shadow ministers did not generally engage with the process) (Riddell, 2019: 48–49).

Oher chiefs have sought to advance the careers of staff through promotions and similar such incentives. Llewellyn and Kate Fall (Deputy Chief, 2010–2015) identified Oliver Dowden (Political Secretary, a senior aide to the PM, 2010–2015) as someone whose advice and organisational skills they valued (Fall, 2020: 76; 121). Consequently, they promoted him to the post of Deputy Chief in 2012 (held alongside his existing post) (Seldon and Snowdon, 2016: 192). Similarly, Powell recorded how he and Blair were initially unsure of David Miliband as Head of the Downing Street Policy Unit (PU) (the section of the Prime Minister's Office which monitors departmental policy work and proposes alternatives for the PM to pursue in fulfilment of their agenda) (Powell, 2010: 96). Powell and Blair originally regarded Miliband as being too junior and, therefore, designated him as *Acting* Head of the PU (Rawnsley, 2000: 26). After the first year in office, they felt that he had disproved their suspicions and, consequently, Powell promoted Miliband to confirmed Head of the PU (Rawnsley, 2000: 26).

Learn how people work

Different chiefs have approached the role, and how it relates to allocating work amongst staff, in different ways. This has involved not only learning how staff work but has, also, included understanding how the political principal concerned (the PM) themselves works. This offers us insight into how the office should learn to work together and cohere around the PM. Whilst the Chief is not a political manager of the PM, their ability to understand the latter's work patterns bears upon how they then instruct and direct staff. Thus, a chief's operational function in this respect is both to be a conduit for the PM's desire to make their office work for them and, subsequently, learning how best to ensure that staff are able to put this into effect. For instance, Powell recounted how he learnt that Blair liked to use weekends to write long notes on his current thinking and strategic objectives (Rawnsley, 2000: 292). Blair circulated these on Sundays and Powell adopted the practice of using them to inform a Monday meeting of senior advisers (Powell, 2010: 102–103). This was then used to establish the tone and goals for the week ahead, guiding staff in understanding the objectives that they were working towards.

Similarly, Heywood realised in Autumn 2008 that Brown's continued dissatisfaction with his Downing Street operation encompassed a feeling that the physical environment itself (with key staff separated out across a series of offices) did not enable the PM to feel sufficiently connected to advisers (Cockerell, 2021: 251–253). This echoed Powell's observation that the haphazard layout of Downing Street obstructed the efficiency of how the team worked together (Brown, 2019: 14). Heywood had heard Brown talk about how he thought that Michael Bloomberg's (Mayor of New York, 2002–2016) use of an open-plan office allowed for this kind of contact (Heywood, 2021: 245). He worked with Brown to design such a space and, in October 2008, the PM and his most senior advisers (including Heywood) moved into the "horseshoe" (Price, 2010: 433). This was a U-shaped series of interconnected desks (with the PM at one end), located in Number 12 Downing Street, that allowed Brown to be in the same physical space as his staff.

These examples underscore the need for chiefs to be the link between the PM's working practice and that of the wider staff. They must serve as the architect of workplace structures and relationships. Consciousness of different practices can alter and align the wider institution towards both delivering for the PM and their agenda and, as importantly, making the PM themselves feel that this is the case.

Motivate

Burch and Holliday (1999: 35) previously made clear that '…personal chemistry is a crucial factor…' in forming a functional and contented Downing Street staff, particularly due to the frenetic and ever-changing workload. This means that those managing the operation must ensure that they both harmonise the team and, in doing so, motivate them to deliver the PM's priorities. Instructive case studies in this can be found in the joint tenure of Hill and Timothy and the subsequent response to this offered by Barwell.

As Timothy (2020: 8) has acknowledged, he and Hill (as, previously, May's special advisors at the Home Office, 2010–2016) had become used to maintaining '…a tight grip on departmental business…' on May's behalf. They assumed that they could replicate this in Downing Street. However, this did not translate well into Downing Street as it meant that they failed to sufficiently delegate to other advisors and civil servants present, leading to the chiefs being 'overwhelmed' and other staff feeling demoralised (Ross and McTague, 2017: 35). For instance, Hill (who had handled May's media relations at the Home Office) undermined the Downing Street Director of Communications (Katie Perrior) and overruled their decisions, due to her unwillingness to relinquish this responsibility (Ross and McTague, 2017: 35). This eventually led to a demotivated Perrior resigning her post on the eve of the 2017 General Election campaign (Seldon and Newell, 2020: 205). It has since been reported that they had a room set aside, close to May's office, which was nicknamed "the Bollocking Room" (Ross and McTague, 2017: 36). This was regularly used for disciplining staff and became a cause for fear and discomfort.

Closeness to the PM is vital for performing the role of Chief (not least as it means that chiefs can claim to speak with the PM's authority). However, this underscores the need to motivate staff. If a chief fails to behave in a manner which encourages and affirms staff, staff will assume that the PM either approves or is insufficiently able to challenge the chief. Therefore, demotivation becomes an engrained factor and much harder to reverse. This is what had happened by the time that Hill and Timothy resigned (carrying some of the blame for the Conservative Party losing seats at the 2017 General Election), with Seldon and Newell (2020: 190) noting that it left staff assuming that the PM was '…incapable of asserting herself…' against the Chiefs.

Barwell's efforts to remotivate May's staff offer us a contrasting account of the impact chiefs can have in this area. By his own admission, Barwell regarded this as one of the most important and immediate tasks he inherited (Barwell, 2021: 38–47). As mentioned earlier, this began with asking Penn to remain as his deputy (recognising that she held staff's trust and, thus, offered him chance to connect with them) (Barwell, 2021: 23; 38–39). Seldon and Newell (2020: 259) recounted how, in his first week in the post, Barwell gathered together all of those staff who reported to him for a meeting in the Cabinet Room and assured them that he recognised the need for change. Subsequent accounts have suggested that these efforts at reassurance remotivated staff, with the outcome being that there was a greater sense of cohesion within Downing Street (Dale, 2017).

Encourage excellence

In order to encourage excellence, it is apparent that there must be trust within Downing Street. The above-mentioned case studies make clear that trust is an essential factor in motivating staff and, subsequently, facilitating them to carry out their roles. The case study of Ed Llewellyn is instructive, here. Between 2010 and 2015, the Conservative Party was in a governing coalition with the Liberal Democrats. This meant that the political teams of Cameron (Conservative leader) and Nick Clegg (Liberal Democrat leader) had to find ways to work together which both delivered government policy and, also, harmonised two political operations that had previously competed with each other. Jonny Oates was Clegg's Chief of Staff. Llewellyn and Oates established trust early on by admitting that both of their bosses leaked and that they, as chiefs, were there to minimise conflict between Conservative and Liberal Democrat advisors (Oates, 2020: 330). By establishing trust based around an ability to be frank with each other, they attempted to make their relationship cohesive and pragmatic. It was this aspect of Llewellyn's work that led Downing Street insiders to refer to him as the person who did the most to ensure the coalition's survival (Seldon and Snowdon, 2016: 236).

Llewellyn also sought to lead by example, encouraging others to develop their own practice. Fall (who shared an office with Llewellyn) recalls, early on in the government, watching as files piled up on her boss' desk every time that he had big issues to address (Fall, 2020: 81). Eventually, she asked him why she was not also receiving them (having assumed that he was automatically supplied with them by civil servants). He replied that he had only received them because he had explicitly requested them, in order that he could be better-informed (and in order to try to pursue Cameron's desire for a more responsive Civil Service) (Fall, 2020: 81). Fall records that she continued to learn from the Chief's practice in this way (Fall, 2020: 81).

Powell offers a further example of how chiefs can recognise, and address, the need for excellence in practice. By the end of Blair's first term, the PM was expressing frustration in the lack of progress made on public service reforms (Riddell, 2019: 140). Consequently, Heywood (then PPS) suggested to Powell that they create a Delivery Unit (DU), which would focus upon measuring progress against key targets (including cutting crime and hospital waiting times) (Heywood, 2021: 108). Powell advocated for the DU with Blair. He then (successfully) argued that Michael Barber (formerly an advisor to David Blunkett, the then-Education Secretary) should lead it. Over the coming years, the DU became a fixture in a Downing Street operation that sought to better-deliver upon the PM's public service priorities (Barber, 2007: 125). In this way, Powell became a leading internal champion for improving structures and staffing in a way that served the PM's needs.

Conclusions

This chapter has addressed the question of "What operational leadership functions does the Downing Street Chief-of-Staff fulfil and how can observation of these contribute to understandings of political human resources and management?" In doing so, it has systematically worked through the criteria (see Table 3.1) set out by Lees-Marshment. Having explored these criteria, we are now able to conclude whether the analysis conducted offers us insight into the operational leadership functions Lees-Marshment also identified. To recap, these were: design the structure and roles within the office; recruit and line-manage staff; delineate and oversee responsibilities; delegate tasks and work areas and; set the office's tone (2021: 119).

Chiefs are, in general, able to have considerable input into the designing of staffing structures. This is accompanied by an expansive role in the recruitment and management of a large number of staff. This includes when they take over part way through a PM's tenure and inherit existing staff. Additionally, they have shown increasing ability to influence the appointment of civil servants, not just special advisors. This was demonstrated early in the existence of the role (with Powell assuming line-management for the PPS) and continues up to more recent occupants (as with Cummings' role in the replacement of a Cabinet Secretary). Conversely, chiefs' influence here can sometimes be countermanded by unexpected sources (as with Stratton's appointment). It is, thus, not an area over which they have unassailable powers.

Delineation of responsibilities, delegating tasks, and setting an appropriate tone for the workplace all seem to be inter-related. For instance, Timothy and Hill's lack of willingness to trust other staff led to a general air of despondency amongst the wider Downing Street team. Ultimately, this created an extra task for their successor, though this did not distract him from being able to introduce innovations such as the Legislative Affairs team. Llewellyn and Fall's relationship, on the other hand, showed how a chief can choose to lead by example and, in so doing, motivate others to develop their own practice.

There were clearly weaknesses in how chiefs used HR practices. For example, Cummings' use of a private 'blog to seek to recruit 'weirdos', albeit with the legitimate desire of widening Downing Street's skills base, could be seen as seeking work around the existing, accountable, HR structures. Conversely, limits to his influence in this aspect of his work were later apparent when he was essentially cut out of the process regarding Stratton's appointment. This waxing and waning of one chief's influence in recruitment (appropriate or otherwise) highlights the fluidity and inconsistency in how chiefs are involved in HR processes. Likewise, Powell's earlier lack of success in trying to engage staff and shadow ministers with pre-government learning exercises is another example of the limitations the role can face in the HR sphere.

Finally, the Chief's role involves encouraging the wider staff (and PM) to be open to change in how tasks are carried out (especially if the alteration leads to greater delivery). Powell's willingness to become a leading advocate for the Delivery Unit and Heywood's physical rearrangement of the office layout both testify to this.

Thus, even a relatively short analysis such as this one demonstrates the emerging and ongoing operational functions of the Downing Street Chief of Staff within the realm of political HR. Not only have individual chiefs had impacts upon this management area but, collectively, the role itself continues (over a quarter of a century since its creation) to embed itself into the institutional practice of management within Downing Street.

Recommendations for academic research

Given the lack of existing research into the Downing Street Chief of Staff, it is unsurprising that a chapter such as this identifies as many avenues for future investigation as those which it resolves. These include those beyond the parameters of a focus upon political management and HR. However, only those that are relevant to that focus are recounted here.

There is clear potential for further examination of how chiefs train and develop staff. This was the shortest section of this chapter precisely because the relevant accounts regarding this could not be uncovered. It seems likely that this could be better-answered by consideration of a wider qualitative data set. To be precise, it indicates an opportunity for interviews and/or ethnographic methods, so that the practise and reflections of those concerned can be more adequately assessed. Such a data set could, in turn, enhance observations on the other five criteria considered, too. For instance, an interviewee might be asked whether a chief's specific practice *did* lead them to feel motivated. It may also then be possible to determine whether this was the result of an individual chief's style or, conversely, due to a wider culture of encouragement and incentivisation (or the opposite). Additionally, such an approach could be used to deepen understandings of how political managers relate to the leaders whom they serve (for example, expanding knowledge of the role a political manager plays in structuring staffing towards being able to deliver the PM's priorities). These are but some of the possibilities for further academic research, with the opportunity for fruitful lessons regarding both political management theory and the specifics of the empirical case study.

Recommendations for practice

Finally, the case study of the Downing Street Chief of Staff presents ground for practice-focused lessons. The chapter has identified:

1 The need for chiefs to be as aware of which staff they need to retain (as with Barwell and Penn) for their existing relationships with staff and institutional memory, as of those whom they wish to dismiss.
2 A need for chiefs to be conscious of the fact that they are often *the* conduit between a PM's desires and the staff's ability to deliver upon them. Being aware of this is vital, as it provides chiefs with another reason to motivate staff and encourage excellence in working practices. It is frequently

accepted that chiefs speak on the PM's behalf, but it cannot always be assumed that chiefs enjoy trusting or motivational relationships with others.
3 The importance of effective, close-working, relationships between political managers, civil servants and elected leaders.
4 The requirement for chiefs to give greater consideration to their management style. There may be merit in examining whether this could be achieved by subjecting what is becoming a constitutionally significant to parliamentary scrutiny (for instance, through a committee). Additionally, they could perhaps be given a more formal job description against which they are regularly appraised (perhaps drawn from the Code of Conduct for Special Advisors) by this committee. If they felt that it was possible that they would be questioned upon it they might pay more attention and it could render them more accountable for the manner in which they reached decisions over both personnel and internal staffing restructures.

Such innovations will not sound particularly innovative to many outside the world of UK politics. However, they would certainly be a step towards greater accountability for political management decisions taken during the occupation of a role that is now more than a quarter-of-a-century old.

Recommended reading

Barwell, G. (2021). *Chief of Staff: Notes from Downing Street*, London, Atlantic Books.
Brown, J. (2019). *No. 10: The Geography of Power at Downing Street*, London, Haus Publishing.
Fall, K. (2020). *The Gatekeeper: Life at the Heart of No. 10*, London, HarperCollins.
Garnett, M. (2021). *The British Prime Minister in an Age of Upheaval*, Cambridge, Polity Press.
Powell, J. (2010). *The New Machiavelli: How to Wield Power in the Modern World*, London: Bodley Head.

Note

1 More detail on why this was necessary is available in "5. Motivate".

References

Ashcroft, M. (2022). *First Lady: Intrigue at the Court of Carrie and Boris Johnson*, London, Biteback.
Barber, M. (2007). *Instruction to Deliver: Fighting to Transform Britain's Public Services*, York, Methuen.
Barwell, G. (2020). How to run Number 10: An insider's guide. Available at: https://www.spectator.co.uk/article/how-to-run-number-10-an-insider-s-guide. [Accessed on January 03 2023].
Barwell, G. (2021). *Chief of Staff: Notes from Downing Street*, London, Atlantic Books.

BBC (2021). *Transcript Dominic Cummings: The Interview, BBC Two*, London, BBC Press Office.

Bennett, O. (2019). *Michael Gove: A Man in a Hurry*, London, Biteback.

Blair, T. (2010). *A Journey*, London, Random House.

Blick, A. (2004). *People Who Live in the Dark: The History of the Special Adviser in British Politics*, London, Politico.

Brown, J. (2019). *No. 10: The Geography of Power at Downing Street*, London, Haus Publishing.

Burch, M. and I. Holliday (1999). The Prime Minister's and Cabinet Offices: An Executive in All But Name. *Parliamentary Affairs*, 52(1), 32–45.

Cockerell, M. (2011). *The Secret World of Whitehall – Episode 3: The Network* [BBC Four] London, BBC Studios.

Cockerell, M. (2021). *Unmasking Our Leaders: Confessions of a Political Documentary-Maker*, London, Biteback.

Dale, I. (2017). The Top 100 Most Influential People On The Right: Iain Dale's 2017 List. Available at: https://www.lbc.co.uk/radio/presenters/iain-dale/100-most-influential-people-on-right-iain-dale. [Accessed on July 13 2021].

Davis, J. and J. Rentoul (2019). *Heroes or Villains? The Blair Government Reconsidered*, Oxford, Oxford University Press.

Fall, K. (2020). *The Gatekeeper: Life at the Heart of No. 10*, London, HarperCollins.

Garnett, M. (2021). *The British Prime Minister in an Age of Upheaval*, Cambridge, Polity Press.

Gimson, A. (2022). *Boris Johnson: The Rise and Fall of a Troublemaker at Number 10*, London, Simon and Schuster.

Heywood, S. (2021). *What Does Jeremy Think? Jeremy Heywood and the Making of Modern Britain*, London, William Collins.

Lees-Marshment, J. (2021). *Political Management: The Dance of Government and Politics*, Abingdon and New York, Routledge.

McDonald, S. (2022). *Leadership: Lessons from a Life in Diplomacy*, London, Haus Publishing.

Oates, J. (2020). *I Never Promised You a Rose Garden*, London, Biteback.

Payne, S. (2022). *The Fall of Boris Johnson: The Full Story*, London, Macmillan.

Powell, J. (2010). *The New Machiavelli: How to Wield Power in the Modern World*, London, Bodley Head.

Price, L. (2010). *Where Power Lies: Prime Ministers v. the Media*, London and New York, Simon & Schuster.

Rawnsley, A. (2000). *Servants of the People: The Inside Story of New Labour*, London, Penguin Books.

Rhodes, R. A.W. and A. Tiernan (2014). *The Gate Keepers: Lessons from Prime Ministers' Chiefs of Staff*, Melbourne, Melbourne University Press.

Richards, S. (2019). *The Prime Ministers: Reflections on Leadership from Wilson to May*, London, Atlantic Books.

Riddell, P. (2019). *15 Minutes of Power: The Uncertain Life of British Ministers*, London, Profile Books.

Ross, T. and T. McTague (2017). *Betting the House: The Inside Story of the 2017 Election*, London, Biteback.

Seldon, A., J. Meakin and I. Thoms (2021). *The Impossible Office? The History of the British Prime Minister*, Cambridge, Cambridge University Press.

Seldon, A. and R. Newell (2020). *May at 10: The Verdict*, London, Biteback.

Seldon, A. and P. Snowdon (2016). *Cameron at 10: The Verdict*, London, William Collins.

Thomas, A. (2020). The prime minister's chief of staff can restore order to the government. Available at: https://www.instituteforgovernment.org.uk/article/comment/prime-ministers-chief-staff-can-restore-order-government. [Accessed on August 06 2021].

Thomas, A. (2022). Downing Street chief of staff. Available at: https://www.institute-forgovernment.org.uk/explainers/downing-street-chief-staff. [Accessed on February 10 2022].

Timothy, N. (2020). *Remaking One Nation: The Future of Conservatism*, Cambridge, Polity Press.

Weller, P. (2018). *The Prime Minister's Craft: Why Some Succeed and Others Fail in Westminster Systems*, Oxford and New York, Oxford University Press.

Whipple, C. (2017). *The Gatekeepers: How the White House Chiefs of Staff Define Every Presidency*, New York, Crown Publishing Group.

4

DECENTRALIZED CAMPAIGN MANAGEMENT

The Motivations, Training, and Recruitment of Leni Robredo Volunteers during the 2022 Philippine Elections

Jean S. Encinas-Franco and Brandon P. De Luna

Introduction

This book chapter focuses on how to manage volunteers in campaigns, focusing on the political campaign volunteers in the 2022 Leni Robredo campaign in the Philippines. Political campaign volunteers are integral in giving life and vigor in electoral cycles. They are considered political human resources defined as "volunteers, candidates, staff, party leaders, and ministers are recruited and appointed to their role; oriented, trained, and developed for it; and supported and motivated to perform to a high level both individually and within their group and organization" (Lees-Marshment 2021, p. 113). The Robredo campaign witnessed unprecedented volunteerism nationwide, which had not been seen in previous elections. It explores their motivations, training, and recruitment. In particular, the chapter aims to answer the following questions: How was the volunteer-led campaign managed? What were the volunteers' motivations? How were they mobilized and trained?

The chapter is organized into six sections: The first section presents the background of volunteerism in the Robredo campaign, followed by an explanation of the volunteers' motivation. Training of volunteers is discussed in the third part, while the fourth and fifth parts, respectively, discussed resources and mobilization. The third part looks at the training of volunteers, while the fourth and fifth parts examine the resources and forms of mobilization, respectively. The chapter concludes with key recommendations and directions for practitioners and studies on political volunteers.

DOI: 10.4324/9781003260677-4

Key literature

Contextualizing political volunteers in the Global South

Volunteers are "someone who contributes time to helping others with no expectation of pay or material benefit to herself (Wilson and Musick 1999)." They differ from political strategists, campaign staff, and consultants, generally covered by the campaign payroll. Volunteers are often mobilized through grassroots organizations to inform and convert voters within specific locations. However, McKenna and Han (2015) point to the decline of local party organizations, and developments in mass media led to less reliance on political volunteers as a crucial component during elections. Social media became the centerpiece of any relevant electoral campaign, where platforms such as Facebook and TikTok became the main medium of communication for candidates to directly reach out to voters (Papakyriakoupoulos, Naranayan, Tessono, and Kshirsagar 2022). Despite these developments, McKenna and Han (2015, p. 32) argue that the emergence of new media, particularly the internet, could have contributed to the reemergence of old-school community organizing, which was thought to be dismantled by mass media.

For example, both Suaedy (2014) and Herdiansah (2022) observed that the emergence of Joko Widodo as a candidate for the 2012 Jakarta gubernatorial elections and 2019 Indonesian presidential elections led to the rise of unconsolidated and sporadic volunteer networks, which gradually transformed into a critical movement to counter elite politics in Indonesia. These volunteer groups evolved into organizations with strong mass bases, representative social categories, and partisan loyalists to the Widodo administration (Herdiansah 2022). During the 2016 Philippine presidential elections, Duterte's online volunteers were observed to be the main drivers of political and community organizing among overseas Filipino workers in Hongkong and the United Arab Emirates (Aranda 2021). Through social media, Duterte volunteers became instrumental organizers to convince their local communities to support former Davao City Mayor Rodrigo Roa Duterte. These case studies suggest that political volunteers have become alternative sources of political power for candidates to utilize during elections.

These studies differ from political volunteers' traditional roles and scope in Western democracies (McKenna and Han 2015). The crucial role of political volunteers during elections, particularly in developing democracies in the Global South, where political parties are weaker, is to counter the dominance of elites in the electoral process (Herdiansah 2022). Therefore, practitioners and political management scholars need to explore the constraints, opportunities, and lessons learned from these organic volunteer mobilizations to assess their respective impacts on political management research, scholarship, and practice in the future.

This chapter is a case study of political volunteerism in the Robredo campaign. Drawing on participant observations, auto-ethnographic accounts of the authors' experiences during the 2022 elections, media reports, and a few key informant interviews among the leaders of volunteer groups campaigning for Robredo's presidential campaign, the chapter hopes to contribute to the understanding of political volunteerism and management in the Global South. The study is also significant in a country where clientelism, bossism, and electoral machinery are the norm in electing its political leaders (Teehankee and Calimbahin 2015), media reports argue that the emergence of the Robredo people's campaign is a hallmark in mobilizing voters against the traditional methods in electoral politics (Subingsubing and Ramos 2022). Notably, the chapter does not claim to account for all volunteer efforts by Robredo supporters. Instead, it is an initial exploration in an area that is arguably novel in recent Philippine political history.

Leni Robredo, the pink revolution, and bayanihan

Local pundits consider the 2022 national elections in the Philippines one of the country's most crucial. Not only was it the first election held during a pandemic, it was also the election that witnessed dictator Ferdinand Marcos' son's candidacy to the highest post in the land. What was at stake was more than 60 million votes in a nationwide election simultaneously held with local elections. During this election cycle, the public witnessed the emergence of more than 2 million volunteers mobilizing for the presidential campaign of former Vice President Leni Gerona Robredo, an independent candidate who is also the chairperson of the Liberal Party of the Philippines (Wee 2022). During the elections, however, Robredo ran as an independent to veer away from the public backlash against the Liberal Party, which has come to be associated with elitist governance, resulting in the loss of its senatorial candidates in the 2019 elections.

On 7 October 2021, then-Vice President Leni Robredo declared her candidacy for Philippine President amid vocal calls from various socio-civic organizations. Following her announcement, multiple informal volunteer groups were organized on social media and on the ground to prepare for the official campaign period, which began in February 2022.

Since February 2022, around 2.2 million political volunteers, mostly youth and first-time voters, have mobilized and organized multiple house-to-house campaigns, sorties, and events culminating in major street parties across strategic locations in the Philippines (Cabato 2022). The Robredo political volunteers are credited with significantly increasing her numbers in survey polls from 6% in October 2021 to 24% in April 2022 (Pulse Asia 2022). While Robredo eventually lost in the 2022 elections with only 16 million votes compared to Marcos Jr.'s 31 million, the volunteer-driven campaign was never before seen in Philippine elections. If any, it demonstrated the emergence of resistance to the authoritarian tendencies of Duterte and Marcos, Jr., and collective advocacy for good governance, which Robredo is perceived to exemplify.

The concept and practice of volunteerism are not new to Filipinos. For this reason, the outpouring of volunteerism for Robredo can be likened to an indigenous form called *bayanihan,* a Filipino word that means "to commune" (Hagman 2011). *Bayanihan* is an indigenous form of volunteerism in the Philippines. Virola, Ilarina, Reyes, and Buenaventura (2010, p. 5) pointed out that volunteerism in the Philippines evolved from "its historical and cultural tradition of sharing." From a foreign concept introduced by Catholicism, Virola, Ilarina, Reyes, and Buenaventura (citing Aguiling-Dalisay, Navarro, and Yacat 2004) argued that Filipino volunteerism was integrated with indigenous concepts such as *bayanihan* (mutual assistance); *damayan* (assistance in times of crisis); *kawanggawa* (charity or philanthropy); *pahinungod* (self-sacrifice) and *bahaginan* (sharing).

Interestingly, the outpouring of organic support and volunteerism in Robredo's campaign came on the heels of the COVID-19 pandemic, which witnessed yet another unprecedented call for all forms of donations in kind and cash. For example, some groups launched a donation drive for health workers without personal protective equipment (PPE). Others gave financial assistance to transport workers who lost their livelihood due to the excessive lockdowns imposed by President Duterte's militarized pandemic response. But the one that received the most media and public attention was the community pantries set up in 2021. These involved soliciting food items (i.e., bread, vegetables, rice) from donors so that the poor and those who lost jobs in the community could avail of them. Therefore, arguing that these activities may have shaped Robredo's supporters is not farfetched.

When such *bayanihan* spirit translates into electoral support, it runs counter to vote-buying that has characterized much of the history of Philippine elections. For this reason, the strong support of volunteers for Robredo surprised her and even her opponents. In an interview, she explained that "I think I just became the symbol,"… "It's like the time was right. The people are now ready. It's like they were full of bottled-up emotions" (Cepeda 2022). She calls it the "pink revolution" or pink wave, about her campaign color and the wave-like drone scenes of massive crowds during her jampacked rallies. The volunteer network is paralleled by the formal political network comprising Liberal Party stalwarts, the 1Sambayan (a group of politicians and civil society groups who publicly selected Robredo as the candidate they will support), and a few regional politicians. However, the volunteer network had sometimes outpaced the formal part of the campaign and had been said to have swayed some politicians to Robredo's side at the last minute.

The political volunteer arm of Leni Robredo can be divided either into formalized political networks or decentralized volunteer movements (De Luna 2022). Decentralized volunteers are groups or individuals who independently created their network to volunteer for the campaign of former Vice President Robredo. While some volunteer groups come from the so-called usual suspects such as church and laymen leaders, civil society groups, and people's organizations, veterans of the parliament of the streets which formed the anti-Marcos movements in the 1970s and 80s, new groups and networks emerged that have not been witnessed in the country's political history since the EDSA Revolution that ousted Marcos, Sr. Suddenly, groups such as Doctors for Leni, Mumshies (Mothers) for Leni, Millennials for Leni Robredo, Mga Gwapo for Leni (Handsome Men for Leni), Teachers for Leni, Farmers for Leni, sprung up, fueled by social media applications such as Tiktok, Facebook, and Twitter. Others were part of groups who convinced Robredo to run when the latter was still reluctant to join the race. Even volunteer groups who used to shy away from politics, such as former diplomats and celebrities, joined the fray (Esguerra 2022). If, in the past, celebrities were paid as endorsers to boost politicians' campaigns (Centeno 2015), this time, they sang, danced, and did house-to-house campaigns for Robredo. Even Filipinos overseas, who can vote, mounted volunteer groups organizing gatherings, donation drive, and even Zumba sessions. A relatively unknown singer catapulted to national fame when she composed a campaign song that became the Robredo campaign's anthem. The song was reportedly played on Spotify nearly four million times (Gomez 2022). Moreover, the presence of volunteers from all walks of life and ordinary people was also a way to deflect criticisms that Robredo and her political slate are elitists whose interests are merely for the wealthy.

Prevent Marcoses' return, democratic and human rights reforms: volunteers' key motivation

Political pundits and local and international media consider the 2022 elections consequential for two reasons. The first is the impending return of the Marcoses to the country's highest political office, thereby threatening the democratic gains of the 1986 People Power Revolution that ousted Marcos, Sr. Marcos, Jr.'s campaign narrative of false nostalgia for his father's reign shocked those who could not believe that Filipinos seem to have forgotten Marcoses' notorious past of profligacy, corruption, and human rights violations. It is branded as false nostalgia due to accusations that the Marcos, Jr. campaign employed disinformation, depicting the Marcos past as "benign," "stable," and an "era of prosperity" for the country. The second reason is that many see the elections as a venue to hold President Rodrigo Duterte's human rights violations and his bungling of the COVID response. The two reasons are not necessarily unrelated because Sara Duterte, Duterte's daughter, is on the ballot as Marcos, Jr.'s vice presidential candidate. In other words, if both win the elections, the country's democratic backsliding would have been ensured. For these reasons, the stakes are arguably clear for Robredo supporters. In a country comprising 85% Catholics, some frame their support as a moral choice since what is at stake are supposedly the values held dear by Filipinos: honesty and truthfulness, life-affirming, etc., which are closely linked with Robredo's commitment to good governance, ethical leadership, and a continuation of the democratic and human rights-based reforms in the Philippines (De Luna 2022).

These values are what a millennial lawyer and a Robredo supporter described, "We're fighting against the current status quo of the Philippines, which is rampant corruption, red tape, [patronage politics] and it's particularly the brand of Marcos politics that we're trying to resist" (Esguerra 2022). She did not mind even if she and her friends hopped on buses to talk about Robredo and her key message, Sa Gobyernong Tapat, Angat Buhay ang Lahat (An Honest Government Yields Prosperity for All).

A young Robredo volunteer, for example, states, "It doesn't feel wrong now. There are people who feel like volunteering revolves around a particular candidate. For me, when I volunteered, it felt as if I was serving the country. So, it doesn't feel wrong that I volunteered. I was happy even though it was tiring" (Alberto 2022). Meanwhile, a group of doctors who call themselves Robredocs asserted the salience of what is at stake in the elections. "We are against any false news. For once, there is a deserving candidate that needs our support. Join us in a once-in-a-lifetime fight." For this reason, it is easy for the volunteers to understand their role and what they can bring to the campaign: "So, that's the power of volunteerism, you need not align or coordinate with the main campaign, for as long as you believe in the cause of the candidate" (Interview, 1 February 2023). Even some people from the Ilocos region, where the Marcoses come from, could transcend their ethnolinguistic affiliation. One volunteer leader in the area says, "They believe that that is not the right manner to govern a country. They know what to push" (Interview, 31 January 2023).

The above discussion suggests that there is a core message in the Robredo campaign that strikes at the heart of Filipinos across generations and classes and sectors. Unsurprisingly, organic support for the campaign has mushroomed without much prodding and motivation from the official campaign. Instead of the latter providing motivation, the massive volunteerism provided a much-needed lifeline in an otherwise poorly funded candidacy with little preparation due to Robredo's belated announcement of running.

Methodology

This chapter is a case study of political volunteerism in the Robredo campaign. Drawing on participant observations, online archival research, media reports, and a few key informant interviews among the leaders of volunteer groups campaigning for Robredo's presidential campaign to explore the volunteer movements' motivations, characteristics, training, and recruitment practices.

Research findings

Training on messaging, Peoples' Council, and digital app

To control the sporadic and decentralized nature of the volunteer groups that mushroomed nationwide, the Robredo campaign held message training, established the Peoples' Council, and a digital application that volunteers and supporters could download for free.

As mentioned earlier, the Robredo team was surprised by the outpouring of volunteer groups around the country and their activities generated on social media. Robredo's campaign team need not direct the message daily nor incentivize them. It was the other way around. The campaign had to make adjustments and coordinate the influx of volunteers. By November 2021, the Robredo campaign had to establish the national Robredo Peoples Council (RPC) to coordinate volunteer efforts in the entire country. The Council is composed of representatives from grassroots movements, professionals, LGBTQIA, and academics. Provincial RPCs also took charge of local efforts, handed out campaign materials, and organized political sorties that Robredo and her team will attend. The Council provided a critical coordinating mechanism to manage donations and the distribution of campaign materials that were either donated by volunteers themselves, which they bought from private merchandisers or those that were provided by the official campaign. During big provincial sorties, they take charge of the program, performances, stage design, security, and mobilizing supporters to attend. These sorties were highly praised for the stage design, provincial identity showcase, and big-named celebrities' performances. This is a far cry from previous elections in which performances were normally paid and the stage design was not taken seriously. Soon, each RPC from provinces and cities would mount a healthy competition on social media as to which sortie was the most attended, most memorable, and had the most intricate stage design. The stage entrance of Robredo and his vice presidential running mate, Francis Pangilinan, was also much awaited as it normally displays products and goods associated with the provincial venue. The massive attendance in the Robredo rallies was a highlight of the campaign, noticed even by the international media, and is often compared to the Marcos, Jr. rallies which had poor attendance coupled with media reports of paid attendees.

Nonetheless, because of the issues surrounding the elections, heated arguments on social media between Marcos, Jr. supporters and Robredo volunteers most often result in personal attacks and classist remarks. In particular, accusations that Marcos, Jr. did not finish college and, therefore incompetent and unfit to be the country's leader, struck a chord among people experiencing poverty who could not afford higher education. Similarly, when pro-Marcos supporters accused Robredo supporters of being paid to attend rallies, some had to brag about their wealth to prove they could not be bought. This situation heightened accusations that Robredo, her slate, and her supporters were elitists, an image further amplified by Marcos, Jr.'s troll army. This is the case even though Robredo herself is middle-class and would often be seen riding a bus to her hometown even when she was vice president. Nonetheless, to a certain extent, this is the downside of a decentralized volunteer network, in which members, on the one hand, have a sense of ownership of their strategies, but on the other hand, they are untethered to the messaging from the official campaign.

To counter the trend in messaging, Robredo and her official team had to strategize. Therefore, during the launching of the Robredo People's Council, Robredo had to make this clear: Be careful in your words, always speak the truth. Defend the truth. Do not say anything that would hurt your fellow Filipino… And always choose to love. Because communication should be used for us to understand each other" (Lalu 2021). For this reason, training on messaging was focused on how to counter the trolls without necessarily earning the ire of people who can still be converted to support Leni. Moreover, when the house-to-house campaign started around February 2022, the official campaign team also initiated training on how to talk to ordinary people. However, it was unclear if some of these trainings were implemented by the official Robredo team or on their own by the volunteer groups. These were a mix of live zoom training and video materials.

At the same time, when Marcos, Jr.'s poll numbers were way higher than Robredo's despite accusations of disinformation, the training of digital warriors began. What these digital warriors did was to identify social media accounts linked to Marcos, Jr.'s camp that disseminate disinformation and report to respective social media companies. Some also identified fake news articles, reminded people they are fake news, and asked social media companies to take them down. Others, on the other hand, expose troll accounts and inform the public. The training was done under the auspices of the official campaign, but some tech-savvy volunteers did it on their own. The idea of digital warriors was first articulated by a Supreme Court Justice who was a key Robredo ally. According to him, this was one way the Robredo camp could combat paid troll farms fueled by Marcos, Jr.'s huge campaign funds.

However, when the campaign shifted to house-to-house visits during the elections, training on how to approach people was also done, with how-to videos disseminated among volunteers. Later, all the training videos, campaign materials, shirt designs, and how to mobilize people and initiate activities were put together in the Leni App. The idea is to generate materials for volunteers to print or make shirts. The app also contains legal issues surrounding campaign rules in the Philippines so that volunteers can spot illegal campaign strategies and posters and undertake their activities free from legal troubles. The app also guides those who wish to volunteer to be poll watchers. In other words, the app became a one-stop shop for everything related to the campaign. The Leni App was downloadable via mobile phones and laptops.

Because of the breadth and scope of Robredo volunteers, some groups had to conduct their training or need not train at all because their contribution to the campaign is tied to their profession or identity. For instance, a volunteer group called itself "Mga Gwapo for Leni" (Handsome Men for Leni) had a one-of-a-kind training for their house-to-house campaign. Because their volunteers were good-looking young men, they were trained to be like celebrities who must be oblivious to public attention. The group's leader narrated that,

> I think the only training we gave was to be very patient. Because we went to one rally in Cavite, when we got off the bus, we literally could not walk because of the sheer volume of people who mobbed us. So we had to train them, to be extra patient. During the training, we told them, "Oh, indeed you are volunteers, but you have to accept the fact that when you get off the bus during the campaign, you have to act like celebrities, so you have to be patient with picture-taking, and going around. But the volunteers are in fact motivated by this. They even joined the sorties because they like to be seen and treated as celebrities.
>
> *(Interview, 1 February 2023)*

On the part of Doctors for Leni, they also need not be trained because their main activity during the campaign is to handle the medical emergency booth during campaign sorties and rallies. Some carried out medical mission activities in various provinces. This is the same case for Lawyers for Leni of which some of the members volunteer to be the campaign team's legal counsel during the canvassing in key cities and provinces.

According to the official Robredo campaign volunteer guide, the currency of its movement is trust; its machinery is the volunteers. Thus, the volunteers are expected to be open-minded, helpful, understanding, and loving to others. This is in line with the official campaign's radical love strategy during the elections.

However, the Robredo official campaign had to respond to the elitist accusations against them by asking volunteers to refrain from classist attacks and controlling the messaging via the Leni app and house-to-house campaign training. But due to the wide differences among the group of volunteers, some had to devise their unique training, while others just had to offer their services for free.

"Ambag" (contribution): resources and networks

One of the most remarkable aspects of the Leni Robredo political volunteer movement is its insistence on not expecting any reward or payment in return for their services, including prominent celebrities. This is amid a stronger political campaign by her erstwhile rival, incumbent president Ferdinand R. Marcos Jr, who was able to catapult to the Presidency with 31 million voters. Local pundits credit the Robredo political volunteer movement as the first in Philippine electoral history, citing its organic growth and movement to convince multiple voter segments across the country.

During President Rodrigo Duterte's administration, and especially at the onset of the pandemic, pro-Duterte netizens would criticize those expressing negative views about Duterte's response to the pandemic and ask them about their "ambag" or contribution to society. They argued that they should not criticize the government so much if they have not contributed much to society. As if in response to this, donations for PPEs, for people who lost their jobs, and food pantries were initiated. Arguably, this may have set the tone for volunteerism during the Robredo campaign.

The "ambag" they shared varied: designing Robredo campaign materials, painting Robredo murals in allowable spaces, donating funds for other volunteer groups without money to spare for house-to-house campaigns, and even putting out advertisements for the campaign. One volunteer group narrated,

> Yes, we needed to put out money. We ran some ads on Facebook to put up the events we will be in, sa Twitter, we never advertised because we were very popular on Twitter. We almost did a lot of content for Instagram and TikTok, but due to limited resources, we just stayed on Facebook and on Twitter. Although we did attempt to open up an Instagram account and a Tiktok account, we didn't have all the money, all the resources, we agreed to just focus on two platforms.
>
> *(Interview, 1 February 2023)*

The group also created campaign materials: "Because we are in the creative industry, we asked a volunteer friend to design our banners. but even the materials we were producing, ...we did not sell, we produced the design, and we sent it nationwide. Then it is up to the others to reproduce them" (Interview, 1 February 2023).

For volunteers with close ties to the formal campaign, resources were combined from the formal campaign and volunteers. For example, an active volunteer in Ilocos Sur transformed her family's house which used to be a bed and breakfast hotel, into a headquarters for volunteers. She discussed,

> We raised our funds but there are those coming from the Robredo Peoples' Council. In the beginning, there were also fundraising dinners organized by 1Sambayan.
>
> *(Interview, 31 January 2023)*

But because they are volunteers, time was their utmost contribution as volunteers. This situation is especially challenging for students. In a media interview, a student volunteer remarked, "I can say that time management is one [challenge]. We are students while some are working, and volunteer work takes a toll on our time. There are times that we are attending classes and/or taking our quizzes or exams, at the volunteer center, some are attending their classes during events or house-to-house campaigns" (Alberto 2022). For others, they had to work overtime since they have a limited number of people: "Really, the main currency in volunteerism is your time and effort. If you're willing to do it. When we were doing ours, we were working during the daytime, and checking all engagement until early in the morning" (Interview, 1 February 2023).

From these forms of volunteerism discussed above, it is not farfetched to say that there are two types of volunteers in the campaign: those who had ties to the official or formal campaign and those that had nothing to do with them. Because the campaign period is limited and knowing that they have to catch up with the electoral poll lead of Marcos, Jr., everyone did their fair share in volunteerism with or without the assistance of the formal campaign.

However, the upside is that volunteerism brings a sense of ownership to the campaign. They are motivated that they would use their time, talents, and resources. However, they could only do so much because they are using their own time and resources. The other downside is that their independence allows volunteers to figure out on their own what message to bring in the campaign, even with the Leni app, which was supposed to curate and unify the messaging.

> No, I think that was our strength, we were purely volunteers. Definitely they know us because the official social media teams were reaching out to us. Sometimes we were helping them spread information about events. But we were never directed by the main campaign, they've allowed us to be independent. That's why when sometimes it's not politically savvy, and the way we communicate is not formal, that's okay because we were never under any official political organization.
>
> *(Interview, 1 February 2023)*

Recruitment and mobilization of volunteers

The recruitment and mobilization of volunteers discussed in this section are two types: those who are purely independent of the official campaign, and those that had ties to them. The following are two vignettes describing how two Robredo volunteer groups were established.

Ilocos Sur for Leni Robredo: there is no Solid North

One of the bases of the Marcos campaign is what local pundits call the "Solid North," a regional bloc of the northern provinces in the Ilocos Region, Cordillera Administrative Region, and the Cagayan Valley (Pawilen 2021). According to latest data from the Commission on Elections, it was found that 89.23% of all election returns in Ilocos Region, 90.74% in Cagayan Region, and 91.37% in the Cordilleras were all for Marcos if he was head-to-head against Robredo (Cimatu 2022). Ethnolinguistic affinity to the Marcoses, a prominent Ilocano political family, could have been a factor in the strength of this provincial bloc. Thus, the Ilocos Region, the home of the Marcoses, is the heartland of its political power. The Marcos camp strengthened their grip on the region winning the governorship, congressional and mayoral elections, respectively (Adriano 2022).

During the 2022 national elections, Robredo received 15,643 votes in Ilocos Sur, a significantly better result than in Ilocos Norte where she only garnered 10,043 votes. It is noteworthy that Robredo also received 2,000 more votes in Ilocos Sur compared to her performance in the 2016 elections, indicating increased support for her despite the province being considered a stronghold of the Marcos family.

The Ilocos Sur volunteer groups were directly aligned with the national campaign. One of their leaders was a former public official with direct ties to non-government organizations closely allied with the formal campaign. The leader, who was interviewed for this chapter, offered her ancestral home as the campaign headquarters, which used to be a bed and breakfast place in the region. During small Zoom meetings with 1Sambayan, a broad coalition of opposition groups allied with Robredo, she already volunteered to be one of the leaders in the region, even before Robredo's candidacy was announced. During these meetings, she met former government officials, NGO leaders, and party-list representatives that would later declare support for Robredo. Later on, she explained that the volunteer groups in Ilocos Sur were organized under the umbrella of the Ilocos Sur Peoples' Council, the regional arm of the Robredo Peoples' Council (Interview, 31 January 2023).

While the presence of Ilocos Sur volunteer groups was extensively covered by the media, thereby giving credence to the, "There is no Solid North" slogan of the Robredo campaign, there were big challenges that the groups had to hurdle. Because incumbent politicians were erstwhile Marcos allies, it was difficult to know which were the real supporters. Some prominent people in the area would attend meetings but will be absent in future ones because someone already talked to them. Even if there was money from the formal campaign to pay for poll watchers on election day, it was also challenging because they did not know whether people were just there for the money. She narrated that, "You do not know whether the pollwatcher you recruited was committed because, at the last minute, we were pressed for time" (Interview, 31 January 2023).

There were also harassments, heckling during public activities, and the so-called "silent" supporters. Some people would not come out because they would be ridiculed by relatives and friends staunchly loyal to the Marcoses. Others fear violence from pro-Marcos political families that have ruled the province for decades. This scenario made it even more difficult to mobilize more volunteers.

Handsome Men for Leni

The group independently created their volunteer network by thinking of a fun name, indicating that some groups have already started calling themselves based on their profession, such as Lawyers for Leni or Doctors for Leni. The founders thought of basing their group name not on one's professional identity but on looks, knowing fully well that this would generate curiosity and fun for netizens. So they thought of the name Mga Gwapo for Leni (Handsome Men for Leni).

> So, we released it, and in one week we were Twitter trending already, Twitter and Facebook trending. And then, within a few days, actually, within a few weeks, we crafted over 111 sub-groups that were formed following our example, such as, Coffee Lovers for Leni, or "Pet Lovers for Leni.
>
> *(Interview, 1 February 2023)*

Their name and social media accounts became viral that even celebrities joined. However, when the house-to-house campaign started, they had to recruit genuinely handsome volunteers to attract people. They were the front liners who would also be present during campaign rallies and hand out campaign materials. It became such a hit that people would swarm them like celebrities. They also did not find it hard to recruit volunteers since their recruits would like to be treated as celebrities and have fun. Soon after, there were groups approaching them that would like to establish other chapters in the Philippines and even abroad. However, their limited resources and time prevented them from becoming a much bigger volunteer group.

> One lesson learned is that if we were ready for mobilization, we would've been bigger and more organized nationwide but we're all Manila-based. The good thing was that we were able to use the digital means to communicate with them and give them the liberty to mobilize on their own.
>
> *(Interview, 1 February 2023)*

They also had to treat all members as volunteers knowing that everyone is using their talents, resources, and time. "Another learning is that in a volunteer organization, you cannot really mandate or put a very tight hierarchy 'cause everyone's a volunteer, you have to learn to engage where everyone's on equal footing'" (Interview, 1 February 2023).

Moreover, they also did not have a long-term strategy because they were reliant on reading online strategy so they can adapt. Nevertheless, they see their independence from the official campaign as a "strength" since they can do what they want and disseminate messages that they want.

From the discussion, it can be gleaned that the two forms of volunteer groups in the Robredo campaign each had their strengths and weaknesses which informed how they recruited and mobilized volunteers.

Conclusion

Overall, this chapter has endeavored to show whether political volunteers were managed or not managed at all, their limits, and possibilities. It also established indigenous origins of volunteerism in the Philippines which were transferred in the campaign arena. Since the Robredo campaign had an overarching and powerful message, it did not train volunteers on the substance of their narrative. However, the key challenge is how to unify messaging, consolidate donors and campaign materials, and ways to respond to Marcos, Jr.'s troll army and genuine supporters. Hence, the official campaign had to manage it by creating mechanisms such as the Robredo Peoples' Council and the Leni App. While on the one hand, independent volunteers have ownership of their cause since they are using their funds, it can also be a limitation in recruitment and mobilizing. Moreover, because the volunteers are not paid, most were juggling their time between volunteering and other activities such as school and work. Furthermore, because it is not really "work" for some, it is easy to give up or stop participating if there are hurdles along the way or fear of violence and harassment.

The Robredo campaign provides a good case for exploring genuine volunteerism in the Philippines—a country renowned for weak political parties and vote-buying during elections. However, it is precisely the lack of strong and institutionalized political parties that made it difficult for volunteers to be managed by the Robredo campaign. Had a prior playbook existed from political parties, it would have provided a script for political management and handling the influx of volunteers.

Recommendations for research

For academic research, the following areas may be explored:

- Comparative analysis of political management of volunteers in Global South countries
- Examine the indigenous origins of volunteerism and how this can be used in managing political volunteers.
- Investigate how volunteer groups can be a force for political reforms in countries with weak democratic institutions

Recommendations for practice

The following are directions for practitioners that they may wish to take:

- Institute a core of professional political managers in the Philippines in the lead up to strengthening political parties.
- Devise ways to compensate volunteer groups in kind or cash (i.e., practicum units for student volunteers, allowances for transportation, mobile phone credit for others)
- Establish mechanisms to control volunteers (for messaging and/or donation). This must come one or two years before the campaign.

Recommended Readings

McKenna, Elizabeth, and Hahrie Han. 2014. *Groundbreakers: How Obama's 2.2 Million Volunteers Transformed Campaigning in America*. Oxford University Press.

Callahan, William A. 2018. *Pollwatching, Elections and Civil Society in Southeast Asia*. Routledge.

Hara, Tamiki. 2019. "Defeating a Political Dynasty: Local Progressive Politics through People Power Volunteers for Reform and Bottom-up Budgeting Projects in Siquijor, Philippines." *Southeast Asian Studies* 8 (3): 413–439.

Lees-Marshment, Jennifer, and Robin T. Pettitt. 2014. "Mobilising Volunteer Activists in Political Parties: the View from Central Office." *Contemporary Politics* 20 (2): 246–260.

Teehankee, Julio. 2017. "Electoral Campaigning in the Philippines." In *Election Campaigning in East and Southeast Asia*, pp. 79–101. Routledge.

References

Adriano, Leilanie. 2022. "Marcoses, Singsons maintain a grip on bailiwicks in Ilocos." *Philippine News Agency.* May 11, 2022. https://www.pna.gov.ph/articles/1174171.

Aguiling-Dalisay, Grace, Jay Yacat, and Atoy Navarro. 2004. "Extending the self: Volunteering as pakikipagkapwa." Quezon City: University of the Philippines Center for Leadership, Citizenship and Democracy.

Alberto, Mary Antonie Joan. 2022. "Defying the Odds: How Youth Volunteers Conquered Campaign Challenges." Los Baños Times. July 8, 2022. https://lbtimes.ph/2022/07/08/defying-the-odds-how-youth-volunteers-conquered-election-challenges/.

Antonio, Raymund. 2022. "Leni App Launched for Robredo's Volunteer-Driven Campaign." Manila Bulletin. February 27, 2022. http://mb.com.ph/2022/02/27/leni-app-launched-for-robredos-volunteer-driven-campaign/.

Aranda, Danna. 2021. "Die-Hard Supporters": Overseas Filipino Workers' Online Grassroots Campaign for Duterte in the 2016 Philippines Elections. *Cornell International Affairs Review* 14 (2): 86–118. https://doi.org/10.37513/ciar.v14i2.618.

Cabato, Regine. 2022. "In the Philippines, Grass-Roots Campaign Takes on the Marcos Juggernaut." *Washington Post*, May 6, 2022. https://www.washingtonpost.com/world/2022/05/06/philippines-election-leni-robredo-marcos/.

Calleja, Joseph Peter. 2022. "Bishop Praises Doctors' Support for Philippine Candidate—UCA News." Ucanews.com. January 5, 2022. https://www.ucanews.com/news/bishop-praises-doctors-support-for-philippine-candidate/95598

Centeno, Dave De Guzman. 2015. "Constructing Celebrities as Political Endorsers: Parasocial Acts, Cultural Power, and Cultural Capital." *Philippine Political Science Journal* 36 (2): 209–32. https://doi.org/10.1080/01154451.2015.1084746.

Cepeda, Mara. 2022. "'I just became the symbol': Robredo says people raring for change sparked pink wave." RAPPLER. April 20, 2022. https://www.rappler.com/nation/elections/robredo-symbol-people-raring-for-change-sparked-pink-wave-maria-ressa-interviews/

Gomez, Jim. 2022. "Philippine Vote: Volunteers Back Reformer vs. Dictator's Son." AP NEWS. May 2, 2022. https://apnews.com/article/entertainment-elections-campaigns-presidential-philippines-2a311393fa1f492835ce20b2031bf36d.

Cimatu, Frank. 2022. "Solid North 'Bus' Zooms on as Political Juggernaut." RAPPLER. June 25, 2022. https://www.rappler.com/nation/elections/solid-north-bus-zooms-political-juggernaut-2022-part-1/.

De Luna, Brandon. "Political volunteers as campaign surrogates: Understanding the role of female UP Diliman student campaign volunteers as surrogates of the Leni Robredo 2022 presidential campaign." (unpublished manuscript, 2022), typescript.

Esguerra, Anthony. 2022. "'Our Generation's Fight': Robredo's Campaign to Stop Marcos Jr." AL JAZEERA. May 7, 2022. https://www.aljazeera.com/news/2022/5/7/our-generations-fight-the-robredo-campaign-to-stop-marcos-jr?fbclid=IwAR0TwOTZIzB2Uq-AJBHCIqiaOMRbwgQ7OGYxI0mivCOyT03wGVFz-66KAMXs.

Hagman, Mimmi Viviana Clase. 2011. *Impact of Youth Volunteering in the Philippines.* Sweden: International Cultural Youth Exchange.

Herdiansah, Ari Ganjar. 2022. "Political Participation Convergence in Indonesia: A Study of Partisan Volunteers in the 2019 Election." *Jurnal Politik* 4 (2): 263. https://scholarhub.ui.ac.id/cgi/viewcontent.cgi?article=1046&context=politik.

Lees-Marshment, Jennifer. 2021. *Political Management: The Dance of Government and Politics*. London: New York Routledge.

McKenna, Elizabeth, and Hahrie Han. 2015. *Groundbreakers: How Obama's 2.2 Million Volunteers Transformed Campaigning in America*. Erscheinungsort Nicht Ermittelbar: Oxford University Press - Books Distribution Services.

Lalu, Gabriel Pabico. 2021. "Robredo Says People's Council Being Created to Unify Different Grassroots Campaigns." INQUIRER.net. November 9, 2021. https://newsinfo.inquirer.net/1512411/robredo-says-peoples-council-being-created-to-unify-different-grassroots-campaigns.

Papakyriakopoulos, Orestis, Christelle Tessono, Arvind Narayanan, and Mihir Kshirsagar. 2022. "How Algorithms Shape the Distribution of Political Advertising: Case Studies of Facebook, Google, and TikTok." arXiv preprint arXiv:2206.04720.

Pawilen, Reidan M. 2021. "The Solid North Myth: an Investigation on the Status of Dissent and Human Rights during the Marcos Regime in Regions 1 and 2, 1969–1986". *Journal Article*. 3918. https://www.ukdr.uplb.edu.ph/journal-articles/3918.

Pulse Asia. 2022. "April 2022 Nationwide Survey on the May 2022 Elections." Pulse Asia Research Inc. https://pulseasia.ph/updates/april-2022-nationwide-survey-on-the-may-2022-elections/.

Subingsubing, Krixia, and Marlon Ramos. 2022. "Robredo: Rare Force and Flair of 'a People's Campaign.'" INQUIRER.net. May 7, 2022. https://newsinfo.inquirer.net/1593333/robredo-rareforce-and-flair-of-a-peoples-campaign.

Suaedy, Ahmad. 2014. "The Role of Volunteers and Political Participation in the 2012 Jakarta Gubernatorial Election." *Journal of Current Southeast Asian Affairs* 33 (1): 111–38. https://doi.org/10.1177/186810341403300106.

Teehankee, Julio C., and Cleo Anne A. Calimbahin. 2015. *Patronage Democracy in the Philippines: Clans, Clients, and Competition in Local Elections*. Bughaw.

Virola, Romulo A., Vivian R. Ilarina, Christopher M. Reyes, and Corazon R. Buenaventura. 2010. "Volunteerism in the Philippines: Dead or alive? On measuring the economic contribution of volunteer work." In *11th National Convention on Statistics*, pp. 4–5.

Wee, S.-L. (2022, May 1). "We Want a Change": In the Philippines, Young People Aim to Upend an Election. *The New York Times*. https://www.nytimes.com/2022/05/01/world/asia/philippines-election-marcos-robredo.html

Wilson, John, and Marc Musick. 1999. "The Effects of Volunteering on the Volunteer." *Law and Contemporary Problems* 62 (4): 141. https://doi.org/10.2307/1192270.

5

THE PROBLEMATIC WORKPLACE CONDITIONS FACING POLITICAL STAFFERS IN CANADA AND THE US

Simon Vodrey

Introduction

The practitioners involved in leading political management activity are crucially important to its nature and effectiveness; yet there is a dearth of traditional human resources practices and training. Additionally, many practitioners in the political management profession come from traditional business backgrounds and therefore, while political and business management are indeed separate entities, the personnel who work in both universes often overlap. This chapter examines how political management can be characterized by a style of management that is dictated by an environment demonstrating great career instability, little institutional knowledge/memory due to high staff turnover, and little money to be made — especially in the Canadian political system given its stricter political fundraising requirements and less frequent electoral contests. It explores three questions: First, to what extent can political management be characterized by a style of management where there is great career instability? Second, to what extent can political management be characterized by a style of management where there is little institutional knowledge/memory due to high staff turnover? Third, to what extent does financial insecurity permeate the practice of political management?

Key literature

The existing literature on the largely unexplored topic of political management correctly points out that political management is not the same thing as business management and that, therefore, business management theories and training are insufficient for wholesale application to the practice of political management

DOI: 10.4324/9781003260677-5

(see Dolan, 2000; Gilley, 2006; Bourgault, 2007; Craft & Howlett, 2012). Yet, it is valuable to apply and adapt literature on business management, HR theory, and public management to politics to inform our analysis of political management. This chapter draws on literature associated with the subjects being examined in the research questions: career instability, institutional knowledge/ memory and its relationship with staff turnover, and financial insecurity.

Career instability has long been a defining feature of life in the political management profession. Much of this stems from the fact that the work of a political practitioner — as an intern, a chief of staff or a principal secretary — is precarious, fast-paced, unforgiving, and lacking predictability at the best of times. The work is all-consuming, the expectations and the stakes are high, and there is very little traditional training to ensure that the political practitioner truly knows how to "do their job" (Agere, 2000; Kaid, 2009; Nelson, 2009). In addition, there are very few safety nets or employment protections for individuals in this line of work (Eichbaum & Shaw, 2011; Lees-Marshment, 2020). Even worse, the argument could be made that politics is becoming more polarized, visceral and unpredictable with each passing election cycle and that this trajectory only compounds the career instability which is considered typical among political management personnel.

An important consequence of the career instability associated with pursuing work in the political management world is the fact that it hobbles the formation, maintenance, and transfer of institutional knowledge/memory (Aucoin, 2010; Abramson, Chenk, & Kamensky, 2016). The high frequency of staff turnover and the tendency to "clean house" after each change of government are primary culprits for this seldom discussed setback. Not surprisingly, it creates numerous problems as the policy issues that political practitioners must juggle become more nuanced.

No discussion of political management can be complete without addressing the flipside of the career instability coin: financial insecurity. When assessing the career instability of political management staff, financial insecurity is often thought to be a natural by-product (Marland & Esselment, 2018; Lees-Marshment, 2020). While there are exceptions to that perspective (for example, the constant cycle of American elections at local, county, state, and federal levels), political management is not generally a lucrative profession. That is especially true in countries like Canada where there are far fewer political races and more stringent rules regarding campaign finance and the kind of work that political practitioners can engage in once they leave government (Inwood, 2008; Good, 2014; Johnson, 2016).

Methodology

This project utilized elite in-depth interviews with Canadian and American commercial and political marketers, political strategists, political consultants, public opinion researchers, lobbyists, and political staffers. Interviewees were selected using a combination of purposive and snowball (or network) sampling whereby the participants were interviewed to learn the extent to which political management can be characterized as a fluid style of management with great career instability, little institutional knowledge/memory due to high staff turnover, and little money to be made. Interviewees with extensive experience in federal level politics in both Canada and the US were prioritized. Interviews were conducted by telephone and ZOOM. During the Winter of 2023, 151 interview requests were sent with a total participation of fourteen interviewees representing a 9.3% response rate. While that response rate was lower than hoped for, those fourteen interviewees (of whom ten were Canadian and four were American practitioners), provided a grand total of 447.13 minutes' worth of conversations representing the seasoned political and corporate management personnel required to answer this study's research questions.

Turning our attention to the empirical contribution that this chapter makes to the existing literature on political management, as was indicated in the introduction, that empirical contribution will examine the key themes revealed in the interviews seen as problematic for skills development among political management practitioners.

Research findings

Challenges for skills development

Employment instability and turnover

The most commonly noted of these themes concerned the very nature of the profession itself: its volatility in both Canada and the US. Turnover of staff is repeatedly referred to as the key culprit in cultivating instability.

Interviewee #12, the CEO of the public affairs wing of a global market research firm and a political and social researcher, wastes no time highlighting why this is particularly the case in the Canadian context, stating that the very use of the term "political management profession" is a misnomer. To use his words, "It's not a profession" (Interviewee #12, personal communication, February 23, 2023). He adds more context by explaining that, in Canada,

> One set of hobbyists replaces another set of hobbyists. And they tend to come out of the lobbying companies or they tend to come out of these small polling companies […] but they're doing it as kind of a hobby. I mean, they're not political management professionals.
> *(Interviewee #12, personal communication, February 23, 2023)*

Interviewee #5, the Chief Strategy Officer at a well-known Canadian government relations and strategic research firm and also a key political advisor who played an integral role in engineering the rebranding of the Liberal Party of Canada (LPC), paints a picture of the situation by describing why the "hobbyist" label espoused by *Interviewee #12* is accurate by noting that, in Canada,

> There [are] fewer people who would do this as a sole profession. In the States […] they can make a business out of it. In Canada, I would say [for] the people who work in that space [it] tends to be one of several lines of business for them. So, if you run political campaigns, it's probably not what you do professionally. Maybe you have another consulting job or you have to do something else. And then when elections come around, you can kind of take a leave or put your other work aside and focus on that.
> *(Interviewee #5, personal communication, February 17, 2023)*

In his opinion, as well as that of numerous other interviewees, political management in Canada is not a full-time profession and therefore it requires practitioners to earn the majority of their income outside of politics. Consequently, he says,

> I work in the polling and research business at […] a company that does some political work (and those are fun projects, and we obviously do a lot of them), but that would be 5% of our line of business or 10% of the amount of business in an election year.
> *(Interviewee #5, personal communication, February 17, 2023)*

Importantly, as some of interviewees noted, employers are less willing than before to give their employees leave to work on political campaigns. *Interviewee #7*, a Canadian political consultant who ran campaigns for Conservative Party of Canada (CPC) candidates nationwide as well as high-profile national leadership campaigns, and who is both partner and director in a full-service boutique marketing firm, captures the core reason when he explains that,

> The culture of the communication professionals' world has changed that you don't have many people in your communications shop anymore. You have [one or] two. And also, it [is] no longer as it was in the '90s [where] prep time's at 5pm, so as long as you get your work done for prep time, you're fine. Now, prep time is always because of social media. The other side of that is whether legitimate or not, there was a perceived advantage to sending your vice president of communication to go work on a campaign. If they won, I don't think it was an advantage inside government. I've never met an elected official that would trade papers for some labor. But I think it was that these companies could then go and say, "Yeah, our vice president of communications was on so-and-so

campaign." And there's no prestige in that anymore. So, there's no advantage to the company in that investment.
(Interviewee #7, personal communication, February 17, 2023)

A similar perspective is voiced by *Interviewee #3,* a Canadian Conservative political strategist, pollster, and researcher, when he reminisces about his role as campaign manager during the 2019 Canadian general election,

It was very, very difficult to get people to take time off, even people in sort of public affairs consulting and everything else because they're busy, and they've got existing clients and everything else. I had at the time five business partners, and I took a six-month leave of absence to go do this, to go run the campaign, and I still came back to having to rebuild relationships with clients and everything else, right? It was not a financially good decision for my business for me to do that.
(Interviewee #3, personal communication, February 10, 2023)

Accordingly, *Interviewee #11,* the President of the Canadian public affairs division of a global market research firm and communications strategist with expertise in policy development, characterizes the practice of political management in Canada as more a "full-time internship" rather than a "full-time profession" (Interviewee #11, personal communication, February 27, 2023). Similarly, *Interviewee #3* says that, "At some level it's a volunteer sport, right?" (Interviewee #3, personal communication, February 10, 2023). According to him, it is also a "volunteer sport" with a short shelf life because, "there's a constant turnover of those 20-somethings. They age out of the process. [...] They're pushed out of the sort of the active campaigning paid ecosystem" (Interviewee #3, personal communication, February 10, 2023). But why does this happen? He quickly answers by reasoning that,

People can't see themselves building a career, they can't see themselves building a business. In the United States, people go, and they start a firm to do this with a few friends, and then they end up hiring junior staff, and you can build a business where you make a very good living. And in Canada, maybe you can get paid well [...] for a few years, but it's very difficult to do that in the long term because there isn't the business for it.
(Interviewee #3, personal communication, February 10, 2023)

Essentially, there is not enough money in the Canadian political system to sustain a full-time political management profession. This crucial deduction will be explored further after turnover is examined more closely.

Interviewee #4, a Republican political consultant and strategist, explains that a high turnover rate among political management personnel is not unique to Canada. It is a well-known component of American political management which he describes as the "no mercy" nature of political management (Interviewee #4, personal communication, February 14, 2023). On this topic, he explains that,

> There is fierce competition to be inside a campaign that has money to spend [...and] you are there to serve one entity and that's your client and your candidate. It's no-excuses. It's kind of like the battlefield. And I've seen it happen in some high-end campaigns. If you didn't get the job done, you go to work the next morning, you find somebody else in your chair. There is no mercy about it.
> *(Interviewee #4, personal communication, February 14, 2023)*

The reason for this is the increasingly zero-sum nature of politics. To use his words,

> To most candidates, when they're running, it's their shot. There's no going back. They either win or they go into retirement or they go out into the wasteland to lick their wounds. They have a maniacal devotion to their own success. If you're an asset to them, you're great. You keep your chair. When you cease to be an asset or where you're not performing to perfection, you no longer have a seat.
> *(Interviewee #4, personal communication, February 14, 2023)*

Speaking about the extremely tenuous nature of political management work in both countries, *Interviewee #1,* an experienced Canadian strategic communications and public affairs specialist who has provided sage counsel in both politics and business and who serves as the President of a well-known strategy shop, asks a serious but rhetorical question: "Why would you ever go into this industry if there wasn't some sort of a safety net?" (Interviewee #1, personal communication, February 7, 2023). *Interviewee #13,* the co-founder and Executive Chairman of a leading government relations, strategic communications, digital marketing firm and a political practitioner with nearly four decades of experience in both Canada and the US, offers an answer when he argues that political management practitioners are "usually doing it for love of politics and that sort of thing" (Interviewee #13, personal communication, March 7, 2023).

Interviewee #5 helps us pivot to the next problematic theme for political management skills development emerging from the interviews when he posits that,

> I think there's a lot of burnout and there's a lot of turnover because these are demanding jobs and high pressure jobs, and they don't last forever so you

kind of have to start to make your succession plan. Either you wait till you lose the job because you're forced to leave or you leave on your own terms and I think there's a natural tendency for people who want to leave on their own terms.

(Interviewee #5, personal communication, February 17, 2023)

However, that "succession plan" is difficult to accomplish in Canada due to the financially constrained nature of the Canadian political environment. *Interviewee #1* sets the stage for that discussion when she states that, after leaving Canadian political management, "you get a lobby ban depending on where you worked. So, in addition to it being high risk [work], you also are limited by what you can do afterwards for a period of time" (Interviewee #1, personal communication, February 7, 2023).

Financial insecurity

The second problematic theme for the development of the political management profession revealed by the interviewees was that political management (in Canada and the US) is characterized by a substantial amount of financial insecurity, a natural by-product of the career instability described in the previous section. *Interviewee #4* offers a prelude to this theme when he explains that,

All campaigns are a business. All good campaigns have a budget. All good campaigns have budget discipline. All good campaigns have to make difficult decisions about the allocation of resources, whether it be personnel, volunteer expenses, advertising, the whole nine yards […] because no campaign ever has all the money it wants. And you have to make difficult decisions.

(Interviewee #4, personal communication, February 14, 2023)

However, the difficult decisions that are spurred by the availability or lack of money on a campaign are much more pronounced in Canada than in the US.

While political management in Canada has always been less lucrative than in the USA, numerous interviewees highlighted how the 2006 Federal Accountability Act (FAA) had a chilling effect. The Act prohibited union or corporate donations, and capped individual donations to political candidates, parties, and constituency organizations at $1,100.00 (Inwood, 2008). It increased the tools for tracking political spending and its sources and it prohibited former elected officials, public servants, or political staffers from working as lobbyists for five years after leaving their positions, thus curtailing the amount of money in Canadian political management and thereby drastically increasing the financial instability associated with the practice (Good, 2014; Johnson, 2016).

Interviewee #7 lays much of the blame for the financial instability in Canadian political management on the FAA when he is asked if he thought that the amount of stability in the political management profession has increased, decreased, or remained constant over the years. He quickly responds that, "It increased significantly with the creation of the Federal Accountability Act" (Interviewee #7, personal communication, February 17, 2023). He then describes in detail how the FAA had widespread consequences for the political management trade, explaining that,

> The unintended consequence of the FAA was the average age of political managers who work for ministers and government and those types of things dropped by about 10 years. It went from mid-30s to mid-20s. And the reason for this is [...that] the number one skill set people who work in politics [or in] the larger industry [of] public affairs [...] have is still being able to network, being able to build quality objectives and agendas, and being able to share their knowledge of government. Not inside knowledge or anything like that but their knowledge of how the wheels and cogs in the system work. That is a value. And if you go and you go work in politics [in Canada], you then can't use any of that knowledge for five years after you leave politics. You're essentially banned from working in the public service industry.
> *(Interviewee #7, personal communication, February 17, 2023)*

He elaborates on how the FAA not only lowered the age of the average political manager in Canada but also changed the career calculus for prospective political management professionals thus setting the stage for increasing the financial insecurity associated with the profession. To use his words,

> And so, if you're 24, yeah, you can do that. You have no dependent. You're just starting your career. Taking a hit on being able to not use your primary skill set for five years can be bad. If you're 34 and you have a young family, the idea of going in, taking what is likely a pay cut because staffers aren't paid well for two years, three years maybe, and then once you're done that, coming out and being horribly unemployable for the better part of five years makes you think twice. And so instead of moving to Ottawa to do service in one form or another, you say, "No, I'd rather stay in the private sector." And so, it's made it a whole lot more unstable. And so, the only two type[s] of people that work in politics are either very young people who have no dependents or very old people who don't care about money because they got more than enough already. Anyone who has to build a life or a profession for themselves takes another path.
> *(Interviewee #7, personal communication, February 17, 2023)*

Generally, "another path" is a path outside of political management and inside the private sector or corporate management sector that excludes political management.

Interviewee #2, a veteran Conservative political consultant and strategist who has worked inside the Prime Minister's Office (PMO) and who serves as a Principal at a nationally known strategic communications firm, even says that political management in Canada is merely a "training ground" (Interviewee #2, personal communication, February 13, 2023). When asked if working as a political management professional in Canada is sustainable, he elaborates how the training ground description fits into the discussion by explaining that,

> I mean, yes, you can sustain yourself [...but] the private sector pays infinitely more. So, for high performing people, there's that. I mean, I think political salaries and government salaries in general have crept up, and the pay and benefits and stuff are on the high end of modest. I think one thing to really think about, though, is there are — and I will put myself in this category — people who went into government, gained a tremendous amount of experience and then leverage that into my career in other places. It can be a training ground for people to go out into the private sector.
> *(Interviewee #2, personal communication, February 13, 2023)*

In comparing the Canadian and American political management playing fields, *Interviewee #12* gives us an important reminder to consider: "And, by the way, I should say since I'm involved in this kind of thing worldwide, the Canadian example is the example. The American example is the real outlier" (Interviewee #12, personal communication, February 23, 2023). He explains why American political management is atypical by noting that,

> There's no other countries that have a permanent political campaign capability that exists that involves the same amount of money or the same amount of resourcing that they have in the United States. It's way beyond anything in any other country.
> *(Interviewee #12, personal communication, February 23, 2023)*

He further claims that, "There really is no political management industry in this country. I mean, and the reason is because the money is all so low. It's all so small" (Interviewee #12, personal communication, February 23, 2023). When asked why that is so, he is quick to respond that,

> Well, it's the lack of money in the campaigns [and] campaign finance rules. But really [...] it's more to do with the fact that it's just not the culture in the country. We've never had a professional political class that can make a living out of just doing campaigns in Canada. It's always been something that was run by volunteers. Now, it tends to be in the professional aspects

of this, like say, for example, if you're in advertising. In the old days, what would happen is you'd work almost volunteer-like on the campaign and maybe you make a little bit of money out of the ad buy or whatever. But you were doing it as a speculative investment in your party winning and you getting a bigger share of the advertising contracts that have been available. But ever since access to information and also changing in the procurement process for everything from advertising to political polling to any type of consulting contribution that you can make to the government, all of that has not really been possible to the same degree as it was. So, as a result, you can't make a living out of it. So, it's a hobby.

(Interviewee #12, personal communication, February 23, 2023)

It is important to point out that there is no legislation like the FAA in the US and, consequently, there are far fewer restrictions on the role money plays in American political campaigning. *Interviewee #1* highlights the freewheeling role of money there when she explains that,

In the States, it's very different [...] the fundraising rules and the elections spending rules are very different. And the rules around lobbying are different. So, we're so restricted here about what we can do, who can donate, can you knock on doors in a general election and get a lobby ban? I can't do debate prep, for example. That's explicitly restricted. If I do debate prep for a candidate, I can't lobby them. In the United States, they don't care about any of that. So, you can make a ton of money.

(Interviewee #1, personal communication, February 7, 2023)

Furthermore, she sums up the key difference about financial insecurity in both countries by stating that American political candidates and political parties themselves "can raise money from corporations, and they can take donations from literally anybody, and we can't" (Interviewee #1, personal communication, February 7, 2023).

Electoral frequency

Besides the FAA, another factor noted by numerous interviewees as contributing to the financial instability associated with Canadian political management concerned the infrequency of elections in Canada. *Interviewee #3* captures the essence of this problem when he explains that, "There's not enough elections, both in terms of number of elected positions and frequency of elections. There's [...] enough to support a few people doing it, but not enough to support an industry" (Interviewee #3, personal communication, February 10, 2023). *Interviewee #5* adds that shorter Canadian general election campaigns create challenges not evident in American presidential races which effectively begin the day after the previous presidential campaign concludes. As he puts it,

> And so, if you're working on that campaign [the presidential race], you've got [...] a longer campaign business line if you know that you're going to be working with a candidate for the next year [...] as opposed to one month or two months in the Canadian context.
> *(Interviewee #5, personal communication, February 17, 2023)*

Those longer campaigns on the American side of the border allow for a greater sense of stability among American political management personnel. Further, as he puts it,

> So, I do think the fact that there are more races and longer races in the US [...and that allows] people who are in the business of working in these fields [to] focus a bit more as opposed to having to sort of juggle other clients and other priorities.
> *(Interviewee #5, personal communication, February 17, 2023)*

Beyond providing a greater sense of employment stability, the higher frequency and longer length of campaigns in the US allow for the development and refinement of a greater degree of specialization among political managers. *Interviewee #7* explains how this can be the case since,

> There are entire companies whose only job is to do not even all of campaigns but all the subsections of a campaign. There are entire companies that only do direct mail elections. There are entire companies that only do phone banking for elections. There are entire companies that only do creative design or ad building for elections.
> *(Interviewee #7, personal communication, February 17, 2023)*

Such specialization is possible because, as he puts it, "There's not 10 minutes that go by that there isn't an election somewhere in the United States" (Interviewee #7, personal communication, February 17, 2023). However, it is impossible in the Canadian context because of the less consistent and less frequent nature of elections. *Interviewee #3* also sheds light upon another inescapable element of political campaigning that is associated with the lower frequency of elections in Canada.

> And the thing I've come over time to realize is probably the most damning of all. The system is too small, so everybody knows everybody [...] and as a result, that means that if you're a, quote-unquote, "professional campaigner" and you do something that the national campaign or the provincial campaign

manager doesn't like, you can get blacklisted and sit out a cycle and there aren't enough cycles and there aren't enough elections to go around.
(Interviewee #3, personal communication, February 10, 2023)

Institutional knowledge/memory

A final theme emerging from the interviews as problematic for skills development among political management professionals concerns the accumulation, maintenance, and transfer of institutional knowledge and memory. They become pronounced areas for concern given the lack of money, career instability, staff turnover and infrequent elections that exist in Canadian political management circles. The creation, curation, and transfer of institutional knowledge and memory among political management practitioners is not guaranteed which can adversely affect the sophistication of the practice itself.

Interviewee #1 initiates our discussion of institutional knowledge and memory and the problems associated with it in political management in a manner that is reminiscent of the career instability discussed earlier when she points out that,

> The first thing that you do when there's a change in leadership is like 50% of the staff are fired, which is ruthless because they were the former leader's people, right? And the dramatic downside of that is you lose a lot of institutional memory.
> *(Interviewee #1, personal communication, February 7, 2023)*

Consequently, institutional knowledge and memory ebbs and flows among political management practitioners. As *Interviewee #2* phrases it, "there's waves of institutional knowledge" (Interviewee #2, personal communication, February 13, 2023). He then walks us through his work history:

> For example, my first really serious job [...] was 2006 in the [Stephen] Harper PMO. Day one [...] you have an empty floor, some bureaucrats advising you and stuff. But, because my political party hadn't been in power [...] since the early 1990s, there wasn't a lot of people that you could call on and ask for advice.
> *(Interviewee #2, personal communication, February 13, 2023)*

As a veteran practitioner, *Interviewee #2* is keenly aware of the ebb and flow of institutional knowledge and memory over time. Referencing the overlapping of both federal and provincial offices, he says,

> But then fast forward a bit, [...and] look at the Ontario government. [The] Conservative government comes in [in 2018 and] there were a lot of

people around who had just worked during the Harper years [...] And so there's a great deal of knowledge, I think, that had gone back and forth. But it could be waves, and it can really atrophy if one party is in power for a long time.

(Interviewee #2, personal communication, February 13, 2023)

A similar perspective is voiced by *Interviewee #8*, the Chief Strategist at a national Canadian political and market research firm, when he posits that,

Institutional knowledge is probably held by a small number of people. There aren't many people who [...] have stayed involved in politics across multiple leaders and multiple generations. So yes, I think institutional knowledge is something that goes missing. And principally, it goes missing when there's a change in leaders because they bring in their own team of new people who are excited to do things differently, and there's a lot of merit in that. That's responding to a need. But usually, it will be a challenge tapping into institutional knowledge. And prudent leaders make an effort to do that in composing their teams.

(Interviewee #8, personal communication, February 17, 2023)

Interviewee #1 is in agreement regarding the consolidation of institutional knowledge and memory with a very small number of political management practitioners. For example,

So, there are some people who have tremendous institutional memory and knowledge because they're the ones that have been doing this [...] for decades, again, for better or worse. And they are the keepers of all that. They've got crazy, amazing stories that are awesome to listen to over drinks, but the institution itself doesn't retain that knowledge and that memory.

(Interviewee #1, personal communication, February 7, 2023).

As *Interviewee #8* and *Interviewee #2* also note, this becomes problematic because most political management practitioners who worked on a campaign do not go on to work in government after an election as compared with public servants who obtained leave to campaign. Should they do so, they often do not remain in that position for long because of the high turnover and burnout rates described earlier in this chapter. Thus, a lack of institutional knowledge and memory can be seen as one of the principal side effects of the high turnover and burnout rates among political management personnel in both Canada and the US. Put differently, continuity can be problematic for political management practitioners — a fact that is compounded by turnover and the HR training challenges that it poses which were discussed previously. Returning to *Interviewee #8* reminds us that, as regards institutional knowledge and memory, incumbency is an important "variable" to consider. As he says himself:

> I think that [...] there's greater institutional knowledge with more success-ful political parties, and that would be a variable in the success of successful parties. So, it's the parties that struggle to win and hold power that turnover much more quickly.
> *(Interviewee #8, personal communication, February 17, 2023)*

Interviewee #13 offers another important consideration to keep in mind when contemplating institutional knowledge in the practice of political man-agement: playing one's cards close to their chest. He explains by distinguish-ing between "institutional knowledge" and "individual knowledge" and says,

> Well, there's little, I would say, institutional knowledge. There is indi-vidual knowledge [...] And there's not a lot of sharing of best practices between the political managers in part because political managers kind of hoard that information and guard it. [They] guard their secrets because if they're [on] any campaign again, they want to make sure that they haven't given everything away.
> *(Interviewee #13, personal communication, March 7, 2023)*

To say that competition can be fierce in politics should come as no sur-prise. Thus, striving to maintain a competitive edge by not broadcasting trade secrets stands to reason. However, doing so can severely hamper the outlook for institutional knowledge.

Interviewee #6, the founder and president of a California-based research firm specializing in elections and public policy and which represents non-profit, government, media, special interest, and corporate clients, allows us to bring our discussion of institutional knowledge and memory to a close and to pivot towards a number of important lessons for political management practitioners and researchers. He helps by reminding us that, in relation to political management practitioners, "when that person leaves their role, they take that knowledge with them and there's nothing left for the next person that runs that congressional campaign or for any other staff. It's just kind of poof, gone" (Interviewee #6, personal communication, February 17, 2023).

Prior to drawing this chapter to a close by describing a number of valuable lessons for both researchers and practitioners of political management and also by recommending a number of helpful resources for those seeking a path into the political management field, it is important to return to the three re-search questions that this chapter sought to answer: First, to what extent can political management be characterized by a style of management where there is great career instability? Second, to what extent can political management be characterized by a style of management where there is little institutional knowledge/memory due to high staff turnover? Third, to what extent does financial insecurity permeate the practice of political management?

First, we can conclude that political management can indeed be characterized by a style of management where there is an abundance of career instability. This career instability is accentuated by the unstable, unpredictable, intense and all-consuming nature of the average political practitioner's working environment.

Second, an institutional knowledge/memory deficit exists in the practice of political management. This is due to high staff turnover and the tendency to replace most staffers when a new government comes into power.

Third, financial insecurity is often an inescapable element of practicing political management. This is especially true in countries like Canada which have far fewer elections than does the US and which have significantly curtailed the amount of large-scale political donations and employment opportunities for former political practitioners by implementing a defacto lobbying ban for several years after leaving politics. That approach impedes the potential to monetize experience gained during time spent as a political practitioner. It should be noted that both of these setbacks are non-existent in the more laissez faire American political environment.

Recommendations for academic research

After weighing the findings from my interviewees, the following recommendations can be made for researchers of political management:

- First, political management research should continue to examine the inescapable career instability that besets political practitioners. The interviewees were unanimous in identifying that element of their profession and the deleterious effect it has.
- Second, the study of political management should also remain focused on exploring the financial instability evident in the pursuit of political management and its adverse impact on practitioners. The vast majority of interviewees — particularly those working in Canada — expressed concern over this common feature of political management.
- Third, and finally, political management research should investigate an often overlooked result of the career and financial instability previously identified as negative attributes of the political management profession: a dearth of institutional knowledge/memory among political practitioners. The logic for further exploring this subject matter rests on its identification by many respondents as being a vitally important variable in the practice of political management that is often essential but ephemeral. Furthermore, it remains unaddressed by much of the literature on the subject of political management.

Recommendations for practice

It should be noted that identifying recommendations for researchers addresses only one relevant audience for this study. Another important audience is, of course, political practitioners themselves. Consequently, the following recommendations represent a selection of best practice principles for political management practitioners to reflect on as they navigate the unpredictable and often turbulent landscape in which they operate:

- First, knowing that political practitioners confront greater career instability than their corporate colleagues, efforts should be made by political management staff to increase their career stability. This will likely be an uphill struggle but it could involve advocating for the creation of trade unions to represent political practitioners as well as consulting with corporate management personnel to determine what HR safeguards could be applicable to political management personnel.
- Second, since political practitioners face greater financial instability than their corporate counterparts, efforts should be made to increase the stability associated with political management. However, that may prove even more difficult than attempting to combat career instability — especially in countries with infrequent electoral contests where the flow of money is strictly regulated and less plentiful than in the past as is the case in Canada. Nonetheless, efforts should be made to secure better pay for political practitioners and the important work that they do.
- Third, accepting that institutional knowledge/memory is in shorter supply among political practitioners than corporate practitioners, an effort should be made to boost its presence in the political world. To cultivate and maintain institutional knowledge/memory, a conscious effort should be made to prevent the wholesale replacement of political staffers when governments change. Again, this may be difficult to achieve, since as was described, political practitioners serve at the pleasure of the politician or party that they work for and their employment is tenuous. Additionally, the aforementioned recommendations for improving career and financial stability could also help boost institutional knowledge/memory because, if implemented, they would address the core reason that many political practitioners do not make a career of their time in political management: the inherently instable nature of the work environment itself.

Recommended reading

The following authors, editors, and their works represent an important point of entry for aspiring researchers and practitioners to consider:

1 *The Routledge Handbook of Political Management* (2009), which is edited by Dennis W. Johnson, and which includes the works of Kaid (2009) and Nelson (2009) referenced earlier in this chapter.

2 Jennifer Lees-Marshment's (2020). *Political Management: The Dance of Government and Politics,* which is published by Routledge.
3 Chris Eichbaum and Richard Shaw's (2011) Political Staff in Executive Government: Conceptualising and Mapping Roles within the Core Executive, as seen in the *Australian Journal of Political Science.*

References

Abramson, M. A., Chenk, D. J., & Kamensky, J. M. (2016). *Getting It Done: A Guide for Government Executives* (2017 ed.). Lanham, MD: Rowman & Littlefield Publishers, Inc.

Agere, S. (2000). *Promoting Good Governance: Principles, Practices and Perspectives.* London, UK: Commonwealth Secretariat.

Aucoin, P. (2010). Canada. In C. Eichbaum, & R. Shaw (Eds.). *Partisan Appointees and Public Servants: An International Analysis of the Role of the Political Adviser* (pp. 64–93). Northampton, MA: Edward Elgar Publishing.

Bourgault, J. (2007). Corporate Management at Top Level of Governments: the Canadian Case. *International Review of Administrative Services,* 73(2), 257–274.

Craft, J., & Howlett, M. (2012). Policy Formulation, Governance Shifts and Policy Influence: Location and Content in Policy Advisory Systems. *Journal of Public Policy,* 32(2), 79–98.

Dolan, J. (2000). Influencing Policy at the Top of the Federal Bureaucracy: A Comparison of Career and Political Senior Executives. *Public Administration Review, 60(6),* 573–581.

Eichbaum, C., & Shaw, R. (2011). Political Staff in Executive Government: Conceptualising and Mapping Roles Within the Core Executive. *Australian Journal of Political Science,* 46(4), 583–600.

Gilley, J. W. (2006). *The Manager as Politician.* Westport, CT: Praeger Publishers.

Good, D. A. (2014). *The Politics of Money* (2nd ed.). Toronto, ON: University of Toronto Press.

Inwood, G. J. (2008). *Understanding Canadian Public Administration: An Introduction to Theory and Practice* (3rd ed.). Toronto, ON: Pearson Canada.

Johnson, D. (2016). *Thinking Government: Public Administration and Politics in Canada* (4th ed.). Toronto, ON: University of Toronto Press.

Kaid, L. L. (2009). Political Management and Political Communications. In D. W. Johnson (Ed.). *Routledge Handbook of Political Management* (pp. 57–66). New York, NY: Routledge.

Lees-Marshment, J. (2020). *Political Management: The Dance of Government and Politics.* London, UK: Routledge.

Marland, A., & Esselment, A. (2018). Tips and Tactics for Securing Interviews With Political Elites. In A. Marland, T. Giasson, & A. Lawlor (Eds.). *Political Elites in Canada: Power and Influence in Instantaneous Times* (pp. 29–47). Vancouver, BC: UBC Press.

Nelson, C. (2009). Ethics in Campaigns and Public Affairs. In D. W. Johnson (Ed.). *Routledge Handbook of Political Management* (pp. 555–563). New York, NY: Routledge.

6

MENTAL HEALTH AND WELL-BEING OF MPs' STAFF

Ashley Weinberg, Estelle Warhurst, and Thomas Fairweather

Introduction

It is estimated there are over 3000 MPs' staff working in and managing approximately 1300 offices across UK constituency and parliamentary locations. Their responsibilities include casework (aiding constituents often in dire need) on behalf of MPs as well as supporting more publicly observable features of political representation carried out by elected politicians, including practical arrangements of staff offices and MPs' daily work. As such, MPs' staff underpin the effective functioning of the politicians who are also their employers and in so doing, perform a vital role in effective governance within the democratic system. Often underestimated, representation of the public is serviced by MPs' staff and contrary to reasonable expectation, consideration of their own well-being in endeavouring to fulfil their role has been overlooked by research – until now.

Concerns about the well-being of UK parliamentary and MPs' staff have been highlighted by high profile investigations. Dame Laura Cox (a politician) and subsequently Gemma White QC (a lawyer) have reported on harassment and bullying and the need for action to address institutionalised issues. Within Parliament, establishment of the MPs' Staff Wellness Working Group (WWG) and Members' Services Team (MST) have raised the profile of well-being, as well as providing forms of human resources support to MPs and their staff. WWG has called for psychological support for staff given increasing caseloads featuring constituents in crisis and experiencing mental health difficulties.

Accordingly, research considered here focuses on surveys of MPs' staff commissioned by WWG, their working experiences and sources of pressure.

DOI: 10.4324/9781003260677-6

The findings of the first survey were shared with the Speaker of the House of Commons in Spring 2022 prior to the establishment of the 'Speaker's Conference' – a periodic inquiry by Parliament into a pressing matter – which highlighted 'employment conditions of Members' staff in order to ensure a more inclusive and respectful working environment'. Based on the findings of the research reported in this chapter, practical recommendations for improved employment practices for MPs' staff were presented to the Speaker's Conference in January 2023.

Key literature

Previous research on mental health in politics

The topic of mental health at work has attained considerable profile following the pandemic. However, the psychosocial dynamics of the political workplace have received relatively modest research attention. Partly this is due to the often 'hidden' nature of political activities away from public scrutiny and to popularly negative public perceptions of politicians (Flinders et al, 2020).

Nevertheless, research on the mental health of national politicians has demonstrated they are just as prone to poorer well-being due to work-related factors as other occupational groups, with the first survey of UK MPs in the early 1990s, as MPs testified to a parliamentary commission established to consider their working practices (Weinberg et al, 1999). Furthermore, the impact of beginning the job of an elected politician raised the question of whether the job should carry a government health warning! (Weinberg and Cooper, 2003). In assessing MPs' psychological well-being, the negative impact of a work-based crisis, has been shown to more than double their prevalence of symptoms of poor mental health from 16% to 40% (Weinberg, 2015), while another study has asserted that compared with employees in similar public roles, 34% of UK MPs report higher frequencies of symptoms (Poulter et al, 2019).

Thus, the potential consequences of undesirable job conditions for elected politicians and their effects on the functioning of democracy has received some scrutiny, but research on the health and well-being of their staff has not. This chapter seeks to address this important omission.

Theoretical model – a framework of political stressors

The focus here will be on sources of pressure – otherwise known as stressors – rather than on symptoms of psychological poor health (for consideration of the latter, please see Weinberg, 2022). The framework described here was developed with reference to the aforementioned studies of MPs and provided a catalyst for an interview-based study of serving and former politicians and

TABLE 6.1 Types and categories of stressor (number of survey questions in parentheses) and illustrative quotes from MPs' staff

	Stressor (number of questions)	Selected response
Public facing	Expectations (mismatched) (2)	'Casework is 99% trying, 1% succeeding'
	Trust (lack of) (4)	'I was attacked by a constituent'
	Political labour (emotion work) (3)	'A necessary evil in casework' 'I have been targeted personally'
Organisation facing	Organisational culture (5)	'Bullying, constant negative feedback'
	Leadership (support from) (4)	'The office manager is great. The MP is a massive bully'; 'I always work remotely and feel forgotten'
	Temporal (1)	'The lack of HR means that one never knows if your boss is just going to sack you'
Individually focused	Lifestyle (4)	'There is an unrelenting tide of incoming casework that has only been increased by the pandemic'. 'Demands on time outside office hours'
	Control (3)	'In one instance, I had to draft a comment from a train as I was coming home from a wedding'
	Skills (4)	'No training in book-keeping or accountancy is provided and we are all expected to fumble through it as best as we can' 'Under-prepared, unsupported and unrecognised'

political staff conducted by the British Psychological Society (Baldwin et al, 2020). While stressors are common to many occupations, there are additional sources of psychological pressure to which politicians are exposed and it is logical to consider how this extends to political workers, including MPs' staff.

The '9-stressor framework' (Flinders et al, 2020) has identified challenging aspects of political work across three main categories (see Table 6.1):

a 'Public facing' – pressures arising from mismatched public expectations and distrust of politics and politicians, as well as the ongoing efforts to convey politically suitable impressions;
b 'Organisation facing' – features that shape working practices in political institutions, including combative culture, leadership styles and the time-limited nature of electoral and media news cycles;
c Individually focused – challenges to balancing work-home life, including long working hours, acquiring and maintaining required skills and achieving healthy levels of control

Methodology

There were two waves in the research. A survey in July–September 2021 assessed the prevalence of poor mental health among MPs' staff and sought to gauge the experience of sources of pressure in their work. This chapter focuses on the latter and it is worth noting that respondents were reflecting not only on the longer term, but also periods during which the UK was 'locked down' during the pandemic. A follow-up survey (December 2022–January 2023) began a process of evaluating potential impact from ongoing well-being oriented initiatives and limited comparison is made where possible.

Measures and procedure

Measures included a brief assessment of emotional responses to the job and additionally the Scale of Political Stressors. The latter assesses the frequency of sources of pressure encountered by MPs' staff and was co-designed as a bespoke measure with representatives from the staff group and parliamentary managers (see Table 6.1). Ethical approval for this research was obtained by the lead author from the University of Salford.

The Scale consists of 30 items covering public facing, organisation-facing and individually focused sources of pressure as suggested by the Framework of Political Stressors. Frequencies were assessed on a Likert scale ranging from 'never' to 'always'. Positive statements included, 'I feel emotionally supported by my MP/office manager/line manager' and 'I make a positive difference to others through the work I do'. Negative statements included, 'I receive email/social media messages from members of the public which are negative in terms of content, personally or professionally' and 'I am concerned for my job security'. In addition, respondents were invited to submit qualitative comments so they could expand on their Likert ratings.

A weblink to the Online Surveys platform was circulated by the WWG and Member Services to all accessible staff working for MPs in Parliament and constituencies. Reminder emails included a link to a parliamentary web-page routinely used by MPs' staff. It is worth noting the survey population did not have a defined size, due to the absence of a confirmed register of all email addresses of MPs' staff. There is apparent variation in organisational record-keeping of email addresses due to the high number of employing MPs ($n = 650$) and frequent turnover of staff, which means that a definitive response rate becomes hard to calculate reliably. This is a recognised issue with conducting research on political staff, but also illustrates the potential for inconsistent employment practices of a nature unlikely to be tolerated in other arenas of work.

Participants

Survey 1 received responses from 217 individuals, yielding an approximate sample size of around 6% of MPs' staff. Almost three-quarters of the sample were women and were based in constituency offices. Approximately half were from the 18–35 age category and one-third had been in the job for less than two years, although the average length of service was 5.3 years. Survey 2 gathered data from 315 (around 10%) MPs' staff and the demographic profile broadly matched that of the baseline survey, with one quarter indicating they had participated in both.

Research findings

How MPs' staff feel about their job

The range of emotions recognised by MPs' staff in relation to their work indicates the complexities and potentially personally conflicting nature of their role (see Figure 6.1). 'Rewarding' and 'emotionally draining' were highlighted most frequently, followed by 'difficult', 'fulfilling', 'proud' and 'stimulating'. It should be noted that respondents had options to highlight each of ten emotions, hence the percentages represent proportions of the total sample.

Compared to the 2021 survey findings (notwithstanding caution about comparability between the samples), the 2023 results (Figure 6.1) indicate a 7% decrease in those selecting 'emotionally draining', and a 5% decrease in the proportion feeling 'under-supported', with a smaller rise in those highlighting 'fearful' reactions.

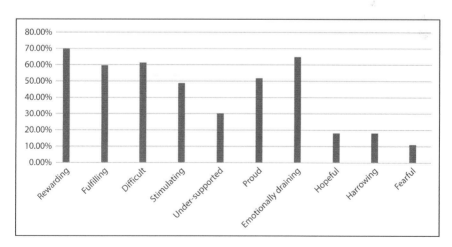

FIGURE 6.1   Emotional reactions reported by MPs' staff reflecting on how the job makes them feel

TABLE 6.2 Rarely or never [this percentage of] MPs' staff feel …

	2021 (%)	2022/3 (%)
Their pay is commensurate with the skills used at work	40.2	43.7
They have opportunities to gain qualifications/training on the skills needed to carry out the job	32	29.4
Supported by their line manager	15.5–18.3	14.9–17.3
Their MP/office manager/line manager shows understanding of the pressures staff experience in their job role	16.3	13.6
Valued in their job role	10.2	10.2

Sources of pressure (stressors) faced by MPs' staff

To consider the prevalence of the full range of job features, descriptive data for each stressor was compiled from the first (2021) survey showing the frequencies with which respondents experience positive and negative aspects of working (see Tables 6.2–6.5). To aid understanding, similarly oriented frequency categories have been amalgamated, i.e. sometimes/rarely/never and always/very frequently/frequently.

Table 6.2 emphasises the proportion of respondents to the survey who rarely/never experience the job features shown – this shows considerable and ongoing dissatisfaction with pay and opportunities for gaining qualifications/ training, as well as less frequent problems with managerial support.

Table 6.3 highlights lower percentages of staff responding to the survey who sometimes/rarely/never experience safety, trust and control at work, as well as a much higher proportion struggling with the common job feature of delivering disappointing news.

Table 6.4 presents nine most frequently experienced aspects of the job, ranging from interruptions – as anticipated in fast-paced workplaces – to concerning high levels of emotional isolation, hostile and unrealistic public expectations, operating outside trained skills, high pressure workloads and conformity to a long working hours culture, stigma around their job role and feeling under-supported. The easing of pandemic restrictions appears to be reflected in slightly lower levels of one reported problem, with a considerable decrease in emotional isolation.

TABLE 6.3 Sometimes, rarely or never [this percentage of] MPs' staff feel …

	2021 (%)	2022/3 (%)
They cope well with delivering disappointing news	40.6	40.4
They have autonomy over how they approach their work	17.8	18.9
They are safe at work	9.5	12.4
They trust others working in their office	9.4	15

TABLE 6.4 Frequently, very frequently, always [this percentage of] MPs' staff ...

	2021 (%)	2022/3 (%)
Experience interruptions when completing tasks at work	81.8	72.4
Feel emotionally isolated in carrying out the job	72.3*	22.7*
Feel expected to perform tasks which are outside of their remit or power to change by members of the public	66.4	56.3
Find it hard to meet the demands of the job within the timescales provided	51.5	48.3
Are required to perform work tasks for which they have received little or no training	49.8	40.1
Tend to hide the nature of their work from people they know outside of Parliament	47.2	39.5
Feel there is more Parliament could do to support their job role	46.4	42.2
Feel that knowing the long hours others work makes it hard for them to cut back on the length of their own working day	46.3	35
Receive email/social media messages from members of the public which are negative in terms of content, personally or professionally	44.2	36.5

* Denotes change most likely caused by easing of pandemic lockdown restrictions.

Table 6.5 features nine less widely experienced – yet frequent for concerning proportions of MPs' staff – job components indicating one-third experience pressure to work at unsociable hours and do not perceive job security. Alongside acceptance that their work supports the image and performance of an MP, respondents highlight the negative impact of working hours on home

TABLE 6.5 Frequently, very frequently, always [this percentage of] MPs' staff ...

	2021 (%)	2022/3 (%)
are contacted over work matters on their mobile phone/ social media at unsociable hours	35.8	31.1
are concerned for their job security	31.3	32.2
are expected to display emotions (in person or in writing) which differ from their own	29.5	25.2
find the working hours of the job make it hard for them to enjoy family relationships/non-work friendships	28.7	24.7
feel under-prepared to cope with the emotions experienced when assisting constituents with traumatic issues	28.3	22.4
say others take credit for work they have done	24.3	18.2
say colleagues in Parliament (e.g. line manager, MP, office or other colleagues) expect them to carry out tasks which are beyond their capacity to do so	19.3	17.1
fear for their own and colleagues' safety	18.7	21
are subject to unreasonable behaviour in the workplace, in person or online	13.6	13.4

life, pressure to act outside their role from political colleagues/managers/ MPs, feeling under-prepared to deal with challenging emotional job content, as well as threats to physical and psychological safety. Although experienced by lower proportions of the survey sample, these constitute serious causes for concern.

In summary, there was a very large decline in respondents 'always', 'very frequently' or 'frequently' feeling emotionally isolated as the pandemic restrictions eased, while over half report unrealistic expectations from the public, while one fifth remain concerned for their safety and job security. Over two-fifths believe Parliament could do more to support their work and nearly one fifth feel rarely or never supported by their line manager. Almost one-third believe they have too few opportunities to gain necessary qualifications/training on the skills needed to carry out their job. Only two-fifths feel consistently their pay is commensurate with the skills used at work.

The daily working experiences of MPs' staff

Qualitative free-text comments from the survey were also analysed. 1517 qualitative comments were provided by Survey 1 respondents accompanying their ratings on the Scale of Political Stressors. The most frequent were in relation to the following: 'I am concerned for my job security' ($n = 106$), 'I feel there is more Parliament could do to support my job role' ($n = 90$), I am subject to unreasonable behaviour in the workplace, in person or online ($n = 76$) and 'My pay is commensurate with the skills I use at work' ($n = 60$). In addition, 128 responses were provided about what MPs' staff regard as the 'most stressful aspect of your work'.

In order to represent the considerable and valuable qualitative data, this section organises respondents' free text comments within the framework of stressors outlined earlier (see Table 6.1) under the main headings of a) public facing, b) organisation-facing and c) individual-focused sources of pressure.

'Public facing' pressures

This section conveys some of the largest challenges to MPs' staff, including to both physical and psychological health. The stressors of mismatched public expectations (sometimes extending to those from colleagues) and lack of public trust are linked and appear to fuel one another: from dealing with death threats and attacks, to online abuse. Trust in their team and support by colleagues, effective managers and MPs appear positive buffers against such worrying unpredictability. Casework yields both challenging and rewarding features of the job, as staff recognise the potential to make positive differences in constituents' lives. However, lack of public understanding of the MPs' power and remit is a major source of frustration for public and staff alike. Accordingly, emotional labour – or political labour in this context – is deployed routinely, however, in attempting to maintain professionalism and manage expectations and difficult news, the potential price paid by staff appears high.

Mismatched expectations

Two-thirds of MPs staff found they were frequently expected to perform tasks outside of their remit or power to change by members of the public. However, 'The [public] assume[s] we can change everything with the assistance of the MP. I call it the magic wand syndrome'; 'I'm expected to stop anti-social behaviour, give legal advice, be a solicitor etc'. This gap results in a clear need to manage expectations, which is both time-consuming and emotionally challenging: 'the MP's office has become the accessible end of the road for many'.

Learning was a key theme for the public and for staff: 'I think a public education piece is needed to help people understand what can be achieved by MPs offices'. However, the role of funding of MPs' offices was raised more than once: 'not...enough staffing budget to cover what should and could be reasonably expected'.

Lack of trust

Almost half of respondents to the survey hide the nature of their work from people they know outside of Parliament: 'I have one or two friends whom I trust, but to everyone else I am just a secretary who works in an office. I rarely tell strangers what I do' contrasts with, 'I'm proud of what I do and share the stresses to manage them'. Equally, there was a desire to avoid potential confrontations, e.g. 'The negativity and hostility towards MPs over the past year has led me to not only not talk of what I do, but actively avoid some social gatherings'.

Awareness and perceptions of risk – whether by MPs or their staff – and strategies for dealing with threats were prevalent in responses, with staff mindful of the murder of Jo Cox MP at her constituency office in 2016. Working from home during the pandemic offset some concerns, however, 'I believe that personal security for MPs staff in the constituencies needs to be taken more seriously'. Most worrying are examples of sporadic extreme violence, 'I was attacked by a constituent who tried to [kill] me, and I was threatened with being killed by another constituent over the phone'; 'I was caught in the Westminster terrorist attack'.

What is striking is the acknowledgement of the potential for an incident, but that 'Thankfully these have not been many in number'. There are occupational sectors which do not accept even a low level of such risk, but the challenge to public-facing work for MPs' staff is clear and was underlined again most tragically: Sir David Amess MP was killed in his constituency shortly after the initial research for this study had been completed.

Political labour (emotion work)

Emotional labour, by which employees are required to convey emotions desired by the work organisation, whilst hiding one's own, has become better understood in recent years. Within the context of politics, this can also include presenting emotions that align with political advantage, hence the adapted term 'political labour'.

Many MPs' staff found themselves on the receiving end of negative comments from the public and some were inured to these by 'not taking things personally' or realising they were directed 'at the government' or indeed their MP. Nevertheless, there were individuals who characterised these as 'abuse' and one pointed to 'regular death threats or abuse'.

Another form of political labour, breaking disappointing news, 'is a necessary evil in casework'. Most respondents seemed accepting of this: 'Over the years, some [situations] have been devastating, but I have been professional and calm'. Coping mechanisms vary: 'It has just become automatic in some cases – I have a range of standard lines for constituents'; 'I find this very difficult and have tried to harden myself.

When it comes to supporting the MP in their overtly political role, 'I am able to put the job above my own views/feelings. This is fundamentally inevitable and expected with our jobs, so isn't a shock'; 'I don't always agree with my MP, but my role is to represent his views'. Ultimately, 'You do not always agree with the direction of the workplace and you need to decide if this means that you are happy to remain working there under those circumstances'.

'Organisation facing' stressors

Qualitative comments in this section underlined the importance of support for MPs' staff and the survey responses pointed to problems for around one-third of staff when considering organisational stressors – although this need not be assumed as the same one-third of staff across all measures. Organisational culture and leadership appeared linked and infused working experiences, whether through enjoyment and feeling valued or conversely reflected in discrimination and bullying. More positive fortunes pervaded the informal dynamics of many teams, which expressed care for co-workers, as well as effective line management and more formalised systems for maintaining regular communications. Where these were absent, isolation had a weathering effect and unreasonable expectations and negatively expressed contact – including discrimination and bullying – threatened to destabilise those affected and also impacted colleagues who witnessed it. Violence and online abuse were evident in extreme communications from the public, but should not overshadow cited cases of staff maltreatment (including by a small number of MPs) and the need for effective systems and standards to address these.

The presence and absence – depending on office circumstances and funding – of the benefits of human resource functions were apparent and associated with perceptions of job (in)security. There seems considerable scope for ensuring access to these functions, which are rightly assumed in most workplaces. The successes of parliamentary groups supporting colleagues and procedures were highlighted, but ensuring parity between constituency and parliamentary offices will help address job insecurity. Foremost appears to be the need for equitable funding in such a way that guarantees reasonable levels of pay and staffing for MPs' offices.

Organisational culture

The word 'team' was mentioned by over half of respondents, largely in recognition of the positive aspects of co-workers, including efforts to enable an inclusive online workspace: 'I far prefer working as part of a team than on my own' versus, 'I always work remotely and feel forgotten by my employer'. The concept of a team serves functions which are beyond the social and co-operative, e.g. 'I enjoy working with colleagues as a result of solidarity from the bullying many in the team face from the MP'.

A 'can do' mentality was clear and for many this had meant an (enforced) opportunity for growth in skills: 'You have to deal with anything that comes up whether you have experience in it or not'. Not surprisingly, healthy work relations and the support of co-workers and managers were important in problem-solving, e.g. 'I've joined a WhatsApp group for other office managers – that has been an incredible source of information and moral support'.

Workplace culture provides a window into expectations of MPs' staff: 'As a Parliamentary Assistant I believe it is your job to do whatever your boss wants, within reason. So long as it is reasonable and fair, and not nasty or degrading or of financial cost to the employee'. However, in terms of unreasonable behaviour from politicians and co-workers, some had experienced bullying or negative acts: 'Some Members and peers can be uniquely rude and unpleasant, although the majority are lovely'. Negative behaviour ranged from unreasonable requests to ill-treatment and as has been evidenced previously in high-profile parliamentary reports, there has been acceptance and tolerance of negative behaviours, whether linked to loyalty, understanding of the strain experienced by an MP or indeed fear: 'It is a mess the way the Whips offices ignore staff and their wellbeing. I think that needs to change and accountability for bad behaviour needs to be there'.

Leadership

There is clear variability in how MPs' staff experience leadership: 'I am conscious that my office manager and MP foster a culture of emotional wellbeing and support, however I am aware that many offices do not.' Feeling valued is not a regular experience for almost one-third of the survey sample: 'I feel valued by constituents but not so much my MP'. This underlines the importance of office managers who oversee the running of MPs' employees, whether good – 'My line manager has been very good at making me feel valued and building my self-confidence'; or bad: 'Recognition, gratitude and reward is pretty much non-existent – basically the reasons I am leaving'.

Communicating a sense of value to the work of MPs' staff is explored differently, e.g. 'the MP will send grateful emails or arrange staff days out'; 'we are taken out for a meal usually'. However, the legacy of a remark or previous criticism can undermine efforts to show appreciation, 'coupled with how constituents treat us, leaves me with low self-esteem about my job'.

The scope for more uniform access to effective human resource practices is also clear: 'I rarely have a proper appraisal, so find it difficult to know if I am doing well in my role'. The importance of effective management again comes to the fore and for some may be the factor, however tenuous, that encourages staff to remain: 'My boss recognises the pressure that I'm under and always acknowledges her gratitude for the work I do'; 'My boss does a good job at it but... is limited in what he can do to make me feel good about things. There are no other perks'.

An effective line manager is appreciated hugely: 'My boss is great. Pressures on him limit the support he can offer me. The intent is there though'; 'My manager is always there for me if I need to discuss anything. I trust her implicitly'. So where do line managers derive their support? 'As an office manager, I would welcome a mentoring arrangement with someone not involved in the organisation who I could turn to for support and advice on issues that I feel I cannot raise with my MP'; 'I would like to be offered group counselling as the topics we are dealing with can be very tough'.

Temporal

'[It's] just a question of time'; 'There simply isn't the time!' The pandemic emphasised this challenge: 'The workload of the past year has not been sustainable with the resource available'; 'Since Covid, even during recess, we have been swamped... we have never been busier. My workload has doubled'. Equally, the perception of a 'career' seemed a distant prospect and was only mentioned by four respondents: 'There is a high turnover of staff in the nature of this job'; 'I am on a fixed term contract which has been extended on a couple of occasions. I don't expect it to last forever'.

In terms of tenure, the tone is understandably pessimistic: 'There is no job security in this role': 'the coming of an election is always looming above our heads'. Those in marginal and safe seats are particularly conscious of such precarity and the lack of control is evident: 'I mean – your job is up for election every few years, when you are legally not allowed to go and campaign to save it. That is demonstrably unfair'. Fears for job security emanated from some MPs' behaviour too: 'MPs can hire and fire whenever they please'. Despite this, a number of MPs clearly engender trust in their staff, e.g. 'if they lose election or decide to step down, my job is gone. But my MP would work hard to help the team move on'.

Individually focused issues

The quantity of work and its unremitting nature, fuelled by rising case-loads, mean that working long hours and internalised pressure to do so leave many exhausted, struggling to take time off (including holidays) and motivating others to leave. Work-life boundaries buckle at the expense of personal relationships as mental space to 'switch off' is squeezed and preyed upon via technology or a particularly demanding MP in an 'always on' culture. Resourcing of sufficient staff numbers is a key issue, currently feeding an unhappy status quo and relying upon unhealthy lifestyle choices, characterised by the long working hours of those willing to remain. Parliamentary funding bodies are reviewed resourcing, although the impact has yet to be assessed.

Capacity to craft the job to suit individuals has merits, although this differs from having sufficient time. Interruptions are part of a busy job, with flexibility and problem-solving essential components in combating unpredictability mediated by 24/7 technology. MPs taking credit for the work of their staff is widely accepted, although there are clear examples of good practice in recognising and sharing team success.

The absence of a formal training path or qualification route is felt from the moment staff start the job. Absence of advance warning of the challenging nature of casework and the need to devise one's own approach to urgent situations clearly necessitates quick thinking. However, this encourages reliance on individuals' ingenuity which would not be considered tolerable in other public-facing occupations taking responsibility for life-changing outcomes. Mental health First Aid training is recognised as pre-requisite for staff working with the public and in supporting one another. The value of teamworking is clear. However, it should be possible for the organisation to provide training, particularly in offsetting the psychological impact of distressing cases including suicidal constituents, addressing the wider need for skills and making it practically possible for staff to take time to attend courses, whether constituency or Parliament-based.

For the skills, adaptability and experience required, there is consensus that the majority of MPs' staff are underpaid and this fuels increased turnover. In other words, cost begets cost. Combined with the demoralising impact, urgent need for the Speaker's Conference to review the working conditions of MPs' staff is clear, carrying potential implications for Parliament's external reputation. While decision-makers may point to public perceptions, improving pay and staff levels should be considered as aiding the public-facing function of a representative democracy.

Lifestyle

Workload appears to be 'managed' within wider notions of a long working hours' culture. Approaches to long hours appear divided between those with robust work-life balance strategies – supported by like-minded managers/MPs – and those feeling unable to do the job if they restricted their hours. The role of office managers in striking the tone was clear: 'As a manager I lead by example – no one should be expected to work an unreasonable number of hours', versus 'I have typically worked the longest hours. It's not due to peer pressure, it's due to sheer workload'. 'I think more education is needed for staff to know it is okay not to always be on and not to be expected to respond to emails throughout the night. We need to train staff that there is no expectation of being awake 24/7. It is unhealthy and leads to other worse issues'.

'The job is never ending' was a recurrent theme: 'There is more to do every day than could ever be done'. This is manifest in how workload is experienced and the impact on staff, as well as the potential knock-on effects for constituents: 'There is always too much work, too much pressure and not enough hours'. This included a plea for help: 'I have no family life. I've barely seen my non-work friends. I'm at breaking point'.

'There is little escape from the computer/relentless emails'. This leads to clear examples of work-family conflict, whereby work matters spill into home life, e.g. '[I'm] often checking e-mails & social media in evenings & weekends'. In turn this lifestyle has affected relationships outside work with both family and friends: 'My relationship with my partner has suffered greatly as a result of my job. He has often complained that I always have time for work and never for him, and I am ashamed to say that he is right, to a certain extent'.

Control

For some, it is unclear and potentially concerning where work begins and ends: 'Sometimes the MP phones me for a social call and talks about work. The boundaries are blurred which I struggle with at times'; 'MP often texts or sends What's App out of hours!'… 'sometimes in the early hours'. This type of intrusive practice is concerning, not least for eroding a sense of agency. Strategies for combating demands for contact or responses may be more open to more experienced or senior staff – 'I have worked out a system of blocking [the MP] before starting a period of leave'.

When it comes to the 'how' of the job, experiences vary: 'I am fortunate to have freedom in my office to approach work as I see fit and am trusted to do a good job, but I am conscious that some line managers or MPs micro-manage their staff'. For a minority, there is a flipside to having such autonomy, e.g. 'Almost too much – there is very little direction or feedback in my choices'.

Interruptions are part of the job, whether constituents, co-workers or the MP, who 'often creates a lot of last-minute work'. 'I often leave work at the end of the day feeling that I haven't actually achieved anything useful, yet I am exhausted because I have not stopped working'.

The importance of co-working and giving credit where due, was also underlined: 'We work as a team generally'. Where the efforts of staff have not been recognised, it 'can be quite dispiriting sometimes but you also know you're not the elected one'; 'the flip side is we are anonymous workers with no acknowledgement of our value or skills or experience'.

Skills

In terms of shaping longer-term learning, one respondent stated, 'Career development is a shambles'; 'I do feel there are other organisations out there that are supportive of their workforce gaining further qualifications'.

This seems shocking given the life-changing nature of casework and need for accurate and appropriate advice and support. However, lack of accessibility of training was linked to a range of factors: time; competing commitments (e.g. 'If I took time to study, I would come back to an even larger stack of casework'); location of courses; lack of cover in small teams for staff; funding, e.g. 'Managers are often reluctant to spend the staff training budget because it gets logged in their expenses – which looks bad to the public'; guidance (e.g. 'I have taken every course available but have no idea if they are relevant or if I am missing important ones'); adequate training capacity ('a huge problem is the availability of these').

The single biggest concern has been limited availability of training for MPs' staff in supporting constituents with mental health difficulties. 'This ranges from small tasks to very emotionally challenging things like suicidal calls or child abuse cases'. 'We do receive a significant amount of calls from people either struggling to cope or who are in crisis. It is very hard to know how best to handle these situations and I am very conscious of this'. This need for training is being addressed by the WWG and Parliamentary Members' Services Team and includes efforts to ensure mental health training is offered as part of the induction package for new staff.

The final theme of pay being commensurate with the skills used indicated a resounding 'No'. This partly explains the high turnover: 'Friends who work easier jobs in the private sector get paid more which is why me and all of my colleagues are considering leaving our roles to take up employment in the private sector'; 'you are working in Parliament, famous all around the world, and you have to scrimp and find yourself waiting for payday'. In this context, scepticism on the part of those who do not see an option is understandable: 'We are massively underpaid for what we do. We are social workers, legal experts, emotional support, someone to abuse'. 'Don't go into politics for the money!'

Overall findings

In summary, it is clear MPs' staff are highly motivated and committed to serving the public, alongside and for democratically elected representatives. This is apparent from the nature and seriousness of the work and from an overarching tolerance of often suboptimal working conditions. These are frequently characterised by job insecurity, lack of career progression and modest renumeration in the face of public hostility and threats of violence and less frequent – but marked – exposure to unreasonable behaviour from some colleagues within the political arena. It is important to note alongside these are positive examples of MPs and office managers who are talented supporters of their staff.

MPs' staff are vital to the efficacy of democratic functioning and as such their well-being has clear implications for their performance and that of elected representatives. Whilst concerning conclusions can be evident in employee surveys, what sets these findings apart is the absence of universal and sufficient safeguards for physical and psychological well-being of MPs' staff. Supported by the organisation of Parliament and its executive officers, there is clear need for a universal human resources function providing effective personnel support available and provided to all MPs' staff as standard. Not only would this build on good practice evidenced by a sizeable proportion of respondents to this survey, but underpin appropriate working practices and hopefully avoid the kind of distress evident in this response: 'Please, help us. Give us the resources we need. I'm at breaking point'.

Based on the findings presented here, recommendations were made to Parliament in a report submitted by the authors to the Speaker's Conference in January 2023. These emphasise strategies for training, support and addressing turnover known to be cost effective and that additional investment should be publicised for what it represents, i.e. resources to support those helping the most needy in society.

In July 2023, the Speaker's Conference published its second report on MPs' staff working conditions. In citing the findings of this research and testimony from parliamentary staff and bodies, it endorsed the need for such steps as discussed here to help improve the efficacy and reputation of the UK Parliament and democracy. At the time of writing, when so many more citizens are turning to the offices of their elected representatives for effective help, it is timely that UK MPs will debate recommendations for changes to staff working conditions that include universal availability of human resource support and training, parity for parliamentary and constituency-based workers and measures engendering respect and recognition. Parliament should be an exemplar for other workplaces; as one survey respondent stated, 'We are the "engine room" of our democratic processes'. It is hoped efforts heralding positive change produce better working experiences and outcomes for MPs' staff, for MPs and their constituents, as well as more effective functioning of representative democracy in the UK.

Recommendations for research

- Findings from this study suggest that the practice of political management has considerable scope for growth in the UK context, notwithstanding valiant efforts by parliamentary services and a good proportion of MPs and their office managers.
- The value of working with the groups under study was highlighted in the successful response to this research and augurs well for future research collaborations.
- It is hoped that analysing qualitative and quantitative data promotes a clear and meaningful insight into the experiences of MPs' staff.

Recommendations for practice

- Value political staff – despite competitive and combative political environments, the role of MPs as employers requires modelling of appropriate behaviour and leadership to ensure optimal team performance. Ensuring parity of treatment of parliamentary and constituency-based staff sends a clear and principled message to MPs' staff.
- Paying political staff a wage commensurate with the skills required will positively impact turnover, reduce loss of valuable co-workers and minimise need for retraining costs.
- Skills training necessary for political staff to work effectively is also important for building healthy and trusting employment relationships, that feed into career development, facilitates engagement and retention in an otherwise insecure employment relationship (with elections always a possibility). Mental health training is a particular need, as turning to the MP is commonly a last resort for seriously ill and potentially suicidal constituents.

- Safeguarding staff is often overlooked, especially if the MP is unafraid personally of potential for danger, e.g. vulnerable constituency office premises, sharing staff personal details with the public. Prioritising physical and psychological safety – in person and online – is paramount in an increasingly volatile and potentially toxic social media-led environment.
- Adopting human resource management practices and principles as standard for all MPs' staff, to help ensure fair and reasonable practices in recruitment, employment and redundancy are available, generating sustainable teams and reducing the potential for causes of grievance.

Recommended reading

Baldwin, A., Pinto, C., Perriard-Abdoh, S. and Weinberg, A. (2020) *Cognitive strain in parliament: How can we reduce psychological stressors to improve policy-making?* Leicester: British Psychological Society. Accessed at: https://www.bps.org.uk/guideline/cognitive-strain-parliament

Flinders, M., Weinberg, A., Weinberg, J., Geddes, M., and Kwiatkowski, R. (2020) Governing under pressure? The mental wellbeing of politicians. *Parliamentary Affairs*, 73(2), 253–273. https://doi.org/10.1093/pa/gsy046

The Constitution Unit (2022) MPs' staff: A study of the 'unsung heroes' of Parliament. Accessed at: https://www.ucl.ac.uk/constitution-unit/research-areas/parliament/mps-staff-study-unsung-heroes-parliament

UK Parliament (2022) Speaker's conference. Accessed at: https://committees.parliament.uk/committee/609/speakers-conference/

Weinberg, A. (2015) A longitudinal study of the impact of changes in the job and the expenses scandal on UK national politicians' experiences of work, stress and the home-work interface. *Parliamentary Affairs*, 68(2), 248–271. https://doi.org/10.1093/pa/gst013

References

Poulter, D., Votruba, N., Bakolis, I., et al (2019) Mental health of UK Members of Parliament in the House of Commons: A cross-sectional survey. *BMJ Open*, 9:e027892.

The Speaker's Conference (2023) Speaker's conference on the employment conditions of Members' staff: Second report. Available at: https://publications.parliament.uk/pa/cm5803/cmselect/cmspeak/1714/online.pdf

Weinberg, A. (Ed.) (2022) *Psychology of democracy: Of the people, by the people, for the people*. Cambridge: Cambridge University Press.

Weinberg, A. and Cooper, C.L. (2003) Stress among national politicians elected to Parliament for the first time. *Stress and Health*, 19, 111–117.

Weinberg, A., Cooper, C.L. and Weinberg, A. (1999). Workload, stress and family life in British Members of Parliament and the psychological impact of reforms to their working hours. *Stress Medicine*, 15, 79–87.

7

PRIME MINISTERIAL MEDIA ADVISERS

Demystifying the Spin Doctor

Karl Magnus Johansson

Introduction

The authority of prime ministers comes in two forms: external and internal. External authority involves the undisputed right of the prime minister to speak for the whole government. Internal authority consists of the right of the prime minister to define the governmental line or to set its message of the day. Both forms of authority are prerequisites for effective participation in media. Both forms are linked through the groundwork laid before public announcements or appearances, and the preparations made before the prime minister or ministers face the media. All this requires an elaborate system of preparation. In politics, arguably, preparation is everything. Prime ministers, indeed all ministers, need support. When they leave, the need remains. This chapter focuses on the support provided by much-needed prime ministerial media advisers, henceforth called PMMAs. More broadly they are communication advisers and their titles may vary. But they are still media advisers in national executives and with the chief executive. They are expressions of something important about political management and governance. What do they do during an average work day? I explore this question empirically through a twofold strategy. First, I survey secondary evidence on PMMAs in a range of countries. Second, I locate the study of the subject in the context of everyday life in Swedish government. The chapter represents an effort to examine the practices pertaining to PMMAs within a given advisory system and a shift in focus from 'spin' and 'spin doctors', loose terms envisioning and mystifying the extraordinary, towards the ordinary. In fiction and non-fiction alike, a mystique surrounds those so-called spin doctors as powerful media manipulators. This is not a work

DOI: 10.4324/9781003260677-7

of fiction. It features real people. I suggest the sharpest lessons lie not in the extremes but in the mundane.

In a nutshell, this chapter aims to understand the practice, to give an account of what PMMAs do in the job, and to show that the media advisory capacity has become a fixture for prime ministers. It also serves to redress a geographical imbalance in political communication (system) research where the focus usually is on Anglo-American-based scholarship and systems. On the theoretical side, I claim that this is a development best explained not as the pursuit of dominance but as a necessary requirement for governments to respond functionally by being responsive to external pressures and to internal coordination problems (Johansson 2022). These pressures and problems are reflected in how institutions are designed to cope and in functional specialization within organizations. This approach is informed by a rational functionalist understanding of organizations or institutions, which then signify a call for efficient functional responses to needs and challenges confronting governments. In this vein, the chapter speaks to research on political management in central government and especially advisory arrangements, but has broader implications for debates about polities and wider politics.

Key literature

Existing academic literature immediately relevant to the subject matter of the present chapter is not vast. Within the broader literature focusing on the role of advisers in politics, also at the very top, the media advisory role has received relatively little attention by political scientists and media and communication scholars alike. Notably, the volume edited by Shaw and Eichbaum (2018) addresses advisory roles but media advisers are only mentioned in the chapter on Germany and, relatively little, in the chapters on Denmark and the UK. This is all the more surprising given the key role of media advisers in those executive systems. The Sweden chapter in that volume does not refer specifically to media advisers but mentions, almost in passing, 'press secretaries'; indeed, the survey does not include political advisers at the prime minister's office because they were negative to the project. This also illustrates the data problem of adviser research. A later volume on ministerial and political advisers, edited by Shaw (2023) and including a special thematic chapter on ministerial advisers and the media, contains more on ministerial media advisers and their role but still relatively little.

This relative neglect of media advisers in this academic field of research is remarkable given the importance of communications to governments and their leaders, not least of the presentation of policy or other matters. A survey of the field of political advisers in the executive branch, by Ng (2020: 514), observes that 'the roles of media advisers remain relatively understudied compared to their policy-based counterparts, with limited exceptions...' Yet media advisers have not gone unnoticed. There is scattered evidence from individual countries, mainly from Anglo-American systems. There are important works describing the roles of the media adviser/press secretary to the prime minister in the UK (e.g., Seymour-Ure 1991, 2003; Kavanagh and Seldon 1999; Blick and Jones 2013; Garland 2021) and Canada (e.g., Thomas 2013; Marland et al. 2017), or of media advisers more widely in Australia (e.g., Phillipps 2002; Tiernan 2007; Young 2007; McKnight 2015; Fynes-Clinton 2017; McLean and Ewart 2020: Ch. 8 and see also Caroline Fisher's chapter in this book), Germany (e.g., Esser et al. 2001; Pfetsch 2008; Althaus 2018; Hustedt 2018), Norway (e.g., Figenschou et al. 2017, 2022; Kolltveit 2021; Bjerkaas and Kolltveit 2023), and Sweden (Johansson and Johansson 2021). Worth noting is also an early illustration from Ireland where an increasing politicization of the role of government press secretary, dating as far back as the early 1980s, has been observed (Horgan 2001: 266). The political dimension of the post became apparent when P.J. [Patrick James] Mara served as government press secretary from 1987 to 1992. He played the same kind of media-advisory role for the Irish prime minister, or taoiseach, Charles Haughey as Bernard Ingham did for Margaret Thatcher.

This literature shows the ways in which government media advisers perform by routines amid intensifying media management by politicians and governments, to cope with the 24/7 media environment. In parts of this literature there is also a concern that *political* media advisers have come to play too dominant a role in the newsmaking (see also, e.g., Street 2021). They operate in a party-political context. Taken together, the literature introduced in this section offer important contributions. However, most existing work is typically limited to individual countries and usually Anglo-Saxon systems and advancing this research agenda requires wider testing of general expectations about the conditions shaping the roles of these advisers in politics and more comparative analysis.

Methodology

The case study covers the centre-right governments from 2006 to 2014 and from 2022, the social democratic–green governments from 2014 to 2021, and the social democratic government from 2021 to 2022. With the exception of the 2006–2010 government, the other governments have all been in the minority. And all have been coalition governments, except the 2021–2022 government. A representative sample of twelve media advisers were interviewed, most with experience of working alongside prime ministers.

Most interviews were conducted together with then-PhD candidate Milda Malling as part of the research project 'Symbiotic leader-media relations? Exploring interaction between prime ministers and the media in Finland, Lithuania, Poland and Sweden', funded by the Foundation for Baltic and East European

Studies (see project website: https://polexmedia.com). All except two had worked in the Prime Minister's Office (PMO) and some of them in a managerial role (one acting press chief and three deputy press chiefs). Unfortunately the head of press, the prime minister's chief media adviser, from October 2014 to October 2022 refused to speak with us. He rarely made himself available for media appearances, beyond his regular interactions with journalists.

When working in the capacity of a press secretary, media advisers were mostly doing ordinary pursuits related to media relations or handling internal communications. One, also based at the PMO, had the title of political adviser for strategic communication, dealing with more long-term aspects of communication but doing press secretary work when needed. Another press secretary also became political adviser, but still mainly working with media-related matters. These examples further illustrate that the boundaries between political and media advisers are not always clear, and suggest that a kind of hybridization of staffing is taking place. Increasingly, we see a mixed category consisting of political media advisers.

Whilst the total number interviewed may seem low, it is to be expected given the well-known challenges securing high level participants for interviews. Moreover, at the time of data collection there were tensions in coalition governments. To supplement the interview data, the chapter collected material from an inventory of PMMAs'/press secretaries' self-presentation online, mainly LinkedIn, and from government documents concerning communications. In addition, internal government documents relevant to communications and especially to coordination thereof were utilised, including information pertaining to the PMO. In the following, I uncover the patterns in the data.

Research findings

Zooming in on the everyday life of prime ministerial media advisers in Sweden

Attention now turns to Sweden, with a particular focus on how PMMAs relate to their work. The aim is to depict what these staffers actually do day-to-day and in the context of the challenges facing them and in their institutional context (see also Johansson et al. 2019; Johansson and Raunio 2020; Johansson and Johansson 2021; Johansson 2022).

Starting with the bigger picture, to put the Swedish case into such context, the heart of the Swedish government and its communication is the PMO. Its press department serves as a hub for government communication, particularly for the coordination of communications among ministers towards the media. Step by step, a strategy aimed at centralizing the flow of government information through the press department at the PMO has been established. A key feature of media management has been the strengthening of institutions and practices including the media advisory capacity at the executive centre. The resources allocated for government communication have grown significantly over the past 60 years; since 1963 when the first government press secretary was employed, with the prime minister. Gradually, working patterns crystallized.

In the past couple of decades, government communication has been highly centralized around the prime minister. All levels of government have a role in its communication but it is an operation increasingly run from the top. Communication has been coordinated to maximize the attention for the issues the government wants to promote. The press department located at the PMO has been upgraded with a strengthened position for the head of press, operating on the direct mandate of the prime minister. The trend has been ever upwards.

Yet, compared with the previous Swedish governments covered in this study, the government which came to office in October 2022 has been partly undoing some of the centralizing strategy. The press secretaries/media advisers are now employed at the ministries, as was the situation before the new and more centralized framework was initiated by the then prime minister in 2014. It was a framework by which government media advisers/press secretaries became more closely linked to the prime minister, through their employment at the PMO. Moreover, it introduced morning meetings on a daily basis led by the head of press at the PMO. That procedure has been relaxed with the new government.

In all, there are certain signs of a relaxation of the tight communications operation. At the same time, the new government operates within the strengthened institutions and that essential structure remains. This government too faces a need to absorb pressure from the media. That requires a management system run from the political centre. Therefore, the centralized approach looked likely to continue.

While relatively less centralized as a centre-right governing coalition consisting of three political parties and relying on an agreement with the nationalist Sweden Democrats, largest of the four cooperation parties but outside the government, a lot is still controlled from the PMO. The agreement also includes principles for external communication. It wants to project control and government unity. According to a centrally placed political media adviser, while the formal employer role rests with the ministries and much is the ministries' own responsibility, the press department at the PMO has overall responsibility for work management, coordinates and 'leads the government's press work'. In the meantime, they worked out routines, for example regarding the meetings. Also worth noting is that the other two leaders of political parties in the government each have a chief press secretary and that these are located at the respective ministry, that is, not centralized to the prime minister's office. In other words, the power over government communication lies at the PMO. Its press department still has the final say in this command structure directly under the prime minister.

The role of the press department is to link the prime minister to the media (and media organizations), and be the main source of advice to the prime minister about how to present his message and the whole range of government policy. The prime minister's advisory needs are thus taken care of by the press department and its head with deputy and additional staff. Added to that are political advisers and, since early 2023, a state secretary for strategic communication to the prime minister. The new state secretary, with a politics as well as a public relations background, would work with the media management team at the PMO. It meant a strengthening of communications around the prime minister, including the longer-term communication and 'storytelling' to make sense of the government's reforms. It is about working to ensure that the constant flow of information from the government works together as a whole, to make all the parts fit together.

The number of politically appointed 'press contacts' in the government amounts to nearly 40. That is not to mention the many others who work with communication in the Government Offices, as well as in other government agencies. The media advisers and other political staffers constitute an important human resource in political management (Lees-Marshment 2020: Ch. 4). Their advisory and informational role at the level of the prime minister is indispensable. The work they do may be mundane but is also consequential for the distribution of resources and power in the executive branch, not least through the greatly increased resources for communication and public relations within the Government Offices. There has also been a restructuring so that resources have become more centralized around the prime minister. Whether or not this government – and future ones – will bring about more or less centralization of government communication remains to be seen.

The contours of the structures of government communication in Sweden are already fairly clear. Now we will learn more about media advisers and what they themselves said in interviews.

Working patterns in Swedish media advisers

This subsection explores the everyday practices of PMMAs through an inventory of interview evidence. The evidence is drawn from a series of interviews with acting or former government/prime ministerial media advisers (PMMAs). In the following, I centre on general tendencies in the interview material and only draw on individual interviews to exemplify common opinions among the interviewees.

The central message from this series of interviews is one of agreement towards the notion of standardized practices. The dominating perception is that that there is a set of routines, which guide the performance of the role and to be effective. This general message is explicitly advanced by most media advisers of different governments and parties, although a common remark is that there is no such thing as a normal day, since there are variations between working days as well as among government media advisers. At the same time, they reported the regular practice of an average day. Interview evidence suggests that they all work quite similar a typical day in the job. Media advisers have a clearly defined position, which has developed professionally over several decades. They have common standards and norms guiding their work and behaviour. A picture emerged.

While much of the news day can be anticipated from early morning, the agenda may have its surprises. Things can be really be moving fast. Any day can bring surprises. Still, they must do what they can to never be unprepared for what might come next. The life of a PMMA, and other governmental media advisers, is a journey across the political and media landscape. They need to follow the news feed in the media, including social media platforms, and relate to some of that.

Government media advisers including PMMAs spend most of their time on media-related matters; less time is taken up by other functions. In other words, there are general responsibilities. They include responding to all inquiries and requests from members of the media, by telephone or in person; to establish and maintain regular contact and relationships with reporters and others (to facilitate achieving the objective of reaching out to the public).

A day in the life of most government media advisers begins early. Most mornings, it appears, they usually start the day by checking social media feeds and websites of the most influential media outlets and that may set an intention for the day. Once they arrive at their office, they have been reading news and social media. Next comes (more) telephoning and texting. After that they may go to meetings. And it can be preparations for, and possible attendance at, press conferences or other events. It is quite a lot of practical arrangements like sending out press invitation, which means keeping in touch with journalists. A normal working day includes contacts with journalists. Different kinds of relationships seem to define the job more than anything else. In the words of one PMMA:

> Relationships are the core of this profession, the ability to build human relationships not only as colleagues but also with journalists [...]. To build external relationships to spread our message [...] requires that we have a relationship somewhere, and it takes longer than you would expect to build these relationships.

One PMMA suggested to meet at 08:00 a.m. 'before the day whirls on', as he had phrased it in an email. In the interview, he explained what it may look like: 'I mean, it is going insanely fast in the news today, now it is really a 24-hour news cycle, it never ends...' He further explained that there is a lot of planning and preparation around the prime minister, much more than there is around all ministers, according to this PMMA. He added that it is more planned with both incoming and outgoing visits like summits in the EU or elsewhere. Then there is a mobile team around the prime minister; a heavy workload and long working days.

Another PMMA provided an example of what may structure the operative work:

> There are many things that a prime minister does that need to be planned in detail. If we are going to visit somewhere, we have to decide where to go, where to stand, where to meet the press, who is going to be present, what will happen during what moment and how the transport will work [...]. I always have to be updated, always reachable, always be in control [...]. And when we are out, we meet a lot of journalists.

In order to plan such public appearances and media relations, meetings are held by political staff. In addition, there are meetings among government media advisers and political staff meetings at the PMO. If a statement involves new policy, it must be coordinated with the policy coordination secretariat at the PMO. Media advisers and political advisers also worked together in teams.

According to one PMMA, it is coordination all the time really, in the prime minister's staff, but also among communications staff:

> I would say that it is more centralized and coordinated in general. But I would also say that it is a product of the spirit of the times and the demands placed on having better control over what the different parts do, the demands for answers and so on. [—] So much of the coordination is developed as a result of the fact that there is a demand as well, that we must be more organized, I think.

With all the news produced and more news outlets, he remarked, 'it is required that we on our part have better control over what goes out.' That involved daily meetings at the PMO to ensure control of government communications. There is a great need to be well organized, because there is a lot in the calendar including meetings to discuss what in media to react to and to coordinate the response or the agenda. In addition, there are meetings meant for more long-term communications planning.

Interviewees gave the same general picture of an increased level of planned communication in the government. A variety of factors are at play, some political and some connected to media development. Among the political reasons are a greater need for coordination in coalition governments and increased awareness of the role of communication in politics. Media-related factors are the increased speed and ever-more media outlets.

One PMMA noted that the prime minister is the person who gets 'most media attention' and is 'most visible'. Contacts are more often initiated by the journalists, he said. There is a practice of background conversations with journalists, as confirmed by this and other interviewees. The media adviser and the journalist often already know one another.

One of the PMMAs working directly for the prime minister explained:

> To talk to journalists, to hand out information and spread the picture we want and the policy we are working for, that is my formal task [...] In my daily work I have professional relationships [...] and talk to journalists all the time to make them understand how we think.

Prime ministers usually have high newsworthiness. A selection must be made among all inquiries and requests from members of the media. This means that the media advisers working for the prime minister exercises a gatekeeper function, as various interviewees noted. This in turn means that they tend to work more reactively than media advisers to ministers with less newsworthiness who therefore need to work more proactively and make more contacts themselves to compete for media attention.

Of course, in the digital age, it is communication on social media every day, which requires a degree of coordination, and variation regarding forms of communication with journalists. But telephoning, texting or emailing are common. Both politicians and staff post content on social media. Media advisers are drawn into social media, themselves and on behalf of their masters, into different social media networks to varying degrees. They do it for professional purposes. They promote the government's agenda and their boss, thereby 'building persona', spread government information, and monitor media. As members of staff, they are in charge of some social media material, such as government budget related content. In interviews, they described how social media impacts on their work. In brief, social media is now a part of their routine and a means to be updated with news flow, trends, and events, but also time-consuming and more unpredictable than traditional media. It means additional functional demands. It adds to the pressure on staff.

Generally speaking, this is a normal working day. Regardless of what is meaningful stimulation for each individual media adviser, the job involves an effort to gain or avoid media attention. The general record also illustrates the mundanity of much of the work.

The professionalizing of media advisers and expansion in their numbers along with other communication professionals in the government reflect the functional pressure from media. In the words of a PMMA, 'a kind of increased professionalization not to give a messy impression' – a mode of expression which incidentally suggests that resources dedicated to communication are a response to necessity demand. This PMMA emphasized the increased speed in media coverage as another explanation for more resources on communication and more coordination within the government: 'Everything is much faster... when something is written on Twitter it can be a news article.' That reflects the need to respond to an intense 24-hour media environment.

As the prime minister's media adviser, you are at the centre of the action as far as the government is concerned. They will also, to varying degrees, deal with issues which may be vast, complicated and interconnected. Certain issues can have great political significance, potentially even deciding the fate of the government in the next election.

Worth noting, in this vein, is also the essentially political nature of their work. Professionalization of government communication is very much about control of information flows from the government and leading political parties. The promotion of good news to journalists and newsrooms and avoidance of bad news is the constant job of the media advisers. This is managed via choosing which information to disclose, and which to withhold, as well as through contacts with journalists. As a result, the media advisers' work is very political in scope. As well as doing routine tasks, they are working for politicians and embedded in political structures. Many of the interviewees emphasized the importance of an understanding of politics. One of them, a social democrat who worked for the 2014–2022 governments, and in the PMO, observed: 'it is, after all, a political environment and a political compass is required, but also political competence.' Interviewees working in the centre-right coalition after the 2006 election emphasized how communication was placed at the political centre. One pointed out that the prime minister explicitly told everyone that, if he is in a meeting and his press secretaries have to get hold of him, then they can enter whatever meeting he has. According to this PMMA, their role goes wider than media relations because as a Swedish press secretary 'you have a very close relationship with a prime minister and a great deal of the external coverage takes place through the press secretary to the prime minister. [—] This applies to everything from media coverage to coverage of the surrounding world in general.' As we were always with the prime minister when he travelled, the PMMA noted, 'very often people called us and, so to speak, we were often the channel in to him.'

In similar vein, another PMMA remarked:

> If you want to have someone who is really good as a press secretary, then it has to be someone who knows politics. [—] It's good if it's a nice person too. It cannot be an introverted person who does not want to answer the phone, but it must be someone who is interested in politics, is knowledgeable about politics, knows the history of politics, knows the party's culture. All parties have different cultures. So that often in politics the press secretary becomes a central station, like the spider in the web.

This is another telling illustration of the close link between politics, policy and communication, as well as of the human element and an appreciation of how valuable these staffers are to the prime minister of the day. The fact that they are entrusted to work alongside, and occasionally speak for, the prime minister at the highest political level is a testament to their power. The functional and instrumental use of them is also an expression of actual needs and practices.

Results reveal the activity patterns in these PMMAs. They are not all alike but exhibit similar working patterns, determined by structures and standards. While they may be pursuing their jobs in a qualitatively different way, I find considerable commonality in how executive media advisers operate. Their work is basically about how to attract or divert attention. In this, the essence of the job is to build and maintain relationships. At the same time, as well as strengthening the centre, media advisers influence who gets access to the corridors of power. This is the gatekeeper role that undoubtedly involves a certain influence.

The chapter's Swedish focus should not obscure its wider lessons about what happens when prime ministers surround themselves with media-savvy staffers and aim for a (more) coherent approach to government communication. In the following, I will highlight what lessons the Swedish experience has for academic research as well as practice, with some recommendations for the future.

Recommendations for academic research

This chapter has explored the question of what government, particularly prime ministerial, media advisers do during an average work day, and shown how that is linked to the contexts and goals of prime ministers and their offices. The chapter serves to advance this research agenda. While most existing research on press secretaries/media advisers takes a 'spin' approach, this chapter rather employs a practice approach, focusing on their varied duties and capturing the realities of their everyday life in government. By zooming in on their working patterns the empirical analysis illustrates how routines structure work. A picture of familiar routines emerges. I find a pattern of professionalized and strengthened political human resources – notably, staff – for government communication. This is not an aberration, but the norm, and has consequences for the development of intra-executive relations as well as government-media relations.

This chapter holds important lessons for the study of political management in different aspects, including for the analysis of governmental institutions and political behaviour. Government is one of the core areas of political management and prime ministerial offices, or offices of presidents in presidential or semi-presidential executive systems, are the highest level of political offices (Lees-Marshment 2020: 15). Typical political manager positions in government and political offices include political staffers involved in communications, such as media relations. The chapter has shown the nature of the role that media advisers play, contributing to our understanding of roles in political offices. It emphasizes the importance and power of media advisers in government and academics might reflect on the implications of this for control and authority given advisers are not elected. Their elected masters operate on advice. Being the prime minister requires advice. More practically, given how important media advisers are as a resource and to sustaining political leaders in power, it emphasizes the need to recruit high quality people into these influential roles; people fit for purpose. After all, as Deutsch (1963: ix) suggested in his book *The Nerves of Government*, 'it might be profitable to look upon government somewhat less as a problem of power and somewhat more as a problem of steering; and it tries to show that steering is decisively a matter of communication.' This book is worth revisiting in the era of communication management and governing through – or with – media, all kinds of media. For governments around the world managing the media is a necessity – not an option.

Still, we know little about media advisers in a particular government policy setting; about what policy influence these political media advisers really have. They may be highly influential given the bond between them and prime ministers. In its next phases, research on this topic should look closer at the question of impact. In similar vein, it remains important to look at what technological innovation and improvement has to offer for political actors and may drive what they are doing.

Recommendations for practice

Communication, in its broadest terms, is a key functional area of activity in political management. This chapter, and its Sweden case analysis, offers real-life examples of what media advisers in governments and particular to prime ministers do. The main lessons this chapter holds for practice are as follows:

- As political media advisers are integral to how prime ministers (and ministers) deal with the media, be conscious that where such advisers have become more assertive tensions may arise with other staffers – whether political or non-political – and that a tendency towards politicization may involve a particular bias in relation to news or other information from the government. Government media advisers who are political appointees are expected to create a favourable impression of the government and its leader when presented to the public. The media advisory role in government is a profoundly political one.
- Similarly, be observant that overly centralized organization and management, driven by complexity and need for functional specialization and involving a hierarchy of roles in the organization, may severely unbalance the relative weight of different categories of staff and create tensions among staffers.

- The advisory system explored in this chapter requires extensive resources, many of which are allocated at higher levels. A critical reflection, aiming to sensitize practitioners to possible implications of resource distribution, concerns the way such resources are allocated and that asymmetries may impair intra-executive relationships.
- At least in Sweden, government communication is little formalized and largely governed by unwritten rules. This is something that varies between countries. Still, it raises questions about the discretion of political operatives and about a possible need to clarify what the role of media adviser actually entails.

While a larger organization tends to lead to specialization, which reflects concerns about functional efficiency as argued in the introduction, little is known about such effects at the lower levels or if attempts are made to really address these issues. The case of Sweden illustrates the problem, well known from various reviews, of insufficient inter-ministerial communication. Therefore, the organization for communications remains a central aspect of efforts to streamline government offices. The overall purpose is to make this activity and the work of the ministries more uniform. Like elsewhere, there is a further development of authority with regard to, among other things, digitalization, which is shaping the content and future of work. But the chapter also carries the caveat that Sweden's lessons from political and media management might not work as a general rule for other countries, although challenges are essentially similar for political management everywhere.

Acknowledgement

The author thanks the editor, Jennifer Lees-Marshment, for comments and constructive suggestions that significantly improved this manuscript.

Recommended Reading

Johansson, Karl Magnus (2022). *The Prime Minister–Media Nexus: Centralization Logic and Application*, Cham: Palgrave Macmillan.

Kolltveit, Kristoffer, and Richard Shaw (eds) (2022). *Core Executives in a Comparative Perspective: Governing in Complex Times*, Cham: Palgrave Macmillan.

Rhodes, R.A.W., and Paul 't Hart (eds) (2014). *The Oxford Handbook of Political Leadership*, Oxford: Oxford University Press.

Seymour-Ure, Colin (2003). *Prime Ministers and the Media: Issues of Power and Control*, Oxford: Blackwell.

Shaw, Richard, and Chris Eichbaum (eds) (2018). *Ministers, Minders and Mandarins: An International Study of Relationships at the Executive Summit of Parliamentary Democracies*, Cheltenham: Edward Elgar.

References

Althaus, Marco (2018). Regierungskommunikation als Herausforderung für die Politikberatung. In Juliana Raupp, Jan Niklas Kocks, and Kim Murphy (eds), *Regierungskommunikation und staatliche Öffentlichkeitsarbeit: Implikationen des technologisch induzierten Medienwandels* (pp. 219–249). Wiesbaden: Springer VS.

Bjerkaas, Sunniva, and Kristoffer Kolltveit (2023). Statsministerens kontor: Kommunikasjonens høyborg i et moderne medielandskap? *Norsk statsvitenskapelig tidsskrift* 39(2): 56–73.

Blick, Andrew, and George Jones (2013). *At Power's Elbow: Aides to the Prime Minister from Robert Walpole to David Cameron*, London: Biteback Publishing.

Deutsch, Karl W. (1963). *The Nerves of Government: Models of Political Communication and Control*, New York: The Free Press of Glencoe.

Esser, Frank, Carsten Reinemann, and David Fan (2001). Spin doctors in the United States, Great Britain, and Germany: Metacommunication about Media Manipulation. *International Journal of Press/Politics* 6(1): 16–45.

Figenschou, Tine U., Rune Karlsen, Kristoffer Kolltveit, and Kjersti Thorbjørnsrud (2017). Serving the media ministers: A mixed methods study on the personalization of ministerial communication. *International Journal of Press/Politics* 22(4): 411–430.

Figenschou, Tine U., Rune Karlsen, and Kristoffer Kolltveit (2022). Between spin doctor and information provider: Conceptualizing communication professionals in government ministries. *Public Administration*, 1–19. Early view. First published 24 June 2022.

Fynes-Clinton, Jane (2017). A matter of trust: The complicated relationship between political media advisers and political journalists. *Media International Australia* 164(1): 128–138.

Garland, Ruth (2021). *Government Communications and the Crisis of Trust: From Political Spin to Post-Truth*, Cham: Palgrave Macmillan.

Horgan, John (2001). 'Government sources said last night…': The development of the parliamentary press lobby in modern Ireland. In Hiram Morgan (ed.). *Information, Media and Power Through the Ages* (pp. 259–271). Dublin: University College Dublin Press.

Hustedt, Thurid (2018). Germany: The smooth and silent emergence of advisory roles. In Richard Shaw and Chris Eichbaum (eds), *Ministers, Minders and Mandarins: An International Study of Relationships at the Executive Summit of Parliamentary Democracies* (pp. 72–90). Cheltenham: Edward Elgar.

Johansson, Elena, and Karl Magnus Johansson (2021). Along the government–media frontier: Press secretaries offline/online. *Journal of Public Affairs*, published online 13 September 2021.

Johansson, Karl Magnus (2022). *The Prime Minister–Media Nexus: Centralization Logic and Application*, Cham: Palgrave Macmillan.

Johansson, Karl Magnus, Milda Malling, and Gunnar Nygren (2019). Sweden: A professionally symbiotic relationship. In Karl Magnus Johansson and Gunnar Nygren (eds), *Close and Distant: Political Executive–Media Relations in Four Countries* (pp. 97–123). Gothenburg: Nordicom

Johansson, Karl Magnus, and Tapio Raunio (2020). Centralizing government communication? Evidence from Finland and Sweden. *Politics & Policy* 48(6): 1138–1160.

Kavanagh, Dennis, and Anthony Seldon (1999). *The Powers Behind the Prime Minister: The Hidden Influence of Number Ten*, London: HarperCollins.

Kolltveit, Kristoffer (2021). Communication advisers in public bureaucracies: Inhabitants of the zone between politics and administration. In Rómulo Pinheiro and Jarle Trondal (eds), *Organising and Governing Governmental Institutions* (pp. 249–265). Bergen: Fagbokforlaget.

Lees-Marshment, Jennifer (2020). *Political Management: The Dance of Government and Politics*, London: Routledge.

Marland, Alex, J. P. Lewis, and Tom Flanagan (2017). Governance in the age of digital media and branding. *Governance* 30(1): 125–141.

McKnight, David (2015). Shaping the news: Media advisers under the Howard and Rudd governments. *Australian Journalism Review* 37(1): 21–31.

McLean, Hamish, and Jacqui Ewart (2020). *Political Leadership in Disaster and Crisis Communication and Management: International Perspectives and Practices*, Cham: Palgrave Macmillan.

Ng, Yee-Fui (2020). Political advisers in the executive branch. In Rudy B. Andeweg, Robert Elgie, Ludger Helms, Juliet Kaarbo, and Ferdinand Müller-Rommel (eds), *The Oxford Handbook of Political Executives* (pp. 501–521). Oxford: Oxford University Press.

Pfetsch, Barbara (2008). Government news management: Institutional approaches and strategies in three Western democracies reconsidered. In Doris A. Graber, Denis McQuail, and Pippa Norris (eds), *The Politics of News: The News of Politics* (pp. 71–97). 2nd ed. Washington, D.C.: CQ Press.

Phillipps, Richard (2002). *Media Advisers – Shadow Players in Political Communication.* Unpublished PhD thesis. Sydney: University of Sydney.

Seymour-Ure, Colin (1991). The role of press secretaries on chief executive staffs in Anglo-American systems. In Colin Campbell, S.J., and Margaret Jane Wyszomirski (eds), *Executive Leadership in Anglo-American Systems* (pp. 381–412). Pittsburgh: University of Pittsburgh Press.

Seymour-Ure, Colin (2003). *Prime Ministers and the Media: Issues of Power and Control*, Oxford: Blackwell.

Shaw, Richard (ed.) (2023). *Handbook on Ministerial and Political Advisers*, Cheltenham: Edward Elgar.

Shaw, Richard, and Chris Eichbaum (eds) (2018). *Ministers, Minders and Mandarins: An International Study of Relationships at the Executive Summit of Parliamentary Democracies*, Cheltenham: Edward Elgar.

Street, John (2021). *Media, Politics and Democracy*. 3rd ed. London: Red Globe Press.

Thomas, Paul G. (2013). Communications and Prime Ministerial Power. In James Bickerton and B. Guy Peters (eds), *Governing: Essays in Honour of Donald J. Savoie* (pp. 53–84). Montreal: McGill-Queen's University Press.

Tiernan, Anne (2007). *Power Without Responsibility: Ministerial Staffers in Australian Governments from Whitlam to Howard*, Sydney: University of New South Wales Press.

Young, Sally (ed.) (2007). *Government Communication in Australia*, Melbourne: Cambridge University Press.

8

MANAGING THE PERFORMANCE OF MEMBERS OF PARLIAMENT

Views from New Zealand

Anita Ferguson and Michael Macaulay

Introduction

The behaviour of ministers and members of parliament (MPs) is rarely out of the news, in any jurisdiction, leaving the impression that politics is often a management-free zone. Even by its own fairly dubious standards, bad behaviour by MPs in Westminster systems appear to have escalated recently: UK witnessed Boris Johnson became the first PM in Britain's history to have been found guilty of breaking the law and in New Zealand, in late 2022, Labour MP Gaurav Sharma was suspended and subsequently expelled following his high-profile accusations of bullying against numerous members of his party. At the same time, National MP Sam Uffindell faced a public outcry and a party investigation following allegations of historical bullying to which he admitted culpability. Indeed, so bad has parliamentary behaviour become within Aotearoa that it was subject to a national inquiry in 2018/2019, which found that "bullying and harassment are systemic in the workplace" (Francis, 2019:7). Electoral accountability lies at the heart of much of this debate, yet the research is largely silent on how to manage the performance of MPs. The public will not vote for MPs they disagree with, whether or not that's to do with policy choices or their own behaviour. This chapter explores an alternative view. Drawing on qualitative research that predates the inquiry into parliament, it shows that New Zealand's MPs and ministers are open to ways in which their own performance can be managed. Interestingly, these views offer a more corporate, dare we say, *businesslike* view than the traditional Westminster model offers. In so doing, the chapter offers insights into accountability and performance, whether or not electoral accountability is a sufficient influence on MP behaviour, and what other forms of performance would be welcomed or rejected?

DOI: 10.4324/9781003260677-8

Key literature

There is comparatively little literature on parliamentarians and performance management. Instead, the majority of research looks at "purple zone" activities (Alford et al, 2017) and political performance management tends to be focused on how ministers manage public servants. Aucoin (2012), for example, investigates the impact of performance management on the impartiality of the public service across four jurisdictions; Di Francesco (2012) assesses the strength of performance management in ministerial departmental leadership (see also Curristine, 2005); and Matthews (2016) investigates various UK governments and how their perspectives on performance management impacted the civil service. Building on this, there is important research on how politicians use performance *information* to manage their departments (Bouckaert and Peters, 2002; Brun and Siegel, 2006; Laegreid et al., 2006; Bjornholt et al., 2016). Bouckaert and Peters (2002) find that performance management has been a key part of the move to modernize the public sector over the past 20 years. Several studies emphasize the value of performance management as a tool to align the goals of politicians and public agencies they oversee (Walker et al., 2013) and, ultimately, to improve organizational performance (Boyne, 2003; Boyne & Chen., 2006). Others are more circumspect. Pollitt (2006), for example, argued that despite the ubiquity of performance information both politicians and the public remain sceptical about its value, reflecting a tension between the reporting of information that is politically useful as opposed to operationally worthwhile (Neale, 2001; Brun and Siegel, 2006).

Literature on parliamentary performance management is much more slight and tends to focus on the hiring and firing of cabinet ministers. While we can expect decisions of this nature to be made based on performance, the literature lacks any discussion about a wider performance process. Rather, it finds the main criteria for appointment is political loyalty to the leader (Dewan and Myatt, 2007). Parliament is an unusual environment in that political leaders must work – almost exclusively – with people they have neither recruited nor selected (Huber and Martinez-Gallardo, 2008). This can lead to issues of "adverse selection" and a paucity of talent (Huber and Martinez-Gallardo, 2008; Berlinski et al., 2010; Not surprisingly, the firing of ministers is also very political (Indridason and Kam, 2008; Berlinski et al., 2010). There are two broad reasons for ministers to be removed from office – "shirking" which occurs when they don't work hard enough or lack the required level of skill or "policy-shifting" when their ideas are seen to be at odds with those of the leadership. Furthermore, governments or prime ministers can benefit politically from firing ministers (Dewan and Dowding, 2005; Dewan and Myatt, 2007) particularly by deflecting blame for a crisis on an individual minister. Dewan and Dowding (2005) suggest that this preference for political expediency over true performance management may serve to keep cabinet ministers on their toes, but others argue that it creates a perverse incentive to do as little as possible in order to avoid the spotlight or any controversy (Dewan and Myatt, 2007).

What is clearly lacking in these discussions is a broader organizational perspective, not least such factors as (1) organizational culture (individual vs organization focus), (2) organizational climate (leader-membership exchange) and the role of politics, and (3) the strength of an organization's human resource management (HRM) system on performance management (St-Onge, 2012). We suggest that such aspects are crucial in understanding experiences of parliamentary performance management.

Organizational culture is the "deep structure of an organization, which is rooted in the values, beliefs and assumptions held by organizational members" (Denison, 1996) and has a significant impact on all aspects of management. An organization's level of focus on employee engagement is the biggest cultural predictor of performance management effectiveness (Haines and St-Onge, 2012; Rusu et al., 2015), organizations that place greater emphasis on employee development and are more likely to have committed employees (Lund, 2003; Haines and St-Onge, 2012). Organizational climate, on the other hand, is concerned with the environment of an organization at a given time and is therefore more dynamic and changeable (Denison, 1996). Haines and St-Onge (2012) found that a positive (strong) employee relations climate was the most significant contextual predictor of effective performance management systems. Liden et al. (1997) found that a positive employee relations climate was generally the product of positive "leader-member exchange" relationships. That is where two-way, trust-based relationships exist within an organization, reducing barriers between managers and their subordinates. Even when feedback may be negative or critical, employees are more likely to respond constructively and work to improve their performance if that feedback is coming from a trusted source (Pilcher, 2012). Conversely, when an organization's employee relations climate is weak, people's perceptions and responses to the goings on around them can vary significantly (Bowen and Ostroff, 2004). If the climate is weak and employees are unclear about what goals are important and what behaviours are expected and will be rewarded, the less likely it is that those goals will be achieved.

HRM is a system of complementary practices which work together to support organizational growth and development (Bowen and Ostroff, 2004). For HRM to be effective, it is crucial that employees see the framework as part of a wider inter-connected system designed to support their own growth and that of the organization (Bowen and Ostroff, 2004; Nankervis, 2006;). Morgan (2006) argues that too often organizations run performance management schemes in isolation from other HRM and other management practices. If employees see that their appraisal is part of a "strategically integrated system of human capital practices" (Haines and St-Onge, 2012), they are more likely to perceive it as important, to respect the process and to behave accordingly. If employees see the wider HRM system as weak or lacking in integrity, performance appraisal is unlikely to deliver desired results (Bowen and Ostroff, 2004). Haines and St-Onge's research (2012) found that a lack of strategic HRM integration was a predictor of weak performance management practices, it was less significant than both climate and culture.

The nature and effectiveness of HRM is especially relevant in a parliamentary context where there is little direct connection between day-to-day performance and promotions, remuneration or even (at the most extreme end) the hiring and firing process. A clear example of this is in parliamentary politics where we would expect MPs to have their performance managed by their particular party leader but where remuneration is fixed and set externally and where the position of individuals within the parliament is determined externally by the voting public. This final point also leads to room for goal conflict as MPs must choose between the wishes of their electorate and those of their political leadership.

Methodology

The bulk of this chapter is based on exploratory research, comprising 19 in-depth interviews conducted between MPs and senior staff from both the New Zealand Labour and New Zealand National political parties (see Table 8.1), of which 18 were finally used. The interviews took place in 2016 but we feel their relevance has only increased since that time.

TABLE 8.1 Interviews conducted between members of parliament and senior staff

	Government	Opposition
R1	X	
R2	X	
R3	X	X
R4	X	X
R5		X
R6	X	X
R7	X	X
R8	X	X
R9	—	—
R10	X	X
R11	X	
R12	X	
R13	X	X
R14		X
R15	X	X
R16	X	X
R17	X	X
R18	X	X
R19	X	

The research was both inspired and aided by the fact that the lead author previously had a career as an advisor in New Zealand Parliament, which also adds an insider research perspective that helped shape the interviews (Wond and Macaulay, 2011). The sampling strategy was purposive, targeting those key respondents understood to have significant first-hand knowledge of their party's performance management system either as someone with responsibility for managing the performance of others or as someone who had received recognition for positive performance or felt the consequences of negative performance. The interviews are evenly split between each of the two major political parties represented in the New Zealand Parliament. Twelve of the 18 respondents (67%) had experience in government, 13 of 18 (72%) had experience in opposition and seven of 18 (39%) drew on experiences from time served in both opposition and in government. Six of the 18 respondents (33%) are current or former ministers and three spoke in their capacity as a member of staff (past or present) involved in their organization's performance management process.

We asked how their parties approach performance management within parliament and whether or not they felt more corporate approaches to performance management would be beneficial in a parliamentary context. We also investigated the contexts that potentially enhance or limit the ability of political leaders to effectively performance manage members of their electorates, and how might political leaders might adapt their approaches to increase the effectiveness of performance management practices.

Research findings

The New Zealand parliamentary performance management process

Performance management in parliamentary political parties is very limited – there is no wraparound system as envisaged by various theorists and as practiced in many corporate organizations. Rather, subsets of MPs within both parties are subject to a performance appraisal process whereby goals or priorities in line with their organization's arching strategy are agreed with their leadership and are reviewed at six monthly intervals.

In government, the prime minister writes to each minister at the start of the year outlining the government's priorities. S/he asks them to write back outlining the work they will do in their portfolio areas to help deliver on the government's objectives as well as any significant additional work they have planned. Once ministers have replied, in consort with their staff and departmental officials, they will meet with the prime minister to agree a way forward. As it was described, there did not appear to be a highly formal and structured process:

When [The Prime Minister] meets with them, s/he also uses that time as an opportunity to talk to them about how they're doing personally and if he feels there are any issues. So for example, the standard way that meeting might take place would be we have senior officials and stuff in the room for the first 20 minutes where we go through some bits and pieces and for the last 10 or 15 he might say, okay right, thanks very much everybody and then it'll just be him and the minister and then he'll go, 'Okay, well how are you getting on?' 'Oh look, I'm a bit concerned about your work-load,' or 'I'm a bit concerned that you've got a bad reputation for beating up on staff,' or 'you've got a reputation for...' this or that. Then they'll have a bit of a discussion about that ....

(R16)

There is no equivalent meeting for other members on the government side of the House, where performance management is characterized as "sporadic, at best" (R10).

In opposition, leaders have over time sought to implement a six-monthly appraisal and review process with limited success. At best, review meetings are held annually with all MPs (not just those in the shadow cabinet or on the front bench).

... And the idea was that we would review that every six months ... The absolute truth, in the interests of academic research truth – it hasn't really worked.... we did an annual one in the end.

(R6)

Finally, list MPs from both parties are required to provide six-monthly re-ports on their activity to their party boards as a means to ensure accountability, though these too appear to be ad-hoc with members from one party reporting that their board was considerably behind schedule as far as "reporting" for list MPs is going.

It was generally agreed by all respondents that political leaders simply do not have adequate time to meet with and actively performance man-age every member of their caucus. Perhaps for this reason, the established convention within both parties is that functions typically associated with a performance management process are carried out by multiple actors. Party leaders are responsible for setting and communicating the strategy to mem-bers, whips deal with day-to-day issues of participation and general HR-like management, the Leader of the House deals with performance in the all-important debating chamber, party boards are concerned with matters of hiring and firing and the chief of staff is a proxy for his party leader in all other matters.

As the leader's proxy, the chief of staff is perhaps the most appropriate person to take responsibility for more formalized performance management but a number of participants voiced concerns about this owing to a perceived status gap between MPs (who are elected) and staff (who are not).

> I'm not sure all my colleagues would be quite as willing to get [performance] feedback from a staff member. … Because we're Ministers and they're not. Because we're out there and they're the Monday morning quarterbacks.
>
> *(R12)*

This reflects interestingly on the purple zone that so many commentators have identified and the perception that the distinction between political and managerial still remains acute for MPs.

Performance evaluation and feedback for MPs

Aside from the appraisal meetings described earlier, there is no evidence of a formal process for performance evaluation on either side of the House. MPs from both parties referred to a lack of routine or regular feedback. The unanimous view was that feedback would generally only be received if performance was particularly negative, with one respondent suggesting: "the absence of negative feedback is an indication that we're on track" (R12). Some chalked this up to an organizational culture of high pressure and a focus on minimizing risks: "It's not a particularly positive environment" (R1). Others identified more systemic reasons, such as the nature of a competitive democracy itself:

> In politics you very rarely get praised for success. It's probably one of the negative parts of [the job] that is difficult, and if you're comparing it to a corporate environment or a normal work environment or family where you try and acknowledge and praise … there's not enough of that.
>
> *(R4)*

Informal mentoring occurs within both parties but the nature and extent of this is down to the individuals concerned: it is relationship-based. This form of positive performance intervention was frequently espoused by senior organizational members but was not referred to at all by their backbench or more junior colleagues. While this does not mean mentoring does not occur, it is clearly less valued by junior members than is desirable. One respondent speculated that, given the competitive nature of the environment, it is not in the interests of senior caucus members to be too supportive of more junior members as ultimately they are all vying for the same limited number of positions.

Feedback from external stakeholders does appear to be a factor for both parties. While this also tends to be ad hoc and opportunistic, it does have an impact.

> When he's in the Koru Lounge or when he goes to meetings and stuff, he'll get people saying, 'Such and such is doing a good job,' or 'Such and such doesn't listen,' or 'Such and such is an arrogant prick,' .... And [he'll follow that up actually. Sometimes if an industry group says, 'oh such and such is being difficult,' He might ... give them a call and say, 'Hey look, you should be aware that this is what's being said. Let's try and deal with it and understand it.' ...So we try not to ignore that stuff.
>
> *(R16)*

Almost by definition, this feedback will relate to ministers or shadow ministers who have clearly defined stakeholders with the ability to influence. Incidences of political leaders receiving feedback on non-portfolio holding members of their team must be far less likely, further increasing the gap in information about the performance of senior MPs relative to those on the backbench. While time-consuming, a more formalized process of feedback from third parties would ensure the work of all members with stakeholders or in their communities was at least able to be recognized.

> I can think of very clear examples where people have been taken out because they stakeholders have made submissions ... and say 'this MP is fucking poison'.
>
> *(R14)*

Incentives, rewards and promotional tracks

The lack of available rewards for good performance or sanctions for poor performance was a strong theme in the interviews. Unlike most organizations' salaries for elected representatives are set by an external body (the remuneration authority), leaving leaders unable to provide financial incentives for good performance. The most meaningful reward is an increased "ranking" within the caucus or cabinet – essentially a promotion (without the pay rise) – but these occur infrequently and are highly political (discussed further later). Challenging work assignments, public praise and opportunities to represent New Zealand or their party at international forums are other valued indicators of good performance. While these rewards – and those above – are valued, a lack of clear process or transparency undermines their effectiveness.

There was also clear evidence of a reluctance to deal with performance issues in a structured or constructive way until they become a "public" issue at which time political imperative took over and action was swift and (sometimes) ruthless.

> If people are publicly incompetent, then it's more likely [SIC] to move them along more quickly.
>
> *(R17)*

MPs who were struggling with their workload or a particular issue spoke of being ignored and becoming isolated. A lack of feedback combined with almost non-existent development support combines to leave some members unsure about what is expected of them, what they can do to lift performance and how to get on the path to promotion.

Unlike other workplaces, however, all unsuccessful applicants remain in the organization. And given the essentially public nature of the application process, their failure is known by everyone who can lead to not just dissatisfaction but destructive behaviour. The inability for political leaders to remove MPs from the parliament if they are not performing is regarded as a major issue and is perhaps the greatest contributor to the lack of performance management – this will be discussed in more detail later in this report.

Performance management occurs to the extent that the environment is conducive to it happening. The parliamentary context is not very conducive, posing substantial threats to a typical approach to performance management. All participants acknowledged the importance of merit in decisions around promotion but demographic and political factors were seen as critical.

> It's not a meritocracy – people get promoted to satisfy wider interests.
>
> *(R2)*

> As long as they're good enough, it's good enough. [It's a question of] are they competent enough? Not are they the best ....
>
> *(R14)*

Respondents painted a picture of political leaders constantly having to manage issues of competence (making sure that they had sufficient skill to drive public policy issues) with those of gender and ethnic diversity, geographic representation and the needs or expectations of their wider organization (outside of parliament).

Issues of gender and ethnicity were most frequently raised as factors most likely to encourage promotion. The prevailing view appears to be that if two candidates for promotion were equally capable but one was a man and one a woman or an ethnic minority, the second was most likely to be successful. The issue of gender bias was raised by all respondents, aside from the female interviewees who would not be drawn on the issue. One commented that, for some members, the idea that one demographic grouping may be favoured over another was a convenient excuse for their own lack of success.

There is a clear tension in both parties between an espoused desire to see the parliament and the ministry reflect the demographic composition of the country and one to believe that all promotions or demotions are based strictly on performance.

> They get promoted [because] of who they were rather than how good they were.
>
> *(R19)*

With discussions on political culture wars currently raging, some respondents were already taking a strong stance on identity politics, citing it as a reason for a lack of promotional progress.

> I am probably the most marginalised sort of person – white, middle-aged male. If I was an ethnic woman, gay person I'd probably have a better chance.
>
> *(R11)*

The appeasement of internal political factions was also a significant factor where promotions were concerned, particularly when the leadership was finely balanced or the environment especially volatile. Respondents reported situations where this factionalization was so extreme that political leaders were more inclined to punish their "friends" rather than their enemies to avoid political fall-out.

> … they were quite a strong group in the Caucus. So [the leader] had to handle them with kid gloves sometimes and they expected to have bums at the Cabinet table, and they got them, and they expected to be listened to in the internal debates and they were listened to. And that was just about politics. It was about interests and just making sure you're keeping that group content. Sometimes it was issues like that that dictated how [the Leader] might respond to an issue. If there was one Minister that she was close to … she could probably be tougher on them and say, 'Look I'm not happy with the way you're doing such and such.' But with the people who are slightly risky … you just had to be careful with him and you didn't want to upset them too much, because you upset them, you upset that little grouping going around them. Then you've got a bit of a festering sore in your Caucus. So it was about balancing those sorts of interests, just keeping things peaceful and on an even keel. A Prime Minister always has to watch their back ….
>
> *(R2)*

The political complications of all aspects of performance management are likely to discourage political leaders unless performance management is absolutely necessary. Leaders appear to make a judgement call that the political risk of carrying a poor performer is less than that of upsetting a rival faction or important demographic group.

> The reason leaders don't reshuffle more frequently is that the people who move down think they don't deserve it and they people who miss out think they should be promoted. Thankless task and in this environment it matters because you need their support and they have the ability to make your life much more difficult than someone in a normal organization who feels aggrieved.
>
> *(R15)*

For this reason, poor performance – at least in terms of portfolio work – is often tolerated.

> Even if they were quite ordinary performers, they could expect to hold their position as long as they didn't cause the leader any grief.
>
> *(R2)*

As previously mentioned, demotions – when they do occur – tend to be a matter of last resort, occurring only when the performance of an MP becomes a public issue and therefore a distraction for the leadership. Punishment in this respect is more about political expediency than bad performance or behaviour. This supports the theme that while it's very competitive to get in to cabinet, once an MP is there, they may only need to expend a minimal amount of effort in order to remain.

> If you've got competent officials around you can get by okay having an ordinary performer sitting in the Cabinet chair.
>
> *(R2)*

> Even if they were quite ordinary performers, they could expect to hold their position as long as they didn't cause the leader any grief.
>
> *(R17)*

All respondents reported incidents of promotions that they perceived to be unfair but also felt that that this lack of fairness was inherent in the political process.

Q: Is it fair?

A: "It's politics." (R14)

There are no avenues for appeal where decisions are regarded as unjust – decisions were viewed as being completely at the leader's prerogative, were frequently made without consultation and were generally communicated just prior to being announced publicly. Further, members did not see it as being in their interests to complain or re-litigate.

Q: Are there grounds for appeal?

A: Shit no! (R6)

> It was hard for me to know … whether it was a message or not. Was it a performance message or was it a message around who I had voted for … But there's actually not much point re-litigating it.
>
> *(R8)*

Despite the fact that the environments they described appeared to be low in trust, many respondents reported either a degree of trust or a qualified trust in their colleagues.

Others were explicit about the lack of trust:

> There's not a lot of trust, no. It's quite a nasty game.
>
> *(R2)*

> You probably don't have too many people you can trust in politics because we've all got different masters.
>
> *(R4)*

Despite the intense and highly competitive environment, all respondents reported a strong degree of collegiality among colleagues, though this may be due to political imperative.

> It's in my personal and professional interest to maintain relationships.
>
> *(R5)*

As is the case with most workplaces, respondents all reported having some colleagues whom they were close to, whom they would talk to most days and get to know personally as well as professionally as well as others whom they didn't have a lot of time for or simply didn't know very well. Relationships between senior and more junior players tended to be based mostly on personality, though there was some discussion about the perception that some senior players were working to forge ties with the backbench as part of a longer-term leadership aspiration.

There were instances of more extreme, anti-social behaviour that would not be associated with the typical office environment. Receiving a dressing-down for perceived bad behaviour in a public or semi-public forum appears to be a favoured form of discipline on both sides of the House.

> Normal people in a normal environment do not bag each other in front of staff – we get that. It's called robust discussion.
>
> *(R18)*

Respondent 5 discussed a situation where he was reprimanded in a caucus meeting by a peer: "*I almost couldn't speak I was so fucking angry. It was a total and utter power play and I thought it was so unprofessional... but that's the dynamic.*"

As with the political considerations outlined above, there was a strong view that levels of trust and collegiality are more present in parties that are not enjoying political success.

> [Collegiality] might party be assisted by the fact that we're polling well. I imagine when a political party's not polling so well, people don't get on so well.
>
> *(R1)*

> You spend most of your time worrying about what people are doing behind your back rather than focusing on what people are doing in front of you. You never felt particularly like everybody was onside.
>
> *(R19)*

Aside from cabinet ministers or frontbenchers, members seldom hear from their political leaders outside of their weekly caucus meetings. While all respondents felt that they could contact their leader if they had a serious issue, they were all reluctant to initiate contact, believing that they could only make a very limited number of approaches to the leadership in their career and should save this for very serious issues. While the view that complaining directly to the organization's leader should only be done is extreme circumstances is likely to prevail in most organizations, most employees have a line manager that they can approach in the first instance. This is not the case in parliament where there are effectively no tiers of management – everyone reports to the leader. This poses two challenges: (1) political leaders have an enormous number of direct reports (currently 60 in national and 32 in labour) making management very difficult and (2) there is a huge gulf between backbench and junior MPs and their leaders which poses challenges for organizational citizenship, performance management and democracy (theoretically all elected members should have equal access to their leaders).

No backbench or more junior respondent reported their leadership pro-actively contacting them to discuss an issue, other than when they were to receive negative feedback. This lack of visibility further increases the divide between the backbench and senior members, who frequently have the opportunity to discuss issues and progress with their leadership.

Electoral accountability vs parliamentary performance

Interview participants discussed a tension between the wants of their electorate and those of their party leadership, which was a particular concern when a party was not polling well. There was a view that some members would focus on winning their seat and therefore securing their future in the parliament even if this was to the detriment of the wider party. Similarly, there is a widely held view that some members focus on the raising of their personal profile at the expense of that of their leadership. It is this kind of goal conflict – between individuals and organizations – that a true performance management process expels.

> There is a major conflict within MMP and that is the constituent vote versus the Party vote – and the value of winning a constituency versus maximising the party vote, or the value of having an individual win a seat versus maximise the vote for the party. Those are major structural conflicts that are non-resolvable.
>
> *(R4)*

When asked if their first loyalty was to their party or their constituency, the split was about even.

The issue of goal conflict – when the goals of the electorate conflict with that of the party – was not as significant as anticipated. Members of both parties reported that while these conflicts did occur, they were manageable. No respondent believed that a conflict of this nature – if managed appropriately – was likely to impact on a member's chance of promotion: "*I was a backbencher so I was nothing*" (R6).

Conclusion

The lack of effective performance management of New Zealand's MPs on both sides of the House is clear. The findings of this research coupled with frequent news reports of bad behaviour of elected officials and the varied and, at times, unpredictable responses of their "management" highlight a gap in both the political management and HRM literature.

A significant impediment to the performance management of our elected politicians is the lack of connection between the various HRM components.

MPs are effectively hired and fired by their local electorates but their day-to-day management comes from their political leaders. Their remuneration (a typical performance indicator) is set by the independent remuneration authority. As leaders ability to performance manage is severely limited as they cannot remove MPs (unless they are only list members), adjust their remuneration or provide many meaningful rewards or consequences for their actions.

The experiences of backbench members both in terms of PM and the wider environment are very different to those of cabinet ministers or frontbenchers. Matters of engagement, trust, internal politics and congeniality are less of a concern if you've already "made it." Further, because these senior people do experience a degree of performance management, they are more likely to know what they need to do to enjoy continued success. Backbenchers, on the other hand, generally have no idea how they are performing or what they need to do to increase performance and their likelihood of promotion.

The parliamentary context is one where, according to research, typical approaches to performance management will be severely challenged. At the time our research was conducted, the culture of our two major political parties is characterized by a lack of trust, limited feedback and poor leader-member exchange. Both organizations are hierarchical with significant difference between the experiences of senior and junior members in terms of performance management and other aspects of organizational life. Our politicians have "many masters" – that is the lines of accountability are complex and therefore so are their motivations. The nature of the system leaves political leaders with a limited ability to either reward good performance or punish poor performance and often provides perverse incentives to tolerate all but the most extreme performance issues.

While senior MPs receive a degree of performance appraisal, more lowly ranked members typically receive nothing. Performance appraisal on its own can be useful but where leaders have little ability to provide consequences, it is meaningless. Given the contextual constraints outlined above, any attempts to introduce a more comprehensive approach to performance management will be fraught, but there are a number of measures that may support improved performance.

While we recognizes that the research has a number of limitations, some of these may actually work in its favour. The sample we spoke with are all largely from a particular sector; our focus on New Zealand shows an inherent bias towards Westminster-style democracies (and indeed a very particular form of Westminster at that). Yet as this sector is so under-represented in terms of discussion on performance, then we hope that our findings have brought several new insights into view. While we cannot reasonably suggest that the purple-zone crosses over from parliament into managerialism, it is very interesting to note that there is a shift towards acceptance of such ideas, which necessitates a potential shift away from simply electoral accountability.

Recommendations for future research

1 There is considerable scope for further research into the performance management of elected officials and the interplay between performance management practices (or the lack thereof) and political or electoral outcomes.
2 Research into political and parliamentary misconduct could take into account HRM approaches.
3 This research highlights the role of appointed political staff in the management of elected representatives which may be worthy of further study.
4 Further research can be conducted into how traditional principles such as electoral accountability play out in real life and to what extent they have been extended.
5 An extension of this research could consider the role of HRM practices in other political contexts – for example, membership organizations.

Recommendations for practitioners

1 HRM approaches can be formally utilized by political parties to reflect the day-to-day reality of how MPs perceive their own performance management.
2 Alongside, traditional mechanisms such as codes of conduct, MPs can have behavioural and conduct issues built into performance appraisals.
3 HRM could be systematized across political party lines and also applied equally to parties in opposition or in government.

Recommended reading

Di Francesco, M. (2012). 'Grand designs? The 'Managerial' role of ministers within Westminster-based public management policy', *Australian Journal of Public Administration*, 71(3), 257–268.
Huber, J., & Martinez-Gallardo, C. (2008). Replacing cabinet ministers: Patterns of ministerial stability in parliamentary democracies. *American Political Science Review*, 102(02).
Matthews, F. M. (2016). Letting go and holding on: The politics of performance management in the United Kingdom. *Public Policy and Administration*, 31(4), 303–332.

References

Alford, J., Hartley, J., Yates, S., & Hughes, O. (2017). Into the purple zone: Deconstructing the politics/administration distinction. *The American Review of Public Administration*, 47(7), 752–763. https://doi.org/10.1177/0275074016638481
Aucoin, P. (2012). New political governance in Westminster systems: Impartial public administration and management performance at risk. *Governance*, 25(2), 177–199.
Berlinski, S., Dewan, T., & Dowding, K. (2010). The impact of individual and collective performance on ministerial tenure. *The Journal of Politics*, 72(2), 559–571.

Bjørnholt, B., Bækgaard, M., & Houlberg, K. (2016). Does fiscal austerity affect political decision-makers' use and perception of performance information? *Public Performance & Management Review, 39*(3), 560–580. http://dx.doi.org/10.1080/15309576.2015.1137766

Bouckaert, G., & Peters, B. (2002). Performance measurement and management: The Achilles' heel in administrative modernization. *Public Performance & Management Review, 25*(4), 359.

Bowen, D., & Ostroff, C. (2004). Understanding HRM-firm performance linkages: The role of The "strength" of The HRM system. *Academy of Management Review, 29*(2), 203–221.

Boyne, G. (2003). Sources of public service improvement: A critical review and research agenda. *Journal of Public Administration Research and Theory, 13*(3), 367–394.

Boyne, G., & Chen, A. (2006). Performance targets and public service improvement. *Journal of Public Administration Research and Theory, 17*(3), 455–477.

Brun, M., & Philipp Siegel, J. (2006). What does appropriate performance reporting for political decision makers require? *International Journal of Productivity and Performance Management, 55*(6), 480–497.

Curristine, T. (2005). Government performance: Lessons and challenges. *OECD Journal on Budgeting, 5*(1), 127–151.

Denison, D. (1996). What is the difference between organizational culture and organizational climate? A native's point of view on a decade of paradigm wars. *Academy of Management Review, 21*(3), 619–654.

Dewan, T., & Dowding, K. (2005). The corrective effect of ministerial resignations on government popularity. *American Journal of Political Science, 49*(1), 46.

Dewan, T., & Myatt, D. (2007). Scandal, protection, and recovery in the cabinet. *American Political Science Review, 101*(01), 63.

Di Francesco, M. (2012). Grand designs? The 'managerial' role of ministers within Westminster-based public management policy. *Australian Journal of Public Administration, 71*(3), 257–268.

Francis, D. (2019) *Bullying and Harassment in the New Zealand Parliamentary Workplace*. Wellington: NZ Parliament.

Haines, V., & St-Onge, S. (2012). Performance management effectiveness: Practices or context? *The International Journal of Human Resource Management, 23*(6), 1158–1175.

Huber, J., & Martinez-Gallardo, C. (2008). Replacing cabinet ministers: Patterns of ministerial stability in parliamentary democracies. *American Political Science Review, 102*(02).

Indridason, I., & Kam, C. (2008). Cabinet reshuffles and ministerial drift. *British Journal of Political Science, 38*(04).

Laegreid, P., Roness, P., & Rubecksen, K. (2006). Performance management in practice: The Norwegian way. *Financial Accountability & Management, 22*(3), 251–270.

Lund, D. (2003). Organizational culture and job satisfaction. *Journal of Business and Industrial Marketing, 18*, 219–236.

Matthews, F. M. (2016). Letting go and holding on: The politics of performance management in the United Kingdom. *Public Policy and Administration, 31*(4), 303–32.

Morgan, R. (2006). Making the most of performance management systems. *Compensation & Benefits Review, 38*(5), 22–27.

Nankervis, A. (2006). Performance management: Theory in practice? *Asia Pacific Journal of Human Resources*, 44(1), 83–101.

Neale, A. (2001). Performance reporting for accountability purposes: Lessons, issues, future. *International Public Management Journal*, 3(1), 93–106.

Pilcher, S. (2012). The social context of performance appraisal and appraisal reactions: A meta-analysis. *Human Resource Management*, 51(5), 709–732. http://dx.doi.org/10.1002/hrm.21499

Pollitt, C. (2006). Performance information for democracy: The missing link? *Evaluation*, 12(1), 38–55.

Rusu, G., Avasilcăi, S., & Huțu, C. (2015). Organizational context factors influencing employee performance appraisal: A research framework. *Procedia – Social And Behavioral Sciences*, 221, 57–65.

Walker, R., Jung, C., & Boyne, G. (2013). Marching to Different Drummers? The Performance Effects of Alignment between Political and Managerial Perceptions of Performance Management. *Public Administration Review*, 73(6), 833–844. http://dx.doi.org/10.1111/puar.12131

Wond, T., & Macaulay, M. (2010). Evaluating local implementation: An evidence-based approach. *Policy and Society*, 29(2), 161–169.

9

THE CHALLENGES OF IMPLEMENTING A NATIONAL PARTY VISION

A Comparative Analysis of Midterm US Senate Elections

Brian M. Conley

Introduction

It is widely accepted by party scholars that US congressional elections have become increasingly "nationalized" (Jacobson, 2015, 2019; Fiorina, 2016; Hopkins, 2018; Sievert and McKee, 2019). The primary evidence scholars cite when supporting the nationalization claim is voting behavior. Curiously, what has not been as closely examined is how parties, or candidates, in the otherwise highly federated US party system have been able to coordinate their activities at a national level. It is an oversight that follows largely from the tendency in the political science literature to overlook the internal, institutional workings of political parties and electoral campaigns, specifically the work unique to the political practitioner – candidates, party leaders, and elected officials – who manage and direct campaigns, parties, and public offices. Such is a key insight of new research in the field of *political management*, which seeks to apply managerial concepts to the strategic and organizational challenges faced by political practitioners as they seek to achieve their political and policy goals. Democratic and Republican Party leaders may increasingly favor a more nationalized politics, but the key question is how successful have they been in achieving this goal?

The goal of this chapter is to address this gap in our understanding by examining the political management challenges that confront both the Democratic and Republican Parties and their affiliated candidates and campaigns. To do so, I look at the degree of message coordination that occurred between the national parties and the campaigns of incumbent Democratic and Republicans US Senators who sought reelection in the 2014, 2018, and 2022 midterm elections. By looking comparatively at Senate incumbents in both parties across the three

DOI: 10.4324/9781003260677-9

midterm elections, I hope to capture not only any variation that existed between the parties in rates of message coordination but also what effect, if any, controlling the White House had on levels of message nationalization within a party.

Key literature

The growing interest in political management has highlighted not only the scope of the managerial obstacles political practitioners must negotiate to achieve their institutional goals, but also the deficiencies of much of the prevailing academic literature and the limited guidance it offers for those in the convoluted world of practical politics.

The existing political management literature provides an array of valuable insights on how to manage the organizational and strategic complexities of running for office, leading political parties, and governing, often drawn from the firsthand experience of political practitioners with decades of experience in politics. But too often the literature fails to provide a broader analytical understanding of how management concepts may be strategically applied to practical politics. Allan Blakeney and Sandford Borins's *Political Management in Canada* (1998) is a case in point. The book abounds with information on a range of topics, from how to set priorities in office to managing budgets, staff, public services, and the media, based largely on Blakeney's extensive experience in Canadian government, notably as the premier of Saskatchewan between 1971 and 1982. Yet it lacks an overarching theoretical framework that might be applied to the myriad managerial challenges that regularly befuddle those in positions of executive authority.

Other research, however, makes only a passing reference to the idea of "political management" without meaningfully engaging with management concepts (Halligan and Power, 1992; Ingraham, Thompson and Eisenberg, 1995; Heatley, 1996). In their comparative analysis of the US presidential appointee process from Ronald Reagan to Bill Clinton, Patricia Ingraham, James Thompson, and Elliot Eisenberg (1995) use the term in a purely descriptive sense, as in "political management strategies," "technique[s]," and the "quality of political management" without explaining what such strategies and techniques might actually look like. Similarly, Alistair Heatley's (1996) otherwise careful account of public administrative practices in Australia's North Territory in the 1970s suffers from what is at best a fragmentary definition of political management. Elsewhere, the concept is either defined or applied so broadly as to cover nearly everything from lobbying to consulting to political campaigns. In his influential book, the *Routledge Handbook on Political Management* (2009), for instance, Dennis Johnson observes that "political management is sometimes referred to as applied politics or applied political science; in the field of communications, it is referred to as applied communications; and in the disciplines of commerce and marketing it is referred to as political marketing" (xiii). Another common fallacy is to uncritically conflate political management with campaign management. In an early essay on the subject, Christopher Arterton (1988) defines "political management" as being "concerned with two core elements: (1) electoral campaign management and (2) government relations and lobbying" (52). It is a definition that appears frequently in the literature, often implicitly. In his article, "Political Science and Political Management," Stephen Craig (2009) raises the important question of whether or not individual political campaigns have any real, substantive effect on the outcome of an election. But curiously, he does so without explaining how political management concepts might help answer the question.

More recently, researchers have begun to identify and address these gaps in our understanding of the concept of political management. They have done so by noting the importance of thinking about political management as a distinct academic field of study requiring not only the articulation of core concepts but also how they may be uniquely applied to the world of politics. Jennifer Lees-Marshment's book, *Political Management: The Dance of Government and Politics* (2021), provides arguably the first step in this direction. "Political management," Lees-Marshment argues, "is about how political practitioners … utilize management concepts and tools involving planning, HR [human resources], reviewing, organizing, and leading to achieve organizational goals, whether that be to win an election or pass a policy in government" (14). It is, "like business management … about getting things done," she writes, and is in this way distinct from political marketing, which focuses more "designing a strategy" rather than the organizational work of implementing. Political management centers on the "nitty gritty … of implementation," she explains (14). But, more importantly, beyond providing definitional clarity, Lees-Marshment identifies "five core areas of political management" that may be used to operationalize and potentially measure its application. They are political planning, political organizing, political human resources, political leadership, and political reviewing. Political planning, she writes, involves "designing and implementing organizational strategy," while political organizing relates to "internal structure and culture," political human resources to "appointing and utilizing staff," political leadership to utilizing power to exercise influence, and political review to critical organizational reflection.

It is a framework that we can use to critically evaluate how much a desire on behalf of the national parties in the US to nationalize elections resulted in higher levels of message coordination in recent congressional elections.

Methodology

To analyze the degree to which either national party in the US has been able to implement a more nationally coordinated message strategy and how this was impacted by party status or whether or not they controlled the White

House, I turn to Lees-Marshment's political management model, particularly the insights she offers on "political planning." Political planning is a key part of a party's overall political management strategy. It involves such vital organizational tasks as developing a coherent, overarching mission for the party; a clear vision concerning immediate political and policy objectives; and specific goals, strategies, and plans that aim to build organizational and strategic cohesion across all levels of the party and ultimately support a master implementation plan.

To assess the parties' ability to craft a coherent, unifying national party vision, I examine the congruence between the policy positions of the Democratic and Republican Parties on the issues of immigration and health care reform with those articulated by incumbent party US Senators during the last three midterm elections in 2014, 2018, and 2022. I look at the 2014, 2018, and 2022 midterm elections in order to control for what effect, if any, a presidential election may have on levels of national message coordination. It also enables me to explore whether in-party status, which flipped from the Democrats to the Republicans between 2014 and 2018 and then back gain in 2022 has an effect on levels of party coordination at the national level. The result was a sample size of 86 campaigns (33 incumbent Republican Senators [12 in 2014, 6 in 2018, and 15 in 2022] and 53 incumbent Democratic Senators [16 in 2014, 24 in 2018, and 13 in 2022]). I first identify and index the key words that defined the national parties' respective immigration and health care policies in each election, as outlined on official party websites and platforms. I then gauge, in terms of percentages, how many Senate incumbents took a public position on the issue on their official campaign websites. I rely on official party and campaign websites as the primary source of my data because, as a growing body of literature highlights, websites offer a uniquely unfiltered and comprehensive view of the policy thinking and positions of parties and candidates alike (Dolan, 2005; Druckman, Kifer and Parkin, 2009, 2020; Painter, 2015). Additionally, I use *ATLAS.ti* to determine the strength of the relationship, calculated in terms of co-occurrence coefficients (c-coefficient), between the policy language of the parties and that of the incumbent party senators who took a position on the issue. The strength of the relationship between the party and incumbents is scored on a scale from 0 to 1, with results closer to 1 indicating a stronger relationship than those closer to 0.

Research findings

What an analysis of the senatorial campaign websites shows is that despite the parties' eagerness to nationalize their messaging in the midterm elections, neither party has been able to effectively coordinate a unifying party message or vision at the national level. The parties do coordinate their activities in a variety of ways and have built the kind of organizational linkages internally that the literature suggests are vital to implementing a nationally coordinated party strategy. But in the last three midterm elections, this activity did not translate into a more national party message or vision for either the Democratic or the Republican Party. Moreover, control of the White House had no discernable effect on levels of message coordination. In fact, an analysis of the policy positions taken by the Senate candidates in the 2014, 2018, and 2022 midterms on the issues of immigration and health care shows that while some policy coordination did occur, and often with a considerable degree of specificity, it rarely involved a majority of the campaigns.

Thus, while the national parties take clear positions on a number of issues facing the country, candidates are quite selective when choosing which of those policies they do and do not publicly endorse or align themselves with on their websites. Indeed, the data suggests that they often chose to opt-out of addressing certain issues promoted by their party. Moreover, even when they do discuss the policy preferences of their party online, they tend to do so in a way that appropriates the language of the party but only as means of developing positions unique to their own campaign and race.

Party visions

In each election, save for the Republicans in 2022, both the Republican and Democratic Parties took clearly articulated positions on the issues of immigration and health care reform – which were remarkably consistent across elections. They were laid out in detail in the party's platforms and on the issue pages of the Republican National Committee (RNC) and Democratic National Committee (DNC) websites. In each election, for example, the Republican Party's position on immigration was largely predicated on a critique of first Obama and then the "Obama-Biden" administration's handling of the issue. In the opinion of Republican leaders, Obama and the Democrats' immigration policies were not only incompetent but also illegal in nature. By essentially adopting a policy of "backdoor amnesty," the Obama administration had "undermined the rule of law," the Republicans argued in 2014 and in the process done real harm to the American worker and the US economy (RNC, 2014a). By 2018, the party's immigration policies had – at the direction of the Trump administration – hardened even further. In a nod to Trump's "America first" rhetoric, the party asserted that "national immigration policy must put the interests of our existing citizens first" (RNC, 2018a). It was to this end that the RNC called in 2018 for a complete halt on all "illegal immigration," and for the "border…[to] be absolutely secured" (RNC, 2018a). The Republican Party did not formally adopt a position on the issue of immigration – or even a new party platform in 2020 – ahead of the 2022 midterms, choosing instead to issue a blanket statement resolving "to enthusiastically support [Trump's] America-first agenda" (RNC, 2020).

Additionally, Republicans remained steadfastly opposed in the 2014, 2018, and 2022 elections to Democratic efforts at health care reform, notably Obamacare. In fact, as the RNC stated in 2014, for Republican leaders "the Patient Protection and Affordable Care Act – Obamacare – was never really about health care" (RNC, 2014b). Rather, "from the start, it was about power, and the expansion of government control over one sixth of our economy." The law represented the "high-water mark of an outdated liberalism," the party exclaimed, "the latest attempt to impose upon Americans a Euro-style bureaucracy to manage all aspects of their lives." It had not only been repudiated in the "court of public opinion," they continued, but was effectively collapsing under "the weight of its own confusing, unworkable, budget-busting, and conflicting provisions." Worse still, in the opinion of Republican leaders, was the way Obamacare had "promoted the notion of abortion as health care" (RNC, 2014b). In response, the Republicans planned to repeal Obamacare once they won a majority in Congress in 2014 and replace it with affordable, "free market" solutions that protect the personal choice of individual patients and their families (RNC, 2014b). After winning the Senate in 2014, and two years later the presidency, the party did press in 2017 to repeal Obamacare but without success. As such, 2018 saw the party once again calling for the "repealing and replacing" of Obamacare and for a "roll back [of] regulations that have prevented market competition" and increased the cost of health care in the country (RNC, 2018b). And, as was the case with immigration policy, the party's 2020 resolution reiterating its wholesale support for Trump's agenda makes no specific reference to health care policy (RNC, 2020).

The Democrats, by contrast, rested their immigration policy in the 2014, 2018, and 2022 elections on calls for "comprehensive reform" of the current system. While Democratic leaders affirmed "America's … long and rich heritage of immigration," they also "recognize[d] that we need to fix our broken immigration system" (DNC, 2014a, 2018b). "Democrats believe America can do better," states the party's 2020 platform (DNC, 2020a). And the policies of the Trump administration after 2016, policies motivated, in the opinion of Democratic leaders, by outright "hatred and bigotry," only made the need for reform that much more urgent (DNC, 2018a). But, they asserted, "the truth is that our immigration system was broken long before President Trump came into office, and his departure alone won't fix it" (DNC, 2020a). The way forward, they contended, was to erect an immigration system built on the twin principles of "responsibility and accountability." The party was dedicated, it explained, "to building a 21st century immigration system that reflects our values, repairs past harms, heals our communities, rebuilds out economy, and renews our global leadership" (DNC, 2020a).

Democrats were equally resolved in the 2014, 2018, and 2022 elections to continue building on what it regarded as a similarly "comprehensive" approach to reforming the nation's health care system; a process that had started when President Obama signed the Affordable Care Act (ACA) into law in March 2010. That year, "President Obama fulfilled a promise that Democrats ha[d] pursued for nearly a century," the DNC claimed, by "making health care available to all Americans" (DNC, 2018c). They did so, Democratic leaders reminded voters in 2014 and again in 2018 and 2022, "despite the unanimous opposition from Republicans" (DNC, 2018c). "At every turn, Democrats' efforts to guarantee health coverage have been met by obstruction and opposition from the Republican Party" (DNC, 2020b). As such, the Democrats resolved in 2020 and 2022 "to … build the health care system the Americans people … deserve: one that finally provides universal health care coverage; reduces prescription drug prices; premiums, and out-of-pocket costs … and tackles the deep-seated inequities in our health care system" (DNC, 2020b).

Candidate positions

These were the ideas, partisan assertions, and policy promises regarding immigration and health care that served as the keywords upon which the national parties committees launched their respective 2014, 2018, and 2022 midterm campaigns. And they were faithfully reiterated by the Senate Campaign Committees. But the same cannot be said for the candidates themselves. Rather, what the data shows is that many candidates chose to either ignore or fundamentally rework the immigration and health care positions adopted by the national parties. And, they did so independent of whether or not their party controlled the presidency.

On the issue of immigration, for example, we have seen that save for the Republicans in 2022, the national parties have articulated detailed policy positions on the issue. Yet, in 2014, as the in-party, only 44% of the Democrats opted to mention immigration on their websites. This was only two points higher than the percentage of Republicans (42%) who discussed the issue that year. In 2018, despite now being in control of the presidency, the Republican percentage ticked up only slightly to 50%. The Democratic percentage dropped to 36%. In 2022, the presidency again switched hands, back to the Democrats. Nonetheless, the percentages of Democrats and Republicans who addressed the issue of immigration was essentially identical, 46% of Democrats to 47% of Republicans.

A similar trend, though not as pronounced, is evident in the positions that candidates in both parties took on the issue of health care. In 2014, 69% of in-party Democrats discussed the issue on their campaign websites but that was several points less than the Republicans, 84% of whom addressed the issue on their campaign sites. However, in 2018, the Democratic percentage, now as the out-party, jumped to 92% and the Republicans dropped to 62%. In 2022, despite another change in party status, the percentages for both parties were, as they had been for immigration, very close: 62% of Democrats to 67% of Republicans.

For immigration, then, the number of incumbent Senators in either party who mentioned the issue never exceeded 50%, regardless of White House control. Senate incumbents in both parties were more likely to publicly address the issue of health care on their campaign websites. Here, too, however, in each election, independent of party status, more than 30% of Senate incumbents in at least one party (31% and 38% of Democrats in 2014 and 2022, and 34% and 33% of Republicans in 2018 and 2022) chose to say nothing on their websites about an issue that was a key part of the national party's agenda.

Moreover, among the incumbent Senators who did take a position on either issue, the degree of actual co-occurrence on their campaign websites of the keywords and phrases that defined national party policy on the issues of immigration and health care was low. Measured in terms of c-coefficients, the results indicate that overall, even when their party controlled the presidency, the manner in which the Senate incumbents described or defined those policies was rarely in close keeping with the party.

If we look at the Democratic candidates who took a position on immigration reform, for example, we see that they were keen to employ many of the same policy phrases used by the party, such as "comprehensive reform," "fix a broken system," "pathway" or "roadmap" to citizenship, and attacks on Trump's "callous" and "cruel" policies. But they refrained from linking them together in the same way that the DNC did in outlining the party's position. In 2014, for instance, the strongest relationship existed between the concepts of "comprehensive reform" and the need to "enforce the law" (.54) and in 2018, between "comprehensive reform" and a "path to citizenship" (.50), and in 2022 between "roadmap to citizenship" and "promote worker rights" (.25). The same held for the issue of health care reform: many Democratic incumbents did use ideas from the party, but the evidence suggests that they brought them together in their own way, creating in the process their own unique policy positions. Overall, the strongest relationship that occurred between the party and candidates across all elections was a mere .48 in 2014 between support for the "ACA" and the principle that health care should be made available to all. In the 2018, the strongest relation was between "cost" and "universal coverage" (.39); in 2022, it was between "cost" and "drug prices" (.30).

Although a similar pattern is evident for the GOP, Republican Senate incumbents did periodically hew more closely with the national party message on both the issues of immigration and health care reform. In 2014, for example, out-party Republican incumbents generally developed their own unique immigration policy positions. But there was one important exception. The relationship between "secure the border" and the claim that Obama's immigration policies had "undermined the rule of law" was quite strong (.83). However, the next strongest relationship was between "harm the American worker" and "secure the border" (.33). However, in 2018, despite now controlling the presidency, there was almost no relationship between Republican Party and candidate messaging on the issue of immigration, save for some congruence between "oppose amnesty" and attacks on Obama (.50). In 2022, something very similar happened: instances where the policy language matched were slightly higher but the strongest overall relationship – between "secure border" and references to the idea of building a wall along the southern border – was lower (.33).

On the issue of health care, Republican candidates overwhelmingly supported the RNC's call for the repeal of Obamacare. But, again, with few exceptions they did so in their own unique policy language and independent of in- or out-party status. Although they referred frequently to the need to "repeal the law," the dangers of "government control" and how the law compromised "patient and personal choice," there was little relationship between these ideas in their policy statement. The strongest association in 2014 was between "expansion of government control" and "patient choice" (.47) and "patient choice" and claims that the law was "unworkable" (.47) in general.

The data does show a tendency among a small group of Republican Senators to exactly mimic the party's health care policy rhetoric. But, again, it appears unaffected by control of the presidency. In 2018, for instance, all of the Republican candidates who discussed health care on their websites – two of six incumbents – linked "patient choice" to a "repeal" of the ACA (1.00). In 2022, two of the ten Republicans who discussed the issue of health care perfectly matched their and their party's critiques of "health mandates and prices" and "repeal of Obamacare" (1.00). These Senate incumbents were perfectly aligned with the national Republican Party in these instances, but they represented only four, or 19%, of the twenty-one Republican Senate incumbents who ran election between 2018 and 2022.

Recommendations for academic research

The experiences of the Democratic and Republican Parties in the last three midterm elections highlight, as political management scholars argue, the challenges that continue to confront the growing number of party leaders, strategists, and candidates in the US who are interested in developing a more unified national party vision. They confront, among other things, the highly federated and decentralized nature of US political parties that has been seen by generations of scholars as the most persistent feature of the American Party System. But, more specifically, any desire for greater coordination within the national parties appears to be curtailed by the limited influence the parties continue to have over the policy choices of their candidates, even when the party controls the presidency. Variations in presidential popularity over time might impact the effect of in- or out-party status, but in the last three midterms, presidential approval ratings for both Democrats and Republicans were essentially the same, at roughly 40%.

As the policy choices of the incumbent Senators examined in this study demonstrate, candidates are more than willing, even when they are the in-party to opt-out or ignore some aspects of the party's message. Indeed, the data suggests that even when they publicly agree with the party, and map out their positions on their campaign websites by appropriating from its policy lexicon, they cast the issue in their own personal or local terms.

The Republicans did display a greater degree of national coordination on the issue of health care in 2018 and 2022. But the trend, which only involved a small number of Senate incumbents, represented only a minor deviation from the broader trend of disengagement. Nonetheless, it might shed light on the circumstances under which increased coordination is possible, and are thus worthy of further study.

Recommendations for practice

To overcome the hurdles that continue to undermine their ability to develop a more unified national party vision, party and campaign officials within both major US parties need to win more internal support for higher levels of national coordination as it relates to not only organizational challenges but also policy formation and messaging. They need, in other words, to more proactively engage relevant party stakeholders – national and state party officials, candidates, and campaign staff – in the political planning process. Specifically, they need:

1 To incorporate key party stakeholders into the information flows involved in developing and implementing a new or updated party mission espousing the party's core values.
2 To include stakeholders, to the extent possible, in the creation of unique vision statement outlining both the party's short- and longer-term policy and political objectives. The vision statement can be used to synchronize both local and national parties and candidate policy messaging.
3 To include stakeholders in the strategic planning necessary to develop and set organizational goals for all levels of the party that focus the party's resources and attention on achieving the organizational and policy priorities central to the party vision.
4 To offer candidates real incentives, particularly in terms of additional informational and financial resources to be involved with rather than opposed to efforts to implement a more coordinated party mission and vision.

Going forward, for both parties, a more coordinated national mission and vision is only going to following from a greater degree of internal coordinated political planning.

Recommended reading

Johnson, Dennis, eds. (2009). *Routledge Handbook of Political Management*. New York: Routledge.
Lees-Marshment, Jennifer. (2021). *Political Management: The Dance of Government and Politics*. London: Routledge.

References

Primary Sources

DNC. (2014a). Immigration Reform. *Democratic National Committee*, accessed at https://web.archive.org/web/20151121081306/http://www.democrats.org/issues/immigration-reform, June 10, 2015.
DNC. (2018a). Immigration. *Democratic National Committee*, accessed at https://web.archive.org/web/20181212081902/https://democrats.org/issues/immigration-reform/, December 12, 2018.
DNC. (2018b). Fixing the Broken Immigration System. Party Platform. *Democratic National Committee*, accessed at https://web.archive.org/web/20190613014431/https://democrats.org/about/party-platform/#boken-immigration, June 30, 2019.
DNC. (2018c). Health Care. *Democratic National Committee*, accessed at https://web.archive.org/web/20181212234351/https://democrats.org/issues/health-care/, December 12, 2018.
DNC. (2020a). Creating a 21st Century Immigration System. Party Platform. *Democratic National Committee*, accessed at https://web.archive.org/web/20221014200728/https://democrats.org/where-we-stand/party-platform/creating-a-21st-century-immigration-system/, October 1, 2022.
DNC. (2020b). Achieving Universal, Affordable, Quality Health Care. Party Platform. *Democratic National Committee*, accessed at https://web.archive.org/web/20221001171232/https://democrats.org/where-we-stand/party-platform/achieving-universal-affordable-quality-health-care/, October 1, 2022.
RNC. (2014a). The Rule of Law: Legal Immigration. Party Platform. *Republican National Committee*, accessed at https://web.archive.org/web/20150612043554/https://gop.com/platform/reforming-government/, June 10, 2015.
RNC. (2014b). Repealing Obamacare. Party Platform. *Republican National Committee*, accessed at https://web.archive.org/web/20150609191059/https://gop.com/platform/renewing-american-values/, June 10, 2015.
RNC. (2018a). Immigration. *Republican National Committee*.
RNC. (2018b). Health Care. *Republican National Committee*, accessed at https://gop.com/issues/health-care, December 12, 2018.
RNC. (2020). Resolution Regarding the Republican Party Platform. *Republican National Committee*, accessed at https://prod-cdn-static.gop.com/docs/Resolution_Platform_2020.pdf, October 1, 2022.

Academic Sources

Arterton, Christopher. (1988, July). Managing Politics, Managing Banking. *Management Review*: 52–53.
Blakeney, Allan, and Sandford Borins. (1998). *Political Management in Canada*. Toronto: University of Toronto.

Craig, Stephen. (2009). Political Science and Political Management. In *Routledge Handbook of Political Management*, ed. Dennis Johnson, 42–57, accessed at https://www.taylorfrancis.com/books/edit/10.4324/9780203892138/routledge-handbook-political-management-dennis-johnson

Dolan, Kathleen. (2005). Do Women Candidates Play to Gender Stereotypes? Do Men Candidates Play to Women? Candidate Sex and Issues Priorities on Campaign Websites. *Political Research Quarterly*, 58 (1): 31–44.

Druckman, James, Martin Kifer, and Michael Parkin. (2009). Campaign Communications in U.S. Congressional Elections. *American Political Science Review*, 103 (3): 343–366.

Druckman, James, Martin Kifer, and Michael Parkin. (2020). Campaign Rhetoric and the Incumbency Advantage. *American Politics Research*, 48 (1): 22–43.

Fiorina, Morris. (2016). The (Re)Nationalization of Congressional Elections. *A Hoover Institution Essay on Contemporary American Politics*. No. 7

Halligan, John, and John Power. (1992). *Political Management in the 1990s*. Oxford: Oxford University Press.

Heatley, Alistair. (1996). Political Management in Australia: The Case of the Northern Territory. *Australian Journal of Public Administration*, 55 (2): 54–64.

Hopkins, Daniel. (2018). *The Increasingly United States. How and Why American Political Behavior Nationalized*. Chicago: University of Chicago Press.

Ingraham, Patricia, James Thompson, and Elliot Eisenberg. (1995, May–June). Political Management Strategies and Political/Career Relationships: Where Are We Now in the Federal Government? *Public Administration Review*, 55 (3): 263–272.

Jacobson, Gary. (2015). Obama and Nationalized Electoral Politics in the 2014 Midterm. *Political Science Quarterly*, 130: 1–25.

Jacobson, Gary. (2019). Extreme Referendum: Donald Trump and the 2018 Elections. *Political Science Quarterly*, 134 (1): 9–38.

Johnson, Dennis, ed. (2009). *Routledge Handbook of Political Management*. New York: Routledge.

Lees-Marshment, Jennifer. (2021). *Political Management: The Dance of Government and Politics*. London: Routledge.

Painter, David. (2015). Online Political Public Relations and Trust: Source and Interactivity Effects in the 2012 U.S. Presidential Campaign. *Public Relations Review*, 41: 801–808.

Sievert, Joel, and Seth McKee. (2019). Nationalization in U.S. Senate and Gubernatorial Elections. *American Politics Research*, 47 (5): 1055–1080.

10

THE CHALLENGES OF PUBLIC POLICY STRATEGY

A Case Study of British Prime Ministers

Pippa Catterall

Introduction

This chapter examines what strategy means in government, focusing on how it is conceived, shaped and co-ordinated across the various bodies delivering public policy and administration. Governments are continually delivering new policies in the form of taxation, legislation, regulation, procurement and other interventions in the public sphere which impinge upon and are often intended to shape the behaviours of people and organisations. The issue considered here is whether these actions are effectively co-ordinated to enact some overall strategic architecture that encompasses means and processes of delivery, planning about where and how to allocate key resources and the goals all this is intended to achieve. As such, strategy is an element in the framework for decision-making and choosing between policy options. So are moral codes and political philosophies, resource availability and requirements, and legal systems. These latter two factors are arguably unavoidable considerations in the design of policy. The importance of strategy, in contrast, not least because of time constraints, is all too often overlooked.

Key literature

This chapter differs from the limited available literature by concentrating on policy strategy rather than political strategy. The literature on the latter, going back to Machiavelli, focuses on how individuals or parties get into and stay in power. Governance considerations of how to gain and maintain support for strategic objectives will nonetheless impinge upon the development of any policy strategy. The electorate do not necessarily need to be enthusiastic to

DOI: 10.4324/9781003260677-10

render certain policies within the bounds of possibility. Policymakers can pursue ideas with low public salience without generating effective and competing counterpublics. However, a strategy is unlikely to go far if it is unleashed on a hostile public for whom the Overton window remains firmly closed, even sometimes in authoritarian systems. Accordingly, the framing of messaging to win support is only one – albeit often major – element in strategising, particularly when it comes to delivering a programme in government.

As Gray (2016) points out, policy strategy has been remarkably neglected by scholars. As a specialist in military strategy, his work only addresses elements of this gap and focuses on leadership. This is not the same as strategy. Leadership involves charisma, vision and a combination of management and rhetorical skills. Byrne et al. (2020) suggest that leadership is about how political actors frame the issues they face and whether and how they decide to act. In portraying much decision-making in British policymaking as essentially reactive, they suggest that environmental factors tend to militate against strategic governmental management. They depict public policymaking as more attritional, or even Sisyphean, than strategic.

Methodology

This exploration of how far this is the case and of how strategy is understood and applied in public policy management draws primarily on British examples. In Britain, after all, the relatively strong position of the prime minister compared to more polyarchic systems like US in theory provides more scope for the development of strategy (James, 2020: 141). These British examples run from Ramsay MacDonald in the 1920s to Rishi Sunak in the 2020s and are deployed to explore wider generic issues about what strategy is in practice, whether it is a desirable facet of government, and how it might be developed, delivered, evaluated and scrutinised. Particular attention is given to the challenges of managing knowledge deficits and the complex and vast range of variables and actors who confront any strategic process in government.

Research findings

It may seem obvious that strategy should be a desirable, if not the key element of applied political management. This does not mean that it is easily achieved. Sir Maurice Hankey, the most important British civil servant of the inter-war years, commented in 1923:

> The real weakness of the existing system is that it does not provide for any central initiative …. The only person who can take any central initiative is the Prime Minister himself, and my experience of several Prime Ministers is that they are always too busy to be bothering with it.
>
> *(Cited in Catterall & Brady, 2000: 170)*

Decades later, Sir Richard Wilson, when he succeeded to Hankey's former position of Cabinet Secretary under Tony Blair, complained that he received idealistic verbiage rather than strategic guidance from the premier (James, 2020: 144). The articulation of strategy is highly dependent on the capacity and capabilities of the few actors who have the necessary authority. This is not just a matter of the personal attributes of the officeholder. If the round of grinding routine punctuated by unexpected crises does not distract heads of government enough, there are always the quotidian demands of responding to party and press (in a democracy) or cronies and clients (in non-democracies).

The machinery of government available may not be designed for providing the central initiative that Hankey considered necessary. For instance, the British administrative machinery developed to deal flexibly with crises, a symptom of a system constructed around the exigencies of global sea-based warfare. The resulting mechanisms were intended to respond quickly to shifting requirements, but not always adept at producing clearly defined strategic goals and the underpinning processes required to achieve them. Strategically identifying and pursuing such goals and processes in peacetime is also more challenging, particularly given the perennial tendency towards competition among principal actors for access to key policy resources like time, money and reputation.

Furthermore, the British machinery of government incentivises a focus on some parts of the policy process at the expense of others. Prestige has historically been attached to processes of policy formulation. In the 21st century, there has been growing recognition of the need to give comparable attention to delivery, exemplified by the Prime Minister's Delivery Unit set up in 2001 under Sir Michael Barber, which has subsequently continued in various guises (James, 2020: 44–45). Nonetheless, these units necessarily function largely as exhortatory bodies since they do not perform actual delivery. Moreover, their very existence testifies to a continuing tendency to regard policy development and delivery as distinct functions rather than ones which should be intimately intertwined in the concurrent and strategic engineering of policy.

Resolving such deficiencies is never easy. Ironically, the most determined attempt to do so in Britain was during the premiership of Edward Heath in 1970–1974. This premiership became so engulfed in successive crises that the instruments Heath hoped to use to plan strategically were generally tainted by the experience. A rare, albeit temporary survivor of the experiment was Heath's Central Policy Review Staff (CPRS), set up in 1971 to develop long-term strategy and co-ordinate policy across government. Taking the view that it had increasingly become a think tank for ideas with which she disagreed, it was scrapped by Margaret Thatcher in 1983.

Thatcher (1993: 277) claimed that a government with 'a clear sense of direction' did not require such a technocratic device. Instead, the strategy prepared for her in opposition focused primarily on tackling the trade unions as a first step towards economic renewal. The device for driving this forward during her first term in 1979–1983 was an ad hoc Thursday Breakfast Meeting of senior ministers. Yet as Sir Geoffrey Howe (1994: 104–108, 147), her Chancellor of the Exchequer, later noted, 'It was characteristic of Margaret's curious lack of organisational insight that these occasions were unprepared and seldom, if ever, exploited for any long-term purpose'.

Having a series of core ideas and beliefs – which in her case were not necessarily as firm or coherent as Thatcher liked to claim – is not the same as having a strategy. Thatcher's instrumental and partial espousal of neoliberalism was often more an exercise in branding than strategising, as exemplified by the number of areas where policy aims collided (Ledger, 2017). Heads of government may arrive in office with visions that they have used to charm the voters or the smaller circle of actors who might need to be squared in more authoritarian systems. However, visions – or manifestoes – and the political narratives that often underpin them are more like (easily breakable) social contracts than strategies.

Furthermore, the challenge of responding to events can militate against even imagining a strategic vision. This can apply equally to routine processes of policymaking. If there is uncertainty about the requirement or impacts of an individual policy, then its transaction costs, in political, financial and administrative terms, will increase. This results in a tendency for decision-making to advance incrementally along more predictable and path-dependent lines, even when most variables are knowable, political controversy muted and the role of external actors limited or non-existent. Knowledge deficits thereby produce a risk-averse unwillingness to attempt strategic thinking. In such circumstances, symbolic grandstanding is often used to give the appearance of a strategy, whilst beneath the rhetoric only minimal changes are attempted. It depends upon how conscious of their knowledge deficits policymakers are. They may be under the mistaken impression that their knowledge is more complete than is the case, even though whole areas of important policy considerations have been overlooked. A classic example is Hankey's ignoring of manpower requirements in War Book planning before 1914.

Policymakers' (misplaced) confidence in the adequacy of the knowledge on which they base their decisions also affects how prepared they are to attempt change. Clement Attlee's Labour government of 1945–1951, for instance, implemented the extensive welfare and economic reconstruction programme sketched out in opposition during the late 1930s, despite the severe post-war circumstances they faced. From an electoral point of view, however, they may have been well-advised to concentrate more on housing policy, a mistake their Conservative opponents successfully chided them over. The strategy arguably needed to be more adaptable once in government to changing needs and popular demands.

Sometimes, individual actions may appear to be recklessly based on knowledge deficits but still be part of an overall vision. Unplanned overseas interventions, such as the Falklands War under Thatcher or the Sierra Leone operation under Blair, are classic examples of actions taken without good foreknowledge of their likely parameters or consequences. However, both became subsequently rationalised into doctrinal views which Blair (2007) at the end of his premiership defined as preparedness 'to project hard as well as soft power' to counter a multiplicity of threats.

As this shows, knowledge deficits affect the enactment of certain policies but they do not necessarily prevent the development of strategy. Indeed, incremental policy implementation could be a sensible strategic response designed to help manage these deficits. Positing a dichotomy between strategic and reactive decision-making in government is therefore unhelpful. Consider an analogy with a building project. In such cases, the variables are generally known, even if their consequences are less readily predictable, with the result that allowance is invariably made for contingencies. With its even greater range of often unknowable variables, policy strategy necessitates similar contingencies be allocated for time, finances, resources, regulatory permissions, and managing actors and stakeholders. How these contingencies are priced will impinge upon how the transaction costs are calculated. These transaction costs are not only just financial but also political and reputational. In turn, resulting calculations by policymakers will determine whether a strategy is worth pursuing or too risky in relation to any predictable benefits.

In examining whether strategy in government is nonetheless possible, it is tempting to explore analogies with project management. The latter involves many of the complexities of government. Delivering effective project management is acknowledged as requiring technical, behavioural and contextual competencies. This includes understanding the knowledge and cultural frameworks influencing the various actors and stakeholders whose conduct affects project management processes. Project management involves strategic considerations such as co-ordination, milestones and timelines. Many of the challenges that impinge on project management are analogous to those encountered in government including:

- Avoiding rent-seeking corruption
- Overcoming administrative and technocratic silos
- Achieving sustainable and readily evaluated outcomes
- Ensuring coherence around goals, decision-making processes and managerial direction and responsibilities

Project management is already a tool of government, not least in discrete areas such as procurement or the delivery of infrastructure. Project teams are also increasingly being used in policy development and delivery. Infrastructure projects, generally with clearly defined goals and processes, often lend themselves to waterfall management techniques. Waterfall project management is a top-down, sequential methodology that developed as one appropriate for projects that need to be tightly controlled and heavily documented, like construction work. Both governments and businesses have nonetheless also applied such techniques in less propitious circumstances, such as Information and Communications Technology (ICT) procurement.

A particular example was the commissioning of the National Programme for IT for Britain's National Health Service by Blair's government in 2002. This was introduced for the benign objective of creating more efficient, effective and user-friendly healthcare systems. As with the litany of ICT procurement disasters that have bedevilled governments everywhere, a core problem lay with the processes adopted for delivering an unhelpfully vague political vision. The goals were never properly articulated. This resulted in lack of clarity about what was being procured or why. Political support was not translated into effective political oversight. Over-confidence fuelled over-ambition. Timescales were wildly unrealistic. Continuous staff turnover exacerbated the knowledge deficits that marked the project from the start. Major considerations, most notably patient confidentiality, were never effectively addressed. A treasury emphasis on price over quality encouraged dependence on suppliers who deliberately lowballed for contracts whilst charging heavily for rectifying poorly written specifications of the kind that typified this project. Many large contracts lacked specificity about the deliverables required. The unfeasible timescales compounded failure properly to map out the project stages or evaluate against expected milestones. Stakeholders and end-users were barely consulted. Inadequate allowance was made for contingencies and setbacks, despite their near inevitability when trying to implement such a large and untried system. These problems were compounded by a centralised, waterfall form of delivery. This was intended to reduce costs, which is ironic given the price of this failed project is generally estimated at between £10 and £20 billion (King & Crewe, 2014: 195–200). Yet, as *Computer Weekly* repeatedly pointed out, the complexity of ICT procurement, along with the rapid pace of change in this field, meant that agile management techniques would have been more appropriate.

In contrast to the focus on deliverable outcomes emphasised in waterfall projects, the various agile management approaches instead focus on adaptability, adjustment and learning by experience throughout the process of delivery. Iterative, incremental development processes intended to reduce risk by not trying to control for all the knowledge deficits and variables from the outset are, for example, a feature of the Scrum technique now widely deployed in British government. The key features of this tool are as follows:

- The composition and effectiveness of the team
- The team's culture, knowledge and capacity for learning
- Engagement between customers and clients
- The ability to adapt during the 'sprints' that are the design and delivery phases used in this technique

Commentaries on implementing agile management in government have so far largely come from management consultancies and in consequence, unsurprisingly, often focus on the allegedly siloed structures, cultures and hierarchies of the public sector. These issues, however, are not necessarily peculiar to government. Nor are problems of securing clear goals and consistent support from management, getting the right teams, or having sufficient resourcing and effectively allocated priorities. The wider administrative environment, whether in the private or public sector, thereby impinges on the successful implementation of agile management. There are also problems of scale to be considered when applying these techniques in government given the range of potential goals and multiplicity of functions – some routine, some developmental – that public policymaking involves.

Both in the private and public sectors, agile management is generally understood as a tool for delivering tasks rather than a strategy mechanism. Nonetheless, it does provide a framework for examining how strategy can be developed in government. After all, the range of tasks any government is trying to accomplish – not to mention the ways in which unforeseen events or agenda-setting by other actors such as nongovernmental organizations (NGOs), the media or even powerful groupings of backbench members of parliament (MPs) might impinge on their activities and priorities – surely requires something analogous with agile management. Yet meetings of senior policymakers can bear more resemblance to gatherings of warring chieftains fighting over the resourcing of their fiefdoms than an agile management Scrum.

This is one of several deficiencies of cabinet government. It is not just that prime ministers are often unequal to the task of establishing the broad direction of travel required by policy strategy, or indeed a successful Scrum. Additionally, there are the constraints that premiers face in picking the team of senior colleagues resulting from the exigencies of political considerations. These problems undoubtedly weaken prime ministerial ability to provide strategic direction. Yet cabinets, as policymaking devices, also compound these problems. Indeed, it is questionable whether cabinet in Britain still functions as a policymaking forum. Since at least the Thatcher years, cabinet has increasingly been characterised as a political reporting rather than a policy determining body with key decision-making siphoned off into more informal ministerial one-to-ones with the Prime Minister or their proxies. Even on a major issue, such as the 2003 Iraq War, the cabinet collectively were only briefed orally for political information purposes rather than consulted. Key discussions then took place instead in small groups of ministers, officials and military officers undermining informed collective political judgement. The result proves another example of policymaking based on knowledge deficits about the grounds for war and its likely consequences. These knowledge deficits also impacted on the lack of planning for peace-enforcement once in Iraq, the long-haul resource requirements and the eventual exit strategy.

Small groupings of likeminded policymakers were preferred because they were seen as more likely to produce action rather than deliberation. Arguably there was a strategic goal but not strategic consideration.

Cabinet committees, whether formal or informal, nonetheless bring together groups of policymakers from different departments and thus co-ordinate areas of policy for both strategic and routine purposes. Committees emerged historically as means of addressing policy areas spanning across departmental boundaries. However, they only serve the development, co-ordination and delivery of strategy if they provide:

- A *clear sense* of the political direction concerning the policy goals towards which the committee is working
- A *clear relationship* between the committee and the departments which implement the resulting policies (Catterall & Brady, 2000: 168)

Without effective political direction, too easily committees become devices for reporting rather than decision-making or fora for inter-departmental disputes rather than their resolution. Despite best intentions, they also tend to proliferate. Depending on the personnel selected, they can either become mired in intractable disagreements or reinforce tendencies to groupthink, giving ill-conceived policies like Thatcher's poll tax an unstoppable momentum by the time they belatedly encounter any opposition from other senior ministers. These problems are exacerbated by the question of who attends their meetings and the tendency of ambitious ministers to try to attend committees they perceive as important, clogging their business and undermining their effectiveness as decision-making bodies (Catterall & Brady, 2000: 162–164).

Prime ministers use deputies to chair some committees but the ones they themselves choose to chair can be used as markers of their key priorities. For instance, after his minor reshuffle in May 2023, Sunak had eleven cabinet committees, chairing six of them himself. Four of these covered national and nuclear security, relations with Europe, and science and technology, whilst the other two dealt with the strained constitutional unity of the United Kingdom and the 'levelling-up' agenda of spreading opportunity and prosperity to all parts of the country inherited from Boris Johnson.

Selecting priorities is not, however, the same as developing a strategy. Instead, Sunak seems more to be dividing up responsibilities by reflecting a long-standing prime ministerial tendency to focus on external and constitutional issues, whilst deputing domestic affairs to the Home Affairs Committee (HAC) chaired by the Chancellor of the Exchequer, which is charged with 'the implementation and delivery of domestic and economic policy' (Cabinet Office, 2023: 11). In effect, this and its various predecessors going back to the Lord President's Committee during the Second World War is a domestic cabinet which acts as a clearing house for the approval of legislation and the allocation of budgets and parliamentary time. It can thus serve a strategic function, though with a formal membership of 23, it may also prove unwieldy.

The other four cabinet committees in May 2023 were chaired by the deputy prime minister. Prime ministers have often relied on such deputies to help them to carry the burdens of office. The effectiveness of such arrangements depends on the personal capabilities of the deputy, how far they share the prime minister's approach to policy and whether they are trustworthy. Paying tribute to a deputy who she felt combined all these virtues at the retirement party for Willie Whitelaw in 1988, Thatcher famously observed 'every Prime Minister needs a Willie' (Aitken, 1988).

The prime minister's deputies in Britain generally have three main roles:

- To deputise for the Prime minister in various routine activities, including chairing meetings in their absence
- To manage a range of policy issues across government and act in the process as the eyes and ears of the prime minister and wield authority on their behalf
- To supplement the whips' advice on political feeling in parliament or the country and advise on decisions

John Prescott as Blair's deputy not only chaired numerous cabinet committees but also acted as a sounding board for the prime minister on what might be acceptable to trade unionists within the Labour Party.

Not all the figures tasked with these functions have held the formal title of deputy prime minister. Nor have all of them managed to fulfil all three, particularly the last, with the same effectiveness as Whitelaw or Prescott. They were both widely respected within their parties and independently significant figures who (no longer) had serious ambitions for the prime minister's own job. The absence of an equivalent figure was immediately apparent under Thatcher after Whitelaw's retirement in 1988 or under Gordon Brown after Prescott instantly followed Blair's resignation with his own. None of the deputies under the succession of Conservative prime ministers since 2010 have had the political heft or independent powerbase of a Whitelaw or Prescott, certainly not Sunak's somewhat anonymous fixer Oliver Dowden.

As one of Whitelaw's cabinet colleagues, Malcolm Rifkind, observed:

It would be highly desirable to have at least one Whitelaw in every British cabinet. Consider the advantage of a senior minister, no longer with personal ambition, able to tell the prime minister, without fear or favour, when he or she was acting foolishly, improperly, or in a manner that would do the government serious damage.

(Cited in Ankomah, 2013)

His point was that the role of deputy head of government is best fulfilled by someone who does not aspire to their boss' role and whose advice can therefore be trusted not to be self-interested. If, like Whitelaw and Prescott, they also come from different socio-cultural settings than the prime ministers they serve they may also be able to help avoid problems such as groupthink.

One type of groupthink is a requirement for policymakers to subscribe to an overarching political framework of ideas and rhetoric. For the Sunak government, as for his three immediate predecessors, that framework is shaped around Brexit and how sovereignty and citizenship are conceived on the right of the Conservative Party. Brexit is not a strategy; rather, it forms the ideational context that determines what stratagems are even possible. It thus, from the moment of the referendum on 23 June 2016, posed a series of dilemmas to successive governments over how to give effect to it.

Among a range of possible options, what leaving the European Union meant in practice was unclear, whilst major considerations – such as the impact on Northern Ireland – were hardly even discussed in the preceding desultory parliamentary debates. Trying to leave her hands untied, new Prime Minister Theresa May with studied ambiguity repeatedly stated, 'Brexit means Brexit' (Richards, 2020: 362). Yet it also meant a whole lot more, subsuming all government policy, eating up huge amounts of parliamentary time and completely derailing any hope May had of making progress on the 'burning injustices' she spoke of on her accession to the premiership (Byrne et al., 2020: 102).

May's ambiguity ensured that – despite windy rhetoric about popular sovereignty – her government and party would interpret Brexit to mean whatever they, rather than the people, wanted it to mean. This ensured that the Brexit outcome would be determined through infighting within the Conservative Party. May's ill-fated attempt to give herself more room for manoeuvre by holding a general election in 2017, in which she instead lost her parliamentary majority, only exacerbated this situation. More fundamental, however, were problems borne of wilful ignorance. This ignorance partly reflected a refusal to grasp how both European and global trade policy worked. Additionally, May early on established 'red lines' around immigration controls which severely curtailed her room for manoeuvre and emboldened the Conservative right (not least to cry foul if they thought that the government was compromising on such matters). This rapidly removed from the table options such as staying in the single market. This in turn constrained May's negotiating position with the European Union and consequently any prospect of the special trade deal the government doggedly and mistakenly seemed to believe feasible. Brexit is thus an example of how a rigid belief system can contort any attempt at strategy. This was compounded by May's tactical mistakes, limiting the policy options available (Byrne et al., 2020: 103–107).

A particular feature of Brexit was the role of stakeholders. Much lipservice was paid to the interests of groups such as farmers or the fishing industry. Nonetheless, over-confidence and (wilful) knowledge deficits combined to ensure that the likely effects of Brexit on these and other economic sectors were not adequately considered. Instead, in practice, one group's interests were treated as paramount in the policymaking around Brexit, those of right-wing Conservative MPs. This resulted in May's privileging of their emphasis – which she shared – on controlling immigration. The political demands of managing this privileged group of stakeholders constantly trumped any public policy strategy for securing the most effective deal.

This same privileged group also shaped the apparent imperative of time management. Being seen to progress, Brexit was always more important for May than planning strategically for managing it well, notwithstanding the multiplicity of stakeholders affected by the outcome. This approach to time management was partly because the complexity of the process was deliberately obscured for political reasons during and after the referendum and partly because the same privileged group demanded speedy delivery on the referendum verdict. The result was that the Brexit process was marked by successive short-term fixes rather than strategic thinking. This approach continued after May was replaced by Johnson in 2019. His determination swiftly to declare that he had delivered Brexit resulted in a deal so threadbare that it not only left uncertainties over the consequences for large parts of the British economy but also prompted Johnson himself rapidly to repudiate a key part of his agreement with the EU in relation to Northern Ireland.

In the case of Brexit, David Cameron brought about a disjunctive moment through a decision to hold a referendum on Britain's membership of the EU whilst preparing inadequately both for the referendum campaign itself or any likely consequences, dooming his own premiership in the process. This disjunction and its aftermath were a negation of strategy rather than its result. Tactical and short-term political goals were repeatedly prioritised both by Cameron and his successors over any kind of public policy strategy. Blaming opponents of Brexit for the difficulties of achieving, it was used to obscure its proponents' own lack of clarity about their objectives or how to achieve them. Whether these proponents could ever have delivered on their Panglossian promises is open to doubt but the lack of strategy and agility throughout the Brexit process certainly did not help. It is almost a textbook case of why having a strategy is a good idea, particularly when attempting such a large scale and ill-defined policy shift. In the process, it is also a textbook example of how politics can prevent any prospect of good strategic thinking.

Trying to resolve this problem through technocratic solutions, as Heath did, has proved to have limited success. Mechanisms and information inputs are among the building blocks that ideally inform the development and delivery of strategy. However, they are elements of strategy, not its substance. Nor do they guarantee success. Consider MacDonald's ill-fated creation of the Economic Advisory Council (EAC) in 1929. This was adorned by some of the leading minds of the age. MacDonald noted:

> When we came into office we found absolutely nothing of the least use to us – no statistics prepared, no experience codified. Had we been in power with the aid of this central body we should have had the whole information at our fingers' end in two days.
>
> *(Jones, 1929)*

However, the danger was that without some kind of clear executive role and guidance, such a body would simply become a talking shop duplicating work already done elsewhere in government. The industrialists and economists who sat on this body offered conflicting advice. MacDonald, despite his initial enthusiasm, was only able to engage with it sporadically. The result was that it operated within a political and policy vacuum with predictable results. In the end, strategy also requires political direction and commitment, a challenge when heads of government are constantly distracted by events or headlines, let alone the crises that buffeted MacDonald or Heath.

MacDonald, like most prime ministers, arrived in Downing Street with a policy and legislative programme. This was the manifesto on which Labour fought and won the 1929 election. Manifestos serve various purposes, not least as indicators of the priorities of the incoming government both to the electorate and to the civil service, who have to design policies or heads of bills to give effect to these ideas. They express what the winning party aspires to do in a more or less choate form but rarely articulate a strategy for achieving these aims. *Labour and the Nation* in 1929 was not a strategy nor was it designed for the crisis that then broke upon the incoming government following the Wall Street Crash. An advisory body like the EAC was always unlikely to be able to make up for this deficiency.

One of the few prime ministers to have arrived in Downing Street with a well-established tendency for strategic thinking was Harold Macmillan. This may be partly because of his successful business career before and after his elevation to the highest political office. Businessmen imported into government have nonetheless often been ineffective, usually because they did not have the political nous and connections that are also required, particularly in peacetime. The failure of Churchill's Overlords experiment in 1951–1953, when he sought to use various non-politicians from business or the military to infuse strategy into government, is a case in point.

Macmillan, in contrast, served a long political apprenticeship before even entering the ranks of junior ministers in 1940. Throughout his political career, from when he was first elected to parliament in 1924 until his premiership between 1957 and 1963, he periodically drafted what he called 'Grand Designs' (Catterall, 2011: xix–xxxii). The first of these, produced in the late 1920s for

Churchill, who was then at the treasury, sketched out an interlocking series of economic measures intended to tackle unemployment, promote industrial reorganisation and modernisation, and improve industrial relations. Macmillan's approach to strategy thus contrasted with that of Churchill himself. The latter, illustrated most starkly by his aspiration to transform the stalemate of the First World War through the imaginative if highly risky and ultimately disastrous Dardanelles operation in 1915, tended to think in terms of single major actions that would prove transformative. Notwithstanding Churchill's reputation as a leader and strategic thinker, these attempts to resolve Gordian knots with single strokes did not always come off, as his ill-fated restoration of the Gold Standard in 1925 also indicates.

It might be argued that Macmillan's very different approach to strategy proved no more successful. As he himself noted in January 1963 about his final Grand Design: 'all our policies at home and abroad are in ruins' (Catterall, 2011: 539). This has generally been understood to refer to the impending failure of Britain's first bid to join the European Economic Community. Yet Europe was merely an element, not the aim, in the overall strategy Macmillan sketched out when drafting this paper in 1960. It was a relatively minor component in the first phase of strategic development, the 'Future Policy' exercise exploring policy requirements across government for the next 20 years that Macmillan charged the Cabinet Secretary, Sir Norman Brook, to superintend in 1959. Joining Europe was simply a means to achieve the overall linked goals of stimulating trade and reducing international tensions during the Cold War, to be delivered through a complex web of devices extending from aid to trade policy. International and domestic elements were linked in this Grand Design: it was intended both to reduce budgetary pressures resulting from military spending and provide external, non-inflationary ways of stimulating the British economy. Meanwhile, tariff reductions would also stimulate economies globally, not least among newly independent poorer countries, thus helping to counter Soviet attempts to woo them. This was all wrapped up in the symbolic language of interdependence. In deploying this term, Macmillan sought to incorporate a communications approach into his Grand Design. This term was intended simultaneously to disguise for a domestic audience the extent to which a Britain with declining international influence had to work with other states to pursue its interests and appeal to those other states by extolling the mutual benefits of co-operation. Strategy, and strategic communication, should be based upon realistic appraisals of how to manage the actions and interests of other actors whose behaviour will impinge crucially upon its chances of success.

It also, like agile project management, should be flexible. Macmillan realised by October 1962 that his attempts to join Europe were likely to end in failure. A core element of the strategy was thus unlikely to be completed. Macmillan then defaulted to a sub-optimal option; the domestic expansion of the economy sketched out in his 'Modernisation of Britain' Cabinet paper that autumn. He combined that with successfully persuading President Kennedy to support alternative means of delivering trade liberalisation (through the Kennedy Round) and reductions in international tensions (through the Test Ban Treaty of 1963). Of course, Kennedy came to support these initiatives because they fitted his own global framework, one which Macmillan did his best to influence. Indeed, this final Grand Design itself had been written following Kennedy's victory in the 1960 presidential election, with Macmillan's relationship to the new president a central element in the strategy. This reflected a clear appreciation of the extent to which the realisation of strategic goals involves persuading or aligning with the potentially competing interests of others.

Recommendations for academic research

As this shows, although other actors can shape or prevent the achievement of strategic goals, this does not mean that articulating a policy strategy should not be attempted. More research in this area could cast light on the environmental factors that militate against the development of strategy. These include:

- The distraction of events
- Internal political conflict
- The political attraction of short-term 'quick wins' and/or symbolic othering (such as Sunak's demonisation of refugees) over the more risky and less quantifiable rewards of longer-term planning required by strategy
- External pressures and actors
- The personal limitations and animosities of heads of government and the proxies through which they operate
- The design of central institutions and of the machinery of government

Policy strategy also needs to be disentangled by researchers from overarching frameworks of ideology or political economy. This includes an appreciation that Thatcher's neoliberalism and Blair's New Labour were more examples of rhetorical positioning than articulations of strategy. There was nonetheless undoubtedly an appreciation of the desirability of strategy in their administrations, hence the emphasis on efficiency under Thatcher and on delivery and 'joined-up government' under Blair (Bogdanor, 2005). This indicates thinking about how strategy can be co-ordinated and implemented across the complexity of government. This approach culminated in the idea of 'total place' under Brown, focused on the better co-ordination of all government spending in a geographical or policy area, a concept that got lost in the ensuing short-termist austerity of Cameron's government.

The concept of 'total place' was intended to produce a proactive reallocation of resources: a shift from reacting to social ills towards preventing them in the first place (Bolden & O'Regan, 2017). It thus combines a strategic goal (prevention and social wellbeing) with a strategic means of co-ordination and delivery (better co-ordination of public services). Short-termism aligned with a political imperative to secure 'quick wins' which can be banked with the electorate is only one factor that works against developing such a strategy. Bureaucratic gatekeeping and institutional inertia are also issues. Furthermore, there is a tendency for both policy and politics *either* to concentrate on goals *or* on processes, whilst combining and co-ordinating the two effectively into an overall strategy is more rarely achieved.

Recommendations for practice

Strategy is desirable in theory but difficult in practice. The burden of providing strategy across a government is also overly dependent on the capabilities and attention span of its head. Few prime ministers have the capacity to sustain strategic visions, even if they have the inclination. Few prepare anything like a strategy in opposition and are then able to sustain it in government. Even fewer are, like Macmillan, given to commissioning forward looks into future strategic requirements and then periodically drafting a new and revised Grand Design. The result is that heads of government, the only figures with the authority to set a strategic direction for the administrations they lead, fall along a spectrum. This ranges from those who are more reactive, short-term, incremental and risk-averse (a classic example being Angela Merkel) to those like Attlee, Blair, Churchill, Macmillan and Thatcher, who thought in strategic terms but in very different ways.

There are various means of tackling these deficiencies. These include:

- Better preparation in opposition for strategical policy management in government. This should include improving the procedures used since the 1960s by the British civil service to prepare oppositions for government by incorporating strategic management in these discussions.
- Closer linkage of policy formulation, communications and delivery in planning strategy.
- Adaptation of agile management techniques to provide a much-needed strategic framework across government.
- Accountability procedures which are extended to focus on scrutiny of government strategy and processes of strategic implementation.

Governments can and do privilege short-termism by claiming that they need to respond flexibly to the concerns expressed by press, parliament and public. However, this is simply an artifice of how accountability mechanisms are configured. The need to agitate to get things on the agenda demonstrates both that governments usually enjoy primacy in setting that agenda, and the corresponding lack of transparency about what that agenda is or for. After all, the only times British governments are required to express and defend their agenda is in the list of planned legislation set out in the speech from the throne and the ensuing set-piece debates in both chambers of parliament. Yet an agenda is not a strategy. Furthermore, a full-scale and highly politicised debate is not the most effective device for scrutinising it. In theory, it would be better to use the occasions, three times a year, when the House of Commons Liaison Committee questions the prime minister on policy by refocusing those occasions on scrutiny of the strategy for the whole of government. If prime ministers had to explain what their strategy is to the Liaison Committee, as well as the policies they are using to deliver it, this might also help to ensure that strategy is not only desirable but is also designed, coordinated, implemented, evaluated and scrutinised.

This need for public policy strategy applies far beyond Britain too. Across the globe, long-term planning is increasingly required to tackle existential crises like the climate emergency. A shift from short-termism to strategic thinking is long overdue.

Recommended reading

Bennister, M., 2022. The Contemporary UK Prime Minister. When the Personal Becomes Political: Agency, Personality, Character, and Celebrity. *Asian Journal of Comparative Politics* 8(1), 35–51.

Brummer, K., 2016. "Fiasco Prime Ministers": leaders' Beliefs and Personality Traits as Possible Causes for Policy Fiascos. *Journal of European Public Policy* 23(5), 702–717.

Greenwood, D., 2023. *Effective Governance and the Political Economy of Coordination*. London: Palgrave Macmillan.

Helms, L. (ed.), 2012. *Poor Leadership and Bad Governance: Reassessing Presidents and Prime Ministers in North America, Europe and Japan*. Cheltenham: Edward Elgar Publishing.

References

Aitken, I., 1988. Points of Order. The Guardian, 29 January, p. 24.

Ankomah, B., 2013. "Every Prime Minister Needs a Willie" Indeed. *New African*, 8 January. https://newafricanmagazine.com/3484/

Blair, A., 2007. Our Nation's Future – Defence. Speech, 12 January. https://webarchive.nationalarchives.gov.uk/ukgwa/+/http://www.number10.gov.uk/Page10735

Bogdanor, V., 2005. *Joined-Up Government*. London: British Academy.

Bolden, R., & O'Regan, N., 2017. Leadership and Creativity in Public Services: An Interview With Lord Michael Bichard, Chair of the National Audit Office. *Journal of Management Inquiry* 27 (1), 45–51.

Byrne, C., Randall, N., & Theakston, K., 2020. *Disjunctive Prime Ministerial Leadership in British Politics: From Baldwin to Brexit*. Cham: Palgrave Macmillan.

Cabinet Office, 2023. *List of Cabinet Committees and their membership*. November. https://assets.publishing.service.gov.uk/media/6582de58ed3c3400133bfc7a/LIVE-Cabinet-Committee-List-November-2023-.pdf

Catterall, P. (ed.), 2011. *The Macmillan Diaries II: Prime Minister and After 1957–1966*. London: Macmillan.

Catterall, P., & Brady, C., 2000. The Development and Role of Cabinet Committees in Britain. In R. Rhodes (ed.) *Transforming British Government: Vol. 1 Changing Institutions*. Basingstoke: Macmillan, 156–175.

Gray, C., 2016. *Strategy and Politics*. Abingdon: Routledge.

Howe, G., 1994. *Conflict of Loyalty*. London: Macmillan.

James, S., 2020. *Prime Minister and Cabinet Government*. 3rd edition. Abingdon: Routledge.

Jones, T., 1929. Minutes of Lunch. 9 December. *Thomas Jones Papers, Class B*, vol. 4, doc. 42, National Library of Wales.

King, A., & Crewe, I., 2014. *The Blunders of Our Governments*. London: Oneworld.

Ledger, R., 2017. *Neoliberal Thought and Thatcherism*. Abingdon: Routledge.

Richards, S., 2020. *The Prime Ministers: Reflections on Leadership from Wilson to Johnson*. 2nd edition. London: Atlantic Books.

Thatcher, M., 1993. *The Downing Street Years*. London: HarperCollins.

11

POLITICAL MEDIA MANAGEMENT, CONTROL, AND TRUST IN A HYBRID MEDIA ENVIRONMENT

Caroline Fisher

Introduction

In political management, it is logical to argue that it is beneficial to have a clear chain of command and control, so that leaders have enough power and authority to achieve their core goals. If political leaders such as prime minister's exert control over the communication system, involving both external actors such as journalists but also internal players and systems such as government departments, it can help them influence the message conveyed to the public.

However, as other chapters show, when core management concepts are applied to politics, it often raises many issues. Part of this concern is normative, arguing that if prime ministers are given too much power, democratic problems arise. The other aspect is pragmatic: while extending control might seem beneficial for political leaders in the short term, it risks undermining the relationship, reputation and trust between the individual politician, the party, the media, and ultimately the public.

This chapter therefore examines the nature and consequences of using political media management tools to extend control in a hybrid media system and the impact it can have on perceptions of trust from the public, political journalists, and the party room. It assesses the case of the leadership and media management style of former Australian Prime Minister Scott Morrison. Drawing on interdisciplinary literature into professionalization and centralization of political media management, trust, journalist source relations and political PR, and analyzing a range of primary sources, it generates important lessons for practitioners and academics about the potential negative impact of over-extending control and centralization on organizational reputation and public trust.

DOI: 10.4324/9781003260677-11

Key literature

This chapter draws on scholarship from a range of fields including political communication, political public relations, journalism studies, and the field of political management to examine the intersection of, and efficacy of, attempts at overt central media management in government.

Previous research highlights that the desire for control over political messaging lies at the heart of all political communication, including the relationship between politicians and the media. The relationship has been variously characterized as symbiotic, interdependent, cooperative, a struggle, and in conflict. The nature of the relationship changes between the two actors as part of the constant negotiation of control over the presentation of information to the public (Ericson et al., 1989). In response to digitalization, the power dynamic has shifted. The news media are no longer the primary gatekeepers and politicians are free to publish their messaging directly to voters across a range of new platforms to meet their strategic goals and without the interference of the mass media (Hermans & Vergeer, 2013). In a hybrid media system where older and newer media forms coexist, intersect, and interact, the power relationship between actors continues to shift as they strategically "create, tap, or steer information flows in ways that suit their goals" which impacts on their level of control over the presentation of information (Chadwick, 2017, p. 4).

The aim of professionalization of government communication "is very much about the control of information flows from the government and leading political parties" to the public (Johansson & Raunio, 2019, p. 142). The trend to professionalization of political communication staff began around the First World War with the rise of the 'press agent' (Lippmann, 1922). As media demands increased with the rise of the 'permanent campaign', so did the need for continual media management apparatus. The rise of digital and social media and the 24-hour news cycle has made permanent campaigning easier and arguably unavoidable. It has also intensified the need for centralized and professionalized political communications operations which require ongoing increases in resources, particularly to the leader's office, furthering the centralization of media operations.

The trend toward centralization of government media around the leader has intensified overtime (Seymour-Ure, 2003). Based on the perceived successes of the centralized media management approach of the Thatcher and Blair governments in UK and Clinton administration in US, similar approaches were adopted elsewhere. As Aucoin (2012, p. 181) noted, the "Australian, British and Canadian governments have become both highly centralized and highly politicized in their media management". In the case of the Harper government in Canada, a command-and-control 'Orwellian' style was adopted to messaging in order to manage the government's brand (Marland, 2016, p. xiv). In Australia, the shift toward more centralized media control was evident during the conservative Howard government (2004–2007) and further still under the first Labor prime ministership of Kevin Rudd (2007–2010). The offices of both prime ministers oversaw media operations attempting to control the news agenda and coordinate all government messaging for consistency (McKnight, 2016). An approach rivalling that of Rudd's was adopted by former Australian Prime Minister Scott Morrison, who is the focus of this chapter.

The more complex and fragmented the media becomes in a hybrid environment, the greater the desire for control (Johansson & Raunio, 2019; Marland, 2016, p. 12). On the one hand, politicians can now communicate directly with their voters and bypass the mainstream media giving them greater control of their messaging. In some cases, they can also set the media agenda by having their social media messages amplified through the mainstream press – former US President Donald Trump was a master at this. On the other hand, once the message is published digitally, the politician loses control and online users anywhere can manipulate it, comment on it, and share it at lightening pace. While politicians gain a degree of freedom and greater control from the mainstream media, their messaging is now competing with a cacophony of other voices for diminishing audience attention. In order to respond to the increasing media demands of the 24-hour news cycle across multiple platforms, "continual communications control is the new reality of governance" (Marland et al., 2017, p. 125). In this digital space, it is also now arguably harder to manage the media activity of restless or rivalrous members of parliament (MPs) and requires strong central control and party discipline to keep the party in line.

There are many benefits to the leader from this centralization approach, such as the coordination, consistency and clarity of messaging, portraying an image of unity and stability, and maintaining the dominance in cabinet. As Johansson (2022, p. 8) plainly states, "leadership is impossible without communication" and access to and a degree of control and coordination of information is pivotal to effective leadership. The personalization of politics (Van Aelst et al., 2012) and the media's focus on elites and political leaders contributes to what Johansson describes as the 'logic of centralization' around the prime minister.

But there are also costs to too much centralized control. "Risk averse communication comes at a price: it accentuates politicization of governance and simplification of information" (Marland et al., 2017, p. 125). It leads to a loss of autonomy in the public service and among colleagues and a loss of trust. From an organizational perspective, "formal control seems to be a double-edged sword. It may complement trustworthiness and trust but can also have a harmful effect on employees' trustworthiness and thus negatively affect trust" (Weibel, 2007, pp. 511–512). The media control of the Blair government led to scandal and an independent review of government communications. The Phillis Inquiry found the degree of control and spin used led to a "three-way breakdown in trust between government and politicians, the media and the general public" (Phillis, 2004, p. 2). In the case of former Canadian Prime Minister Stephen Harper, it was assessed that too much control, not just of messaging, but across all aspects of government had been bad for democracy (Marland, 2016). This manipulative behavior led to a conviction "*in absentia* of abuse of power" (orig. italics) during a trial into a Senator's expense claims (Macdonald, 2018, p. 88). In his judgment, Justice Vaillancourt said:

> The precision and planning of the exercise would make any military commander proud. However, in the context of a democratic society, the plotting as revealed in the emails can only be described as unacceptable.
>
> *(Macdonald, 2018, p. 89)*

In Australia, the controlling leadership style and media management practices of the former Labor Prime Minister Kevin Rudd led to him losing the faith and trust of his parliamentary colleagues and the leadership. When Rudd came to power, he was praised for his savvy media management, "yet, in a relatively short time, the same media management skills are identified as a prime cause of a disastrous downfall" (McKnight, 2016, p. 109).

Trust

Falling levels of trust in politics in recent decades has raised concerns for democracy (Levi & Stoker, 2000; Stoker et al., 2018). It is generally accepted that trust is an essential part of the democratic process. That trust in public institutions, in elected representatives and officials, in each other, and the information we receive is integral to a cohesive, inclusive, and prosperous society. Globally, the 2022 Edelman Trust Barometer finds that trust in government continues to decline and more people see both government and media as divisive forces in society rather than unifying. The media play an intrinsic role in the portrayal of government and individual politicians which influences public perceptions of trust in the political system. How the media report on politics is influenced by the relationship between journalists and politicians and how ethical, professional, open, and honest they are with each other. Perceptions of poor conduct and unfair treatment between journalists and media advisers can erode trust, which impacts on the amount and type of information media advisers are prepared to give to journalists and how the media report on politicians and politics to the public. This is important in the context of the case study in this chapter focusing on the media management style of former Australian Prime Minister Scott Morrison.

As will be discussed, the controlling style of former Prime Minister Scott Morrison, initially resulting in election victory, turned to a thumping loss of power and trust.

As Johansson (2022) states, a range of contingent structural factors play into the degree of centralization around the leader, including their personality, idiosyncrasies, and the domestic political context. That wider context includes whether they are leading a coalition or majority government and wider economic and social settings. I would add to that the health of the news media environment in which the politician is operating. Each of these elements prove to be important in the analysis of the media management style of the former Australian Prime Minister Scott Morrison.

Methodology

The chapter conducts a case study of the Australia Prime Minister Scott Morrison by collecting and analyzing diverse primary sources against the key themes identified in the literature. It draws on public records and published accounts of Morrison's term of government such as news and feature articles, commentary, inquiry reports, published profiles, and books about Morrison and his government. The chapter also includes interviews with Australian federal parliamentary press gallery journalists. Twelve senior press gallery journalists from a wide range of news outlets were approached to participate in an anonymous interview. Four agreed to participate. The interviews were conducted in December 2022. They were recorded via Zoom and took between 30 and 60 minutes, depending on the journalist's time pressures. The transcripts were auto transcribed and then checked against the recordings for accuracy. All comments used in the chapter have been anonymized.

Research findings

Case study of former Australian Prime Minister Scott Morrison

Scott Morrison became Australia's 30th prime minister and leader of the Liberal Party of Australia in 2018. Drawing on his previous career in tourism and marketing, he beat predictions to win the 2019 election after leading a highly disciplined and successful election campaign which featured a strong use of social media micro-targeting against the opposition.

However, Morrison's political success was short-lived. His prime ministership was dogged by a range of external events out of his control, including natural disasters such as devastating summer bushfires, followed by the global COVID-19 pandemic, and extensive floods. There were also several political scandals including allegations of rape against a member of cabinet and of a female Liberal staffer by a colleague in a minister's office in parliament house. The charge against the male staffer was dropped. But on top of this, the self-proclaimed 'bulldozer' sought to significantly and substantially extend his control over government apparatus and the media. For example, he created a one-person Cabinet Office Policy Committee – of which he was the only permanent member. It was protected by cabinet in confidence and so any meeting he attended was protected from external scrutiny (Middleton, 2023). He also had himself sworn in to five portfolios while he was the prime minister without telling cabinet, the parliament, or the public. This secretive grab for power has become emblematic of Morrison's controlling style in government and toward the media.

The Morrison government was roundly rejected by the Australian public in the 2022 federal election, losing key seats to Labor, the Greens, and Independents and installing a majority Labor government under the leadership of Anthony Albanese.

This case, and Morrison's leadership style, is therefore a strong example of the nature and ultimately negative consequences of exerting too much leadership control in politics.

Media control

It is of course normal for prime ministers to try to manage the media. The importance of this has radically changed over the past 60 years in response to the professionalization of communication and major shifts in media technology such as television and social media platforms. This has led to an increasing focus on leaders and expectations of what they can achieve, along with a large injection of resources into centralized media operations (Strangio et al., 2017). For example, in Australia, under the war-time prime ministership of John Curtin (1941–1945), the relationship with the press was simpler, more intimate, direct (without a phalanx of staffers), and open. As veteran Australian political journalist Michelle Grattan described it:

> [the press] had loads of first-hand prime ministerial time and attention. They were privy to a huge amount of what was in the prime ministerial in-tray and inner thoughts, and were accorded prime ministerial confidence to a degree that is staggering to anyone covering politics today.
>
> *(Grattan, 1998)*

Today, the degree of centralization and control of media operations in the office of the prime minister is much greater still. Prime ministerial offices boast a large staff of media and communications advisers, which results in less direct contact between the media and the leader and far less access to information.

In comparison to previous leaders, Murphy and Ricketson (2023) say Morrison gave few long-form interviews to the print media and was reluctant to appear on the public broadcaster. They argue this gave an impression of wanting to avoid scrutiny for his government's actions but he had an appetite for commercial TV and radio.

Morrison's controlling character was evident before he became prime minister. Early signs of his desire to restrict media access were on display earlier when he was just a minister. In 2013, he became immigration minister and in charge of 'operation sovereign borders' stopping refugees arriving in Australia by boat. To control all information flow, he refused to engage in discussion with the media about 'on water matters'. The media blackout was deemed necessary to deny people smugglers with sensitive information. During their interview for this chapter, one senior member of the parliamentary press gallery said the clamp down on information was so strong "we had the joke of 'on water matters wouldn't be discussed'" (Anonymous 2). Also, on display during his time as Minister for Immigration was a combination of "Morrison being secretive and controlling but also proactively using the media and using his friends" (Anonymous 2). This was echoed by another senior political reporter who said his approach as immigration minister "was very secretive and very controlling. We were always trying to find different ways of trying to get to the truth … and it did carry through to his time as prime minister" (Anonymous 4). Morrison also had a history of strict control over media activity from his departments. In 2015, when Morrison was the Minister for Social Services, it was reported that the 50-strong communication section responded directly to just two of 390 media requests in a six-month period, with the rest being referred to the minister's office (Thomson, 2015).

Once he became prime minister, Scott Morrison continued to run a very tight media operation. As one political journalist said:

> Well, I think it was very controlling. And that follows a pattern of an increasing desire by governments to control information flow, to control what spin goes with decisions to fill the media space… but his whole style, as a politician was to be dominant and controlling and that extended to everything, not just the media strategy.
>
> *(Anonymous 2)*

This tendency was acknowledged by Morrison himself. In a defining television interview during the 2022 federal election campaign, the prime minister said, "I know that Australians know that I can be a bit of a bulldozer when it comes to issues, and I guess you guys [the media] know that too".

One of the key devices for controlling the media was to control the message, informed by his years in marketing and tourism. His emphasis was on presentation, the performance, and 'the game' (Kelly, 2022) rather than policy substance. As one press gallery reporter saw it "he just maintained that real campaign director's mindset. It's sort of like, here's the desired package at the end of it. And let's work back from the desired package" (Anonymous 3). The emphasis on image resulted in him playing fast and loose with the truth.

Books about his mendacious tendencies document the 'lies and falsehoods' that litter his prime ministership (Keane, 2022).

His penchant for meddling with the truth undermined media trust in the information provided by his office. As one political reporter put it: "I would say unaccountable, really. I don't think that unless it was some basic information about where the leader was going to pop up anywhere you could really trust what they were saying" (Anonymous 3).

One of the biggest lies was in relation to where he was during the devastating 2020 bushfires that burnt across the east coast of Australia. While communities were defending their homes, Morrison went to Hawaii with his family for a holiday and he wasn't honest with the media about it. He even lied about telling the opposition leader that he was going overseas, which was revealed in parliament (Martin, 2021). Photos emerged of the prime minister drinking beer in Hawaii while Australia burned, which damaged his standing with the Australian public. His lies about his whereabouts also damaged his relationship with the federal parliamentary press gallery:

> I think it set a tone for 90% of the press gallery, knowing that these offices wouldn't necessarily tell the truth. Knowing that the press secretary you're talking to is telling the truth is fundamental to how press secretaries and journalists just do their jobs. You know, you can get away with not quite giving the full answer. But you can't get away with telling someone something that's not true.
>
> *(Anonymous 1)*

One of the key devices for control of the media was to play favorites with media outlets that served his electoral purposes and relegate everyone else to the bottom of the pile. As one reporter put it: "It's simple. They hold access in exchange for favorable coverage. And outlets who didn't give any favorable coverage didn't get access. It was very, very clear" (Anonymous 1). The strong preferential treatment for particular newspapers owned by News Corp was seen by one political reporter as 'fairly aggressive' and tailored particularly to the needs of the tabloid *Daily Telegraph* audience. "There was also a very clear conduit between the PMs office, the prime minister himself and [reporter] Simon Benson at *The Australian*, most particularly, but to the paper more generally, as well" (Anonymous 1).

The personal conduit between the prime minister and the reporter Simon Benson at *The Australian* newspaper was so strong, that two journalists interviewed for this chapter recalled Morrison making a public reference to it. In a speech at the annual mid-winter ball held by the parliamentary press gallery, the prime minister said "'Simon, this is the first speech I haven't had to give you in advance' or something to that effect", indicating the 'total access, total trust' between the prime minister and his favored reporter (Anonymous 3).

For others, such as political reporters who worked for smaller news outlets or publications in electorates that were not deemed politically beneficial, the experience of dealing with the prime minister's media office was 'always a struggle', 'like dealing with a brick wall', and an 'exhausting battling to get the basics'.

> I mean, obviously, there are relationships and I understand favorites and stuff like that. But if you're the leader of a party, you are either governing the entire country or you are trying to govern for the whole country, and to just sort of completely block out vast swathes of the nation because of either your history or your ...political worldview. It's just sort of bizarre to me. I don't think [former Liberal prime minister] John Howard would have done that. I just don't think that it's the way to go. I just think you have still got to communicate on a basic level and some of this stuff is just like basic level stuff. They thought 'that population never votes my way, so I'm just not going to communicate with them'. That's ridiculous.
>
> *(Anonymous 4)*

To some extent, playing favorites and focusing on news outlets that are the most politically advantageous to the government is not unusual. In a busy political office, making those choices represents a degree of triage to manage the large number of media enquiries flooding in. Morrison's media office has been described as "an active shop, mainly professionally, mostly courteous, sometimes helpful" (Murphy & Ricketson, 2023, p. 77). For others, Morrison's approach was deemed to be different. The approach was described by members of the press gallery as 'transactional', 'manipulative', and 'vindictive'. It got personal and was seen as another tactic to try and control certain reporters. For example, the prime minister went on the attack during a press conference in which he was being asked about allegations of sexual harassment and assault in his government. The prime minister didn't like the questioning and tried to turn the tables back onto the journalist by making a false accusation about another reporter being the subject of a workplace harassment complaint. He warned the attending press that people living in 'glass houses' needed to be careful (Maiden & Graham, 2021). That the prime minister had this argument at hand suggested he may have been given pre-prepared material to use against the journalist. Such an approach was seen by members of the press gallery as bordering on intimidation. Scott Morrison later apologized to the reporter in a public statement saying he shouldn't have allowed emotion to get in the way and:

> I deeply regret my insensitive response to a question from a News Ltd journalist by making an anonymous reference to an incident at News Ltd that has been rejected by the company. I accept their account.

Another example of this approach to control involves a former female Liberal staffer who alleged she was raped in a minister's office in parliament house by a colleague political reporter and former Liberal Party staffer, Peter Van Onselen told the ABC members of the prime minister's media staff were negatively backgrounding journalists against the alleged victim's partner in an attempt to control the narrative. "That might not technically be victim blaming, but I tell you what, it's grubby", Van Onselen told ABC Radio National (Murphy & Ricketson, 2023, p. 77). An inquiry into the claims by the prime minister's chief of staff, John Kunkel, did not find enough evidence to prove this did occur but it also did not conclude that it did not happen (Grattan, 2021). In his report to the prime minister, Kunkel concluded:

> While I am not in a position to make a finding that the alleged activity took place, the fact that those allegations have been made serves as an important reminder of the need for your staff to hold themselves to the highest standards.

The media control extended to other ministerial offices and the bureaucracy. Journalists recalled having to wait, often for long periods, to get a comment cleared by the prime minister's office (PMO):

> I've lost count of how many times I had a conversation with someone … and they'd say, 'We're just waiting for PMO to clear this. We're just waiting to clear this'… It was just a view in that office that they knew best. They knew how best to control the media.
>
> *(Anonymous 1)*

While ministers were not prohibited from speaking to the media, they were wary about putting anything on the record that hadn't been cleared by the PMO first. But the level of autonomy varied. Some ministers had much greater freedom over the media engagement than others:

> On the whole, they were pretty constrained and therefore their media operations were pretty constrained by the center, but there are breakouts from time to time and the Prime Minister will be pissed off with that.
>
> *(Anonymous 2)*

For the press gallery, dealing with the bureaucracy was even harder than trying to get information from ministers. Two journalists from the press gallery described a closed feedback loop between the department of the prime minister and cabinet and the PMO. One said "the external view was that it was very much a fused entity. It was sort of hard to see where the degree of separation was between the department and the PMO" (Anonymous 3).

Another reflected the media's relationship with the public service has progressively diminished over time as media operations have increasingly come under the control of the PMO, a phenomenon not restricted to Morrison's prime ministership:

> The public service has been, I think, basically cut off from the media. Except where people do have some personal relationships, but it's been cut off from the media for years.
>
> *(Anonymous 2)*

Morrison also tried to control access to information in other ways. During the pandemic, he established the Cabinet Office Policy Committee, of which he was the only permanent member. It was protected by cabinet in confidence and so any meeting he attended and related documents were protected from scrutiny. This move again highlights a tendency toward secrecy and control by a prime minister who "routinely jettisoned the conventions of the Westminster system except when they allowed him to keep things secret or otherwise afforded political advantage" (Middleton, 2023, p. 32).

The ultimate display of Morrison's controlling style was revealed after losing the federal election in 2022. It provides a cautionary tale about exerting too much control in politics. The prime minister had given his favored political journalist, Simon Benson and his colleague Geoff Chambers, exclusive fly-on-the-wall access during the COVID-19 pandemic. The account was published in the book called *Plagued: Australia's two years of hell – the inside story*, which was designed to reveal the complexities of decision making and leadership of the Morrison government at a time of crisis. A promotional article in *The Australian* newspaper included an excerpt from the book that mentioned Morrison had himself sworn into two portfolios by the governor-general as a demonstration of his leadership during the pandemic. It took another journalist to dig further to find out there was a third ministry and to point out this represented a significant breach of convention.

Further investigations by the new government revealed Morrison had himself sworn into five portfolios without telling four of the incumbent ministers, the parliament, or the public what he had done. In a press conference, Morrison explained he did it to provide a safety net in case one of the ministers became severely ill with COVID-19, which was unnecessary because provisions already exist to replace ministers in such situations at short notice. The other reason he gave was to protect against one of his ministers taking 'unilateral action' that may threaten the national interest, which strongly implied a lack of trust in the ability of his ministerial colleagues and reflected his desire to be in charge (Speers, 2022). Morrison's penchant for control had been on display throughout his political career but was greatly facilitated by the COVID-19 pandemic, which gave leaders across the world increased powers to limit personal freedoms and functions of government as they grappled with the health crisis. As high-profile journalist Paul Kelly (2022) summarized it:

> The bottom line here goes to Morrison's sense of power. His instinct to concentrate power was accentuated by the pandemic. Convinced of his own judgment, the focus of government decision-making revolved around himself and his office while the cabinet declined as an effective decision-making instrument.

From a media management perspective, Morrison's attempt at controlling the narrative by the use of favored journalists backfired. It can be argued that the authors of the book '*Plagued*' were too close to the prime minister and unable to see the consequences of what Morrison had done. They had lost their independence, were blinded by the spin of their friend, and stopped asking critical questions in a time of crisis. As a result, they missed one of the biggest stories of the year and damaged their reputations. Morrison, lulled into the safety of working with a friendly journalist, revealed his secret power grab and ultimately lost control of the narrative and the trust of his colleagues and the nation.

The negative impact went beyond the individual political leader, however. The revelations of the secret ministries caused further damage to the Liberal Party which was already crushed by losing the federal election and the government's poor handling of a range of issues from natural disasters to gender equality. In the lead up to his loss of the 2022 election, state and federal Liberal female MPs began to speak out publicly against Scott Morrison. Federal NSW Senator Concetta Fierravanti-Wells told the parliament that Morrison was "An autocrat, a bully who has no moral compass", it was "his way or the highway" and he was "not fit to be prime minister" (Tingle, 2022). Federal Liberal MP Julia Banks left parliament because of the bullying and intimidation of women in politics (Karp, 2018). NSW Liberal MLC Catherine Cusack announced she could not vote for the re-election of a Morrison government having earlier announced she would not run again. She later condemned the "secret power grab" of five ministries during the pandemic by "the most powerful man in the land [who] exploited a health crisis to extract yet more personal power" (Cusack, 2022). The former Minister for Home Affairs Karen Andrews, whose portfolio Morrison secretly shared, called for his resignation from parliament (Evans, 2022). In her book about Morrison's demise, author and journalist Niki Savva, who is also a former Liberal staffer, said his political colleagues "knew he was secretive and that he lied; that he was stubborn; that he bullied people; that he even sought advice but seldom took it" (Savva, 2022, p. 6).

There were also broader impacts on government and democracy. An Independent Inquiry by the Hon. Virginia Bell into Scott Morrison's multiple ministerial appointments found the lack of disclosure was "apt to undermine public confidence in government" and once the secrecy was revealed it was "corrosive of trust in government" (Bell, 2022, p. 6). More broadly, during the three years of his prime ministership, Morrison lost the trust of the Australian people and the election. When he was elected as prime minister in 2019, a longitudinal survey of Australian political opinion, the Australia Electoral Study found 47% of voters said they trusted him as prime minister. In 2022, it had fallen to 29% and he became the least popular leader since the study began in 1987 (Cameron & McAllister, 2022, p. 5).

Recommendations for academic research

The case study demonstrates that if political leaders exert too much control, it can backfire. It showed that Australian Prime Minister Scott Morrison's favored relationships with the parliamentary press gallery, his secret self-appointment to five ministries, and his manipulation of the truth reflect a controlling leadership style that backfired and contributed to his election loss in 2022. He is not alone. Former Australian Labor Prime Minister Kevin Rudd lost his leadership as a result of exerting too much control and the former Harper prime ministership in Canada was judged in the harshest terms for its attempts at control and manipulation. As media technologies continue to change and pose new threats and opportunities to political communicators – such as artificial intelligence (AI), chat bots, and deepfakes – the desire for increased control of the message will likely also continue.

Control is an area that deserves in-depth research. While a certain degree of control and centralization is necessary for government media operations to function effectively, there is a degree of control that is counterproductive, contributing to an erosion of trust and even electoral defeat. Further research is needed to better understand where the sweet spot lies between centralized and coordinated media operations and respectful, accountable government.

Politics does not occur within the defined boundaries of narrow academic fields. There is much to be learned from related and intersecting fields of political studies, political management and marketing, political communication, and journalism studies. By taking this multi-disciplinary approach, this chapter aims to give a fuller examination of the impacts of media control on democracy.

Recommendations for practice

There are several important lessons for practitioners from this research:

1 Build and maintain relationships with the media and colleagues based on respect for professional autonomy and the truth rather than control to help boost perceptions of trust in government and political leaders and improve electoral success.

2 Reconsider the validity of tight centralized control in the hybrid media environment from the perspective of external media messaging, media and public trust, and internal cohesion. Exerting too much control over messaging and access to information can build animosity and resentment toward you.
3 Consider the long-term impact of how political management is used. Actions to exert control may appear to have short-term benefits but in the long term may give rise to multiple negative consequences such as loss of organizational reputation and trust, which will not only risk losing an election but also make it harder for the party to rebuild its reputation under a new leader.
4 Carefully consider the quality of the information you are releasing to the media and the public. Misinformation and lies undermine public and media trust in the political process that is difficult to recover. Avoid lying at all costs.

Recommended reading

Chadwick, A. (2017). *The Hybrid Media System: Politics and Power* (2nd ed.). New York: Oxford University Press.
Fisher, C. (2018). News sources and journalist/source interaction. In H. Örnebring (Ed.), *Oxford Encyclopedia of Communication (Journalism)*. New York: Oxford University Press.
Johansson, K. M. (2022). *The Prime Minister–Media Nexus: Centralization Logic and Application*. Cham, Switzerland: Springer.
Levi, M., & Stoker, L. (2000). Political trust and trustworthiness. *Annual Review of Political Science*, 3(1), 475–507.
McNair, B. (2018). *An Introduction to Political Communication* (6th ed.). Abingdon, UK; New York: Routledge.

References

Aucoin, P. (2012). New political governance in Westminster systems: Impartial public administration and management performance at risk. *Governance*, 25(2), 177–199.
Bell, V. (2022). *Inquiry into the appointment of the former prime minister to administer multiple departments*. Canberra: Office of Prime Minister and Cabinet, Australian Government.
Cameron, S., & McAllister, I. (2022). Trends in Australian political opinion: Results from the Australian Election Study, 1987–2022. Canberra: Australian National University.
Chadwick, A. (2017). *The Hybrid Media System: Politics and Power* (2nd ed.). New York: Oxford University Press.
Cusack, C. (2022, August 19). Scott Morrison is relentlessly eroding Australians' faith in democracy – and laughing about it. *The Guardian Australia*. https://www.theguardian.com/australia-news/2022/aug/19/scott-morrison-is-relentlessly-eroding-australians-faith-in-democracy-and-laughing-about-it
Ericson, R. V., Baranek, P. M., & Chan, J. B. (1989). *Negotiating Control: A Study of News Sources*. New York; Milton Keynes, UK: Open University Press.

Evans, J. (2022, August 16). Former home affairs minister Karen Andrews calls on Scott Morrison to resign from parliament over secret power grab, as former PM apologises. *ABC News*. https://www.abc.net.au/news/2022-08-16/karen-andrews-says-morrison-should-resign-as-he-apologises/101336646

Grattan, M. (1998, April 20). *The Prime Minister and the Press: A Study in Intimacy*, John Curtin: A Man of Peace, a Time of War. Perth, Western Australia: John Curtin Ministerial Library, Curtin University.

Grattan, M. (2021, May 25). View from The Hill: Morrison's top staffer doesn't find colleagues briefed against Higgins' partner but reminds them of 'standards'. *The Conversation*. https://theconversation.com/view-from-the-hill-morrisons-top-staffer-doesnt-find-colleagues-briefed-against-higgins-partner-but-reminds-them-of-standards-161512

Hermans, L., & Vergeer, M. (2013). Personalization in e-campaigning: A cross-national comparison of personalization strategies used on candidate websites of 17 countries in EP elections 2009. *New Media & Society*, 15(1), 72–92.

Johansson, K. M. (2022). *The Prime Minister–Media Nexus: Centralization Logic and Application*. Cham, Switzerland: Springer.

Johansson, K. M., & Raunio, T. (2019). Government communication in a comparative perspective. In K. M. Johansson and G. Nygren (Ed.), *Close and Distant: Political Executive-Media Relations in Four Countries* (pp. 127–148). Göteborg, Sweden: University of Gothenburg, Nordicom.

Karp, P. (2018, August 29). Liberal MP Julia Banks to quit parliament, citing 'bullying and intimidation'. *The Guardian Australia*. https://www.theguardian.com/australia-news/2018/aug/29/liberal-mp-julia-banks-to-quit-parliament-next-election-citing-bullying-and-intimidation

Keane, B. (2022). *Lies, Lies and Falsehoods: The Morrison Government and the New Culture of Deceit*. Richmond, VIC: Hardie Grant Books.

Kelly, P. (2022, August 20). Scott Morrison's secret ego trip has damaged the Liberal brand. *The Australian*. https://www.theaustralian.com.au/inquirer/scott-morrisons-secret-ego-trip-has-damaged-the-liberal-brand/news-story/8aa959f424bebd17d33659d719b4a276

Kelly, S. (2022). *The Game: A Portrait of Scott Morrison*. Collingwood, VIC: Black Inc. Books.

Levi, M., & Stoker, L. (2000). Political trust and trustworthiness. *Annual Review of Political Science*, 3(1), 475–507.

Lippmann, W. (1922). *Public Opinion*. New York: Harcourt, Brace & Co.

MacDonald, L. I. (2018). *Inside politics*. McGill-Queen's Press-MQUP.

Maiden, S., & Graham, B. (2021, March 21). Scott Morrison apologises for 'wrong' toilet claim to News Corp journalist. News.com.au. https://www.news.com.au/national/politics/scott-morrison-apologises-for-wrong-remarks-about-news-corp-harassment/news-story/ab0fefeeaa8ab36fed99806684c3cfe9

Marland, A. (2016). *Brand Command: Canadian Politics and Democracy in the Age of Message Control*. Vancouver, BC; Toronto, ON: UBC Press.

Marland, A., Lewis, J., & Flanagan, T. (2017). Governance in the age of digital media and branding. *Governance*, 30(1), 125–141.

Martin, S. (2021, November 22). Morrison under fire for falsely claiming he told Albanese he was travelling to Hawaii in 2019. *The Guardian Australia*. https://www.theguardian.com/australia-news/2021/nov/22/morrison-under-fire-for-falsely-claiming-he-told-albanese-he-was-travelling-to-hawaii-in-2019

McKnight, D. (2016). The Rudd Labor government and the limitations of spin. *Media International Australia*, 159(1), 108–117.

Middleton, K. (2023). Delegating democracy: Parliament in the Morrison era. In M Grattan, Brendan McCaffrie, and Chris Wallace (Ed.), *The Morrison Government. Governing Though Crisis, 2019–2022*. Sydney: UNSW Press.

Murphy, K., & Ricketson, M. (2023). The Morrison government and the media. In M Grattan, Brendan McCaffrie, and Chris Wallace (Ed.), *The Morrison Government: Governing Through Crisis, 2019- 2022*. Sydney: UNSW Press.

Phillis, B. (2004). *An Independent Review of Government Communications: Presented to the Minister for the Cabinet Office*. Cabinet Office.

Savva, N. (2022). *Bulldozed: Scott Morrison's Fall and Anthony Albanese's Rise*. Brunswick, VIC: Scribe.

Seymour-Ure, C. (2003). *Prime Ministers and the Media: Issues of Power and Control*. Hoboken, NJ: Blackwell Publishers.

Speers, D. (2022, August 18). Scott Morrison gave two reasons for secretly taking on five ministerial roles. But his lack of trust is what's most extraordinary. *ABC News*. https://www.abc.net.au/news/2022-08-18/scott-morrison-secret-ministerial-roles-lack-trust-extraordinary/101343202

Stoker, G., Evans, M., & Halupka, M. (2018). *Bridging the Trust Divide – Lessons from International Experience* (Democracy 2025, Issue). Canberra: MoAD.

Strangio, P., Hart, P., & Walter, J. (2017). *The Pivot of Power: Australian Prime Ministers and Political Leadership, 1949–2016*. Melbourne: Melbourne University Publishing.

Thomson, P. (2015, August 27). Scott Morrison exercises tight media control in Department of Social Services. *Sydney Morning Herald*. https://www.smh.com.au/public-service/scott-morrison-exercises-tight-media-control-in-department-of-social-services-20150827-gj9001.html

Tingle, L. (2022, March 31). Senator Concetta Fierravanti-Wells launches blistering attack on Scott Morrison. ABC| 7.30. https://www.youtube.com/watch?v=2SsZZvn4rNM

Van Aelst, P., Sheafer, T., & Stanyer, J. (2012). The personalization of mediated political communication: A review of concepts, operationalizations and key findings. *Journalism*, 13(2), 203–220.

Weibel, A. (2007). Formal control and trustworthiness: Shall the twain never meet? *Group & Organization Management*, 32(4), 500–517.

12

THE STRATEGIES AND SKILLS POLITICAL LEADERS NEED TO MANAGE GLOBAL CRISES

John Connolly and Robert Pyper

Introduction

This chapter examines the skills and political management strategies required for negotiating global crises at a national level. In contemporary politics the forces of globalisation and complex interdependencies have highlighted the need for national political leaders to manage crises emerging from global threats, including pandemics, cyber-terrorism, climate catastrophes and economic destabilisation (Kreuder-Sonnen and White, 2022). Political managers of the future must reflect on the skills and competences required for leadership through the challenges and complexities of crisis management. Politicians need to grapple with the tensions between an 'it won't happen to me' mentality (aided by groupthink in government) and investing often scarce resources in preparing for long-term threats (Drumhiller, 2022). It is within this context that the chapter provides an overview of the main tasks, tensions and challenges for political leaders in times of crisis which are key to political management. The chapter covers three case studies: (1) New Zealand Prime Minister Jacinda Ardern's management of the Covid-19 pandemic; (2) German Chancellor Angela Merkel's management of the 2015 European Union (EU) refugee crisis; (3) Prime Minister Theresa May's management of the 2018 Salisbury poisonings in the UK.

Key literature

The crisis management literature emphasises that dealing with crises represents opportunities for political leaders to gain popularity. In this respect, crises can be seen as 'politicised critical junctures' (Boin and 't Hart, 2022:14), which can either represent gateways of opportunity or pave the way for

DOI: 10.4324/9781003260677-12

imminent or gradual political failure (Edelman, 2013, McConnell, 2010). Success or failure is dependent on executing effective political management strategies, which include providing reassurance to the public that not only is action being taken but that politicians can be trusted to lead them through troubled waters (Boin and 't Hart, 2022).

This literature stresses the importance of 'framing', which is another way of describing the strategies to define the nature of problems, capture the narrative and communicate solutions to them (Brändström and Kuipers, 2003). The political management of the uncertainties, risks and threats is about shaping public discourse and the channels for doing this might be via media (or various kinds), campaign literatures and speeches within parliamentary settings. Political management is also a feature of post-crisis politics via inquiry processes (Stark, 2019). No matter the venue for communication, it is the narratives through the use of political language, and even blame shifting, that will be the key concern of crisis managers in order to minimise the risk of being subject to ridicule or being on the receiving end of 'gotcha!' politics (Flinders, 2020). Politicians will be aware that managing crises is key to their popularity and reputations.

Managing the operational elements of crises tends to be the job of emergency services and/or officials within bureaucracies (such as those in civil service departments or agencies). Crisis responders might involve actors from industry and other non-governmental organisations who need to mobilise resources to bring crises under control. The politician, on the other hand, tends to be the crisis leader (the figurehead) who is responsible for leading crisis communications. The actions and words of political leaders can have a major role in shaping levels of public support about the legitimacy of government actions (Karyotis et al., 2021). Leaders who can get the temperature of the public mood right are able to use a crisis to their benefit in terms of their political careers. Lilleker et al. (2021) show how political turbulence and instability can make crises feel worse for the public and if the crisis at hand is not managed effectively it can further expose and add fuel to the fire of existing leadership deficiencies. Symbolic exercises, such as appearing at press conferences, calling for 'lessons to be learned' inquiries, and acts of public reassurance, are elements of crisis ritualisation processes by leaders managing these situations (Dzhurova, 2020). Crises themselves take on various identities and they can have inter-sectorial implications within policy systems (Rothstein et al., 2022). A major political management tension to work through relates to the nature of the political environment in which a political leader is situated. Indeed, constitutional arrangements shape forms of accountability and political decision-making can be affected by judicial, parliamentary and wider democratic features of the state (Rothstein et al., 2022). Analyses of leadership provide useful framing mechanisms for understanding the political management of crises. Heifetz (1994) examines adaptive and transformational leadership, both 'with' and 'without' authority, in ways that contribute to our understanding of the political management challenge in a crisis situation. Lees-Marshment has identified a number of key elements of political leadership: 'develop skills …be authoritative … be transformational …persuade …collaborate …delegate… adapt' (Lees-Marshment, 2021: Chapter 5). Each of these has the potential to enhance political management of crises, but she specifically cites the significance of skills development in effective crisis management (Lees-Marshment, 2021: 162–65). The three main components of political leadership specific to crises, to which other tasks are linked, are crisis communication, decision-making and post-crisis governance (Boin and 't Hart, 2022).

The next section provides a concise methodology for the chapter.

Methodology

This chapter draws together the academic literatures of crisis management and applied political management. Refracting insights from these literatures allows for the examination of the political management skills required by national leaders for managing global crises. The chapter provides practical political management lessons from crises and provides a toolkit that can be applied to various crises and at different levels of governance (e.g. transnational, national, regional and local).

The chapter is structured as follows. First, summarised case studies of crises will be contextualised by identifying the political leadership components in the management of crises, including discussion of the tensions and issues that surround them. The crises considered are:

• The leadership of New Zealand Prime Minister Jacinda Ardern when managing the early stages of the Covid-19 pandemic.
• The German Chancellor Angela Merkel's management of the 2015 EU refugee crisis.
• The political leadership of Prime Minister Theresa May in relation to the 2018 poisonings of Sergei and Yulia Skripal by Russian military agents in Salisbury in the UK.

The final section of the chapter draws together the political management skills required to manage crises with global dimensions, which includes a transferable political management toolkit.

Research findings

The political management of crises: tensions and challenges

Table 12.1 highlights the main tasks (or challenges) for political leaders in times of crisis and the associated tensions.

Table 12.1 shows that political leaders need to manage several tasks, but these are not straightforward, not least given the politics and constitutional

TABLE 12.1 Political management and leadership challenges and tensions

Task type	Challenge	Tension
Sense-making	• Comprehend the nature of the complexities and understand what is going on. • Run crisis simulations and crisis prevention exercises to tuneup systems and personnel and equip them to define the nature of threats quickly.	• Relies on adequate, tried and tested pre-crisis training and scenario testing at scale. • Crisis training unlikely to be adequately scaled to cover all eventualities. • Groupthink mentality in government can generate a shared sense of invulnerability, reducing investment in crisis preparation.
Getting the right team in place	• Mobilize the right people to get the most appropriate internal and external groups in place. • Be inclusive and get the right intelligence at the right time.	• Adoption of a transparent and deliberative approach to informing crisis management processes to understanding stakeholder groups assumes governments know who holds the best information and the stakeholders (including media) have a positive relationship with government.
Crisis decision-making	• Have a vision for recovery and assert the values of the political party, government and broader society.	• Neither crises nor political actors exist in a vacuum and knowing when to act can be a political gamble. • Adversarial political systems, and government unpopularity can create risk-averse behaviours and fear of miscalculations.
Multi-directional coordination	• Know *where* crisis decision-making should be located, given that legal and political responsibilities might transcend levels of governance.	• Relies on political leaders having the right strategic, advisory and bureaucratic support to enable a culture of institutional resilience. Relationship coordination across political boundaries can be strained by competing political interests and ideologies within different levels of the governance system.
Meaning-making	• How politicians can frame through narratives the key issues for long-term political sustainability and enhancing the legitimacy of public institutions. • Political actors implement effective meaning-making strategies (via tools like slogans) to shape public trust and behaviour.	• Relies on political leaders being good communicators and being able to explain how they intend to resolve uncertainties and establish a path to stability. • Increased populism, political polarisation and declining trust see crises dangers experienced differently across communities, resulting in competing concepts of successful resolution.

(Continued)

TABLE 12.1 (*Continued*)

Task type	Challenge	Tension
Communication	• Reconcile the internal and external dimensions to ensure that institutional actors have the information about what is happening within government, and societal actors (such as media, public and industry) have confidence that the crisis is being resolved.	• Requires resilience to be embedded in the culture of government. Coordination depends on information sharing and systemic/process integration. Crises based on politicised conflicts can make it very difficult for political leaders to have accurate information about unfolding events.
Accountability	• Explain *why* and *how* events unfolded and defend actions within forums of accountability, including parliamentary settings. • Combine the accumulation of credit with avoidance of culpability.	• Relies on the cooperation of political leaders, who must respect democratic mechanisms and not circumvent accountability conventions (such as ministerial responsibility). • Accountability mechanisms can be partisan, have limited legal instruments at their disposal or even be corrupted depending on the integrity of political leaders (which is difficult to guarantee).
Learning	• Linked to accountability. Each has symbolic dimensions, with effective post-crisis political management relying on communicating commitments to change and visions of reform (policy and organisational) based on crisis experience.	• Post-crisis reform requires learning the 'right' lessons, but learning does not equal reform. Effective change requires on-going political commitment, adequate accountability, governance capacities, resilience cultures, stable political administrations, institutional memory retention and effective public management.

Sources: Original table but informed by Boin et al. (2013), Drennan et al. (2014), Connolly (2016), Stark and Head (2019) and Connolly and Pyper (2020).

conditions that impact on crisis managers. Nonetheless, despite governance complexities, there are lessons for political management that can be drawn from examples of crises. This is where the chapter now turns.

Health crisis: New Zealand PM Jacinda Ardern and the early stages of the 2020 Covid-19 pandemic

Crisis narrative

New Zealand's first recorded case of Covid-19 was on 28 February 2020 (Ministry of Health, 2020). The response by the New Zealand authorities was shaped by the government's 2017 pandemic influenza plan and the crisis management intention was to 'flatten the curve' to minimise the health impact of the disease (Summers et al., 2020: 3). During the early stages of the pandemic, and subsequently, Prime Minister Jacinda Ardern was the political figurehead for the pandemic response and enjoyed favourable media coverage and public support at home and overseas for her political management and leadership approach to the crisis. The civil service benefited from experienced officials who coordinated the response across government and society. The authorities implemented restrictions including a national lockdown in March 2022, with the overall approach by the government being 'to go hard and go early' (Stockman, 2021).

From February 2020 self-isolation and quarantine restrictions for travellers were implemented. By March cases of Covid-19 were increasing and, like many countries, PM Ardern announced a national lockdown and a national state of emergency, with the public being told to stay at home via a 'Stay Home – Save Lives' campaign. Only petrol stations, supermarkets and medical facilities remained open. The initial lockdown was Level 4 (the highest level) and partial lockdown (Level 3) was in place until May 2020. The government supported the economy by providing a lump sum subsidy that essentially acted as a minimum salary payment for employees (OECD, 2020). Although the government did not work to an elimination strategy for Covid-19 in the initial weeks of the pandemic response (i.e. the focus on flattening the curve), PM Ardern changed the crisis management approach to focus on an elimination strategy to protect public health and the health system. The seven-week lockdown was a success, resulting in polling data that indicated high levels of 'public trust in government, social cohesion and a sense of national pride' (Stockman, 2021).

Political skills deployed

A critical dimension to PM Ardern's successes from a political management perspective was her *sense-making* skills linked to ability to *communicate* risk. Her public health communications were led by the science, and, moreover, she captured the crisis narrative by framing the crisis as a public health emergency (Baker and Wilson, 2022). *Sense-making* was also shown through the establishment of a transparent framework for decision-making – the government's alert level framework (Unite Against Covid-19, 2022). The New Zealand civil service implemented a tried and tested crisis management system – Coordinated Incident Management System (CIMS) – which is the framework for effective coordinated incident management across responding agencies (National Emergency Management Agency, 2022). This system has been crucial for *multi-directional coordination* across government and beyond. New Zealand's unitary and centralised system of governance produced lower levels of intergovernmental conflict (Bromfield and McConnell, 2021).

PM Ardern also sought to take a principled approach to protecting public health based on scientific advice and her sincere style helped to politically manage the introduction of unprecedented national restrictions. She *got the right team in place* by introducing scientific advisory groups to support the crisis response. The PM's ability to tell the story of the pandemic to the public and to gain support for crisis measures was testament to her *meaning-making* abilities. A common assessment of PM Ardern's approach within the international press is provided by Friedman (2022): 'Her leadership style is one of empathy in a crisis that tempts people to fend for themselves. Her messages are clear, consistent, and somehow simultaneously sobering and soothing'. The communicative successes of PM Ardern have also been due to her presence and combined use of press conferences, national broadcasts and social media streaming.

The political management successes, and global reputation of competence of PM Ardern, was also indicative of her preparedness to be held politically *accountable* for the actions of the government. There was a lack of evidence of political blame shifting, unlike what could be seen in other countries, including the UK (Karyotis et al., 2021). There was multi-party agreement for her crisis *decision-making* during the acute phase of the crisis when the national restrictions were first introduced, although this became fragmented at later stages of the pandemic response (Baker and Wilson, 2022). Evidence of crisis *learning* was linked to the ongoing adaptations of crisis measures during the crisis management process. Examples of learning during the crisis included the establishment of new border management systems, the establishment of a contact management system and vaccine rollout/passes. PM Ardern secured a landslide victory for the governing Labour Party in October 2020, which reflected the PM's popularity during the early stages of the pandemic.

Political management lessons: scope and limitations

A learning point for Ardern, and her government, from the pandemic response is to anticipate human rights issues when making decisions to restrict freedoms, including the decision-making processes. Ardern's government was legally challenged on human rights grounds (Andrew Borrowdale v Director-General of Health and Attorney-General). Borrowdale, a lawyer based in Wellington, contested that the lockdown restrictions were *ultra vires* i.e., ministers exceeded the reach of the emergency powers conferred by the Health Act 1956 (Act) and that the restrictions were inconsistent with freedoms of movement under the Bill of Rights Act (Human Rights Law Centre, 2020). The Court of Appeal ruled that ministers acted lawfully but that the Director-General for Health, Dr Ashley Bloomfield, had wrongly delegated his powers to officials. The learning here is that even when acute crisis management actions are taken, political leaders need to put human rights dimensions to the forefront of political management, as well as ensuring that decisions are made at the appropriate levels of authority.

As noted earlier in this chapter, the focus of this case study narrative concerns the early stages of the pandemic, which was a resounding success for PM Ardern – until August 2021. It is the case that New Zealand was held up as a 'poster country' for political management of the Covid-19 pandemic, yet it is important to acknowledge that there were major challenges as the crisis progressed. Up until August 2021, New Zealand had recorded approximately 2800 cases and only 26 deaths but the delta variant of the disease usurped the elimination strategy to one of suppression. By mid-October, there were 2099 cases of the delta variant and PM Ardern justified the shift to a suppression strategy due to the availability of vaccines (Megget, 2022). At the same time, Ardern's initial 'zero Covid' policy also had concurrent public health consequences in terms of the rise in respiratory illnesses due to the lack of exposure to bugs and aided by social distancing and sanitising (McClure, 2021).

Although there is arguably some justification for the 'living with Covid' communication approach, the problem is that there was significant inequity with vaccine coverage, particularly with regards to indigenous groups. Moreover, it is evident that there were public health infrastructure and systemic issues, not least the absence of a dedicated national public health emergency agency, but this was resolved by the introduction of a Public Health Agency (PHA) for New Zealand in July 2022.

PM Ardern's popularity waned after the October 2020 election, with opinion polls in August 2022 indicating that her centre-left Labour Party at its lowest level of support in five years due to a lack of grip on crime as well as major economic and social policy challenges (McKenzie, 2022), and she eventually resigned as Prime Minister in January 2023. In short, although the political climate has moved on to focus on non-Covid issues in New Zealand, other public policy concerns meant she has been 'pulled away from being the face of the pandemic' (McClure, 2022). Overall, it is sufficient to argue that PM Ardern was a unifying figure during early response to the Covid-19 pandemic and the associated political management skills she demonstrated will, on balance, be the source of considerable admiration and interest by political leaders for years to come.

Migration crisis: German Chancellor Angela Merkel and the 2015 EU refugee crisis

Crisis narrative

The origins of the 2015 refugee crisis lay in a series of conflicts, mainly in Syria, but also in other regions including sub-Saharan Africa, and Afghanistan, from which increasing numbers of desperate people sought sanctuary in Europe. The migrants applied for asylum at initial entry points mainly in Italy and Greece, or, in large numbers, travelled north to seek entry to other

European states. Estimates of the numbers involved vary considerably, but there is a general consensus that these rose from increasing hundreds of thousands in 2012, 2013 and 2014, to around 2 million in 2015. For the German Chancellor, Angela Merkel, this global catastrophe brought huge political, social and economic challenges as she tried to manage the impact of the refugee crisis within her own country, where the numbers seeking asylum rose to over 1 million (Marten, 2021: 191), and to coordinate a united response across the EU. In doing so, she faced serious obstacles from opponents in her own party and governing coalition, the ranks of the opposition in Germany, including the increasingly vocal far right, and the leadership of other EU states who either opposed migration outright, or objected to Merkel's specific proposals for assimilating the refugees.

Although, as noted below, Merkel was required to make some compromises in her management of the crisis, the outcome which emerged by 2016 was broadly aligned with her objectives of securing a sensitive response to a massive humanitarian challenge, ensuring that Germany granted asylum to the vast majority of those who had crossed her borders, and obliging other EU member states to take appropriate shares of the migrants.

Political management skills deployed

Throughout the crisis, Merkel showed herself to be particularly adept at deploying the political management skills associated with *sense making* (which includes quickly grasping the significance of the crisis) and *meaning-making* (framing a convincing narrative around the events). Apparently passive as the crisis became increasingly acute in the spring and summer of 2015, while some European countries closed their borders to refugees and opposition grew within Germany, Merkel was carefully analysing the developments before breaking her silence. When she did so, at the end of August 2015, it was to assert that Germany had both a humanitarian duty to help the refugees and an economic opportunity to integrate new workers as taxpayers who would ease a growing pensions crisis in the state, and also argue for a change in EU policy to allow migrants to be registered and processed in countries other than those where they had initially landed (Marten, 2021: 188–89). Her political management approach was encapsulated in the phrase 'Wir schaffen das!' – 'we can do this!' (Qvortrup, 2021: 79–80). It should be noted that some critics believe that while Merkel's *communication* of the crisis narrative was strong in relation to the humanitarian elements, she faltered somewhat when explaining the perceived economic advantages to Germany of assimilating large numbers of migrants (Marten, 2021:192).

Merkel acted swiftly to *get the right team in place* to manage the crisis both at the national level, and in her negotiations with EU partners. Immigration policy, and the task of arranging accommodation for the refugees, was to be coordinated through a special unit in the Chancellor's office, headed by Peter Altmaier, Chief of Staff of the Federal Chancellery, while the Interior Minister, Thomas de Maiziere, was deployed as Merkel's link-man with the EU member states, charged with responsibility for maximising burden-sharing (Qvortrup, 2021: 323–24). This approach aided the tasks associated with complex *multi-directional coordination* to manage policy, administration, infrastructure logistics, employment, health and social care challenges at the levels of the state, the local authorities, and the EU.

Merkel's generally adept *crisis decision-making* can be illustrated with reference to her announcement of Germany's policy at the end of August (see above), and the follow-up which culminated in her adopting a tough negotiating stance within the EU, involving the threat of forcing the refugee issue to a qualified majority vote as a means to securing the agreement of the member states (the latter did so, with the exception of Romania, the Czech Republic, Slovakia and Hungary) to a quota system (Qvortrup, 2021: 321–33).

The *accountability* and *learning* aspects of Merkel's political management of this crisis can be seen in the subtle adjustments to her policy in the last weeks of 2015. She implicitly acknowledged her accountability to sceptics within her own party, and across the governing coalition, by exhibiting her willingness to learn from the realities of the refugee crisis within Germany, and agreeing that there would be limits to the country's capacity to assimilate migrants. Specifically, only Syrian refugees would be granted immediate asylum, while others could be processed at immigration centres (Qvortrup, 2021: 324).

Political management lessons: scope and limitations

Angela Merkel's deployment of core political management skills during this crisis, which had global origins but significant implications for national policy-makers, was generally astute and assured, and provides a model for political managers at all levels. At the end of her tenure as Germany's Chancellor in 2021, she argued that her prediction about successfully managing the crisis had been correct, the refugees were accommodated socially and economically without a significant rise in internal tensions (notwithstanding some political gains enjoyed by far right parties at certain points), although it has been noted that measuring outcomes in relation to the assimilation of migrants is inherently difficult (Nostlinger, 2021).

There were some limitations to Merkel's management of the crisis, nonetheless. As noted above, her communication skills were arguably more adept in some areas than others, and occasionally neglected the need to bring others along with her own viewpoint. Linked to this, some critics argued that Merkel's relatively closed decision-making process, in which she maintained silence on key issues before announcing policy, created some unnecessary problems with her domestic and EU allies who were taken by surprise by her announcements (Marten, 2021: 189–90; 192). Political managers must strike a balance between calm reflection and quiet analysis, and keeping other key actors involved and informed in the interest of minimising conflict over policy.

Security and public health crisis: United Kingdom PM Theresa May and the 2018 Salisbury poisonings

Crisis narrative

This crisis involved two extremely serious instances of poisoning by a nerve agent subsequently identified as Novichok (Prime Minister's Office, 2018), with consequential public health management challenges and, due to Russia being quickly identified as the likely source of the nerve agent, a major security and diplomatic crisis. On 4 March 2018, Sergei Skripal, a former Russian military intelligence officer who became a double agent for the intelligence services of the UK, and was now living in Britain following a 'spy swap', and his daughter Yulia who was visiting the UK, took ill while sitting on a public bench in Salisbury (Harding et al., 2018). They spent several weeks in hospital before recovering. A major incident was declared, Skripal's home was isolated, members of the public were checked for symptoms, and three police officers required treatment. A discarded perfume bottle containing the same nerve agent was picked up some time later in Salisbury by Charlie Rowley, who innocently gave it to his friend Dawn Sturgess. Sturgess fell ill in the nearby town of Amesbury on 30 June, and died on 8 July, while Rowley survived his encounter with the poison (Dodd et al., 2018). In each case, the matter was handled as a major public health incident, and triggered involvement by Scotland Yard's anti-terrorism unit. It took almost a year for the local sites to be declared free of contamination (Morris and Bannock, 2019).

During the following weeks and months, Prime Minister Theresa May led a coordinated effort from her government to identify the members of the Russian intelligence service said to be responsible for the poisonings, link these men to the political leadership in the Kremlin, expel over 20 Russian diplomats from the UK, freeze Russian state assets, and work bilaterally with allies and multi-laterally within NATO and the United Nations to secure an international response to Russian aggression involving sanctions and expulsion of diplomats (Walker and Roth, 2018).

Political management skills deployed

Theresa May effectively deployed a range of political management skills appropriate to this crisis. She rapidly *made sense* of the initial reports from Salisbury, informed Parliament of the initial facts, subsequently updated the Commons that no credible explanation had been provided by the Russian government, and that the matter would now be pursued as an attack by Russia on the Skripals, which threatened the lives of other British citizens and was an 'appalling act against our country' (Prime Minister's Office, 2018). She *got the right team in place* to deal with both the public health and diplomatic elements of the developing crisis, including assigning key leadership roles to the Foreign Secretary, the Home Secretary, the Health Secretary and the leadership of the security and intelligence services, as well as ensuring that there was effective liaison with Scotland Yard and the Crown Prosecution Service in relation to charges and arrest warrants for the suspects.

The Prime Minister made *timely, well-focused decisions*, starting with the summoning of the Russian ambassador to the Foreign Office on 12 March, and continuing through the expulsion of Russian diplomats, the suspension of bilateral contacts, strengthening of UK defences including enhanced powers of detention and monitoring, briefing of allies and the United Nations, and reviewing the application of Unexplained Wealth Orders against Russian residents in the UK (Allan, 2018). Having established the *right team*, PM May maintained a firm grip on the challenge of *multi-directional coordination* across government departments, Scotland Yard, Parliament, local institutions (including the South Wiltshire Recovery Coordinating Group), foreign allies and international organisations. Overcoming an initial reluctance to become involved on the part of the French government, and the isolationist and pro-Russian instincts of US President Trump, May deployed effective political management skills to build an international coalition against Russia (Casalicchio, 2018). She deployed effective *communication* skills in order to create a *meaningful* narrative around the events in Salisbury and the resulting fallout, with ongoing media briefings which combined reassuring public health and security information with the government's story of the unfolding events within the UK and beyond. Her astute political management of the communication dimension was epitomised by her steely approach to confronting the Putin regime in defence of British values, human rights and Western interests. This stance was epitomised in her cold personal meeting with Putin during the 2019 G20 Summit in Osaka, during which she confronted him with the evidence of his government's malfeasance (Stewart, 2019).

Throughout the crisis, effective *accountability* (in its various forms, including the most basic explanatory strain, and also the stronger forms encompassing commitments to amendatory actions in policy and practice) was secured via regular statements to Parliament, and post-crisis *learning* opportunities covering the public health, security and policy dimensions were put in place. In the latter context, the experience gained during the Salisbury crisis by the Director of Public Health for Wiltshire Council led to her appointment as a Deputy Director of Health and Wellbeing with Public Health England, with responsibility for leading the response to the Covid-19 outbreak (Kelly, 2020).

Political management lessons: scope and limitations

Throughout the Salisbury poisoning affair, Prime Minister Theresa May exhibited a full set of political management skills appropriate to effective handling of this crisis, the origins of which lay beyond her direct control. However, during her Premiership, she was much less adept at politically managing other crises. She performed relatively poorly during the initial phase of the crisis caused by the Grenfell Tower fire in London in 2017, when she visited the site but failed to meet residents and survivors of the catastrophic blaze, attracting criticism for a perceived lack of empathy, and she subsequently admitted that this was an error (Walker, 2018). It is possible that she learned some lessons from this failure when politically managing her response to the Salisbury crisis the following year. May struggled throughout the event that was to define her period in office, and ultimately lead to her downfall: the process of securing the UK's departure from the EU on terms which were acceptable both to the EU and to a majority with the UK Parliament. The strengths she had shown in the Salisbury crisis were either missing, or deployed inconsistently during her failed political leadership in the Brexit process. The latter originated not from a global crisis beyond her control, but from the internal politics of the UK, and of her own political party, and her failures in this case were particularly obvious in relation to the key political management skills of decision-making, coordination and communication.

Recommendations for academic research

- The political management skills we have covered in this chapter have an applicability beyond the specific level of national political leadership.
- There is considerable scope for further research into the deployment of the skills by political managers in sub-national, local and regional settings, as well as within political parties and other political organisations.
- Research of this kind would expand and enrich the literature base for political management and create further linkages across to studies of crisis management and leadership.

Recommendations for practice

- Examining the challenges associated with the political management of national crises which have global dimensions make it possible to develop some core recommendations for practice, applicable to the work of political managers in a range of different contexts.
- Crises are a natural and recurring aspect of the political environment, and those who have responsibility for managing and leading in political contexts, whether this is primarily within parties, elected bodies, or governing institutions at local, regional, national, transnational or international

levels, can benefit from accessing a clear and easily comprehensible set of guidelines which will enhance their capacity to manage their way through these events.

- We argue that there emerges an effective transferable toolkit for political management of crises, at all levels and in a range of contexts. This toolkit comprises the eight tasks we have set out above ('sense-making', 'getting the right team in place', 'crisis decision-making', 'multi-directional coordination', 'meaning-making', 'communication', 'accountability', 'learning').
- While some of these tasks are clearly sequential (e.g. 'sense-making' comes first, and 'learning' later), some may be deployed flexibly, and at different points in a developing crisis, depending upon specific circumstances, while others, including 'communication' should be seen as ongoing throughout the event. The practical challenges and work of political managers facing the (inevitable) crises which occur in their spheres of operation can be managed more strategically through the deployment of this toolkit.

Recommended reading

Boin, A., Kuipers, S., & Overdijk, W. (2013). Leadership in times of crisis: A framework for assessment. *International Review of Public Administration*, 18(1), 79–91.

Connolly, J., & Pyper, R. (2020). Public servants and corporate governance failures: Developing for the future by learning from the past. *The Palgrave Handbook of the Public Servant*, 1–19.

Edelman, M. (2013). *Political Language: Words That Succeed and Policies That Fail*. Amsterdam: Elsevier.

Lilleker, D., Coman, I. A., Gregor, M., & Novelli, E. (2021). Political communication and COVID-19: Governance and rhetoric in global comparative perspective. In *Political Communication and COVID-19* (pp. 333–350). Abingdon: Routledge.

Wodak, R. (2021). Crisis communication and crisis management during COVID-19. *Global Discourse*, 11(3), 329–353.

References

Allan, D. (2018). Managed confrontation: UK policy towards Russia after the Salisbury attack, *Chatham House Research Paper*, London: Chatham House.

Baker, M., & Wilson, N. (2022). 'New Zealand's Covid strategy was one of the world's most successful – what can we learn from it?', Available at https://www.theguardian.com/world/commentisfree/2022/apr/05/new-zealands-covid-strategy-was-one-of-the-worlds-most-successful-what-can-it-learn-from-it

Boin, A., Kuipers, S., & Overdijk, W. (2013). Leadership in times of crisis: A framework for assessment. *International Review of Public Administration*, 18(1), 79–91.

Boin, A., & 't Hart, P. (2022). From crisis to reform? Exploring three post-COVID pathways. *Policy and Society*, 41(1), 13–24.

Brändström, A., & Kuipers, S. (2003). From "normal incidents" to political crises: Understanding the selective politicization of policy failures. *Government and Opposition*, 38(3), 279–305.

Bromfield, N., & McConnell, A. (2021). Two routes to precarious success: Australia, New Zealand, COVID-19 and the politics of crisis governance. *International Review of Administrative Sciences*, 87(3), 518–535.

Casalicchio, E. (2018). 'Theresa May Visits Salisbury in Wake of Poison Attack on Russian Ex-Spy', *Politics Home*, 15 March.

Connolly, J. (2016). *The Politics and Crisis Management of Animal Health Security*. Routledge.

Connolly, J., & Pyper, R. (2020). Public servants and corporate governance failures: Developing for the future by learning from the past. *The Palgrave Handbook of the Public Servant*, 1–19.

Dodd, V., Morris, S., & Bannock, C. (2018). Novichok in Wiltshire death "Highly likely" from batch used on Skripals. *The Guardian*, 9 July.

Drennan, L. T., McConnell, A., & Stark, A. (2014). *Risk and Crisis Management in the Public Sector*. Routledge.

Drumhiller, N. K. (2022). Advice, decision making, and leadership in security crises. In *Oxford Research Encyclopedia of Politics*.

Dzhurova, A. (2020). Symbolic politics and government response to a national emergency: Narrating the COVID-19 crisis. *Administrative Theory & Praxis*, 42(4), 571–587.

Edelman, M. (2013). *Political Language: Words That Succeed and Policies That Fail*. Amsterdam: Elsevier.

Flinders, M. (2020). Gotcha! Coronavirus, crises and the politics of blame games. *Political Insight*, 11(2), 22–25.

Friedman, U. (2022). 'New Zealand's Prime Minister May Be the Most Effective Leader on the Planet' *The Atlantic*, Available at https://www.theatlantic.com/politics/archive/2020/04/jacinda-ardern-new-zealand-leadership-coronavirus/610237/

Harding, L., Morris, S., & Bannock, C. (2018). How Salisbury case went from local drama to international incident. *The Guardian*, 10 March.

Heifetz, R. A. (1994). *Leadership Without Easy Answers*. Cambridge Mass: Harvard University Press.

Human Rights Law Centre. (2020). *New Zealand High Court finds COVID-19 lockdown measures to be justified under human rights law (but partially unlawful on other grounds)*. Available at https://www.hrlc.org.au/human-rights-case-summaries/2020/8/19/new-zealand-high-court-finds-covid-19-lockdown-measures-to-be-justified-under-human-rights-law-but-partially-unlawful-on-other-grounds

Karyotis, G., Connolly, J., Collignon, S., Judge, A., Makropoulos, I., Rüdig, W., & Skleparis, D. (2021). What drives support for social distancing? Pandemic politics, securitization, and crisis management in Britain. *European Political Science Review*, 13(4), 467–487.

Kelly, G. (2020). How the Salisbury poisonings prepared us for a pandemic. *The Telegraph*, 16 June.

Kreuder-Sonnen, C., & White, J. (2022). Europe and the transnational politics of emergency. *Journal of European Public Policy*, 29(6), 953–965.

Lees-Marshment, J. (2021). *Political Management. The Dance of Government and Politics*. Abingdon: Routledge.

Lilleker, D., Coman, I. A., Gregor, M., & Novelli, E. (2021). Political communication and COVID-19: Governance and rhetoric in global comparative perspective. In *Political Communication and COVID-19* (pp. 333–350). Abingdon: Routledge.

Marten, K. (2021). *The Chancellor. The Remarkable Odyssey of Angela Merkel.* London: William Collins.

McClure, T. (2021). 'New Zealand children falling ill in high numbers due to Covid 'immunity debt'', *Guardian*, Available at: https://www.theguardian.com/world/2021/jul/08/new-zealand-children-falling-ill-in-high-numbers-due-to-covid-immunity-debt #

McClure, T. (2022). 'New Zealand seeks to repeat world-beating Covid response in face of surging cases', *Guardian*, Available at: https://www.theguardian.com/world/2022/jul/16/new-zealand-seeks-to-repeat-world-beating-covid-response-in-face-of-surging-cases

McConnell, A. (2010). Policy success, policy failure and grey areas in-between: A framework to help capture complex policy outcomes. *Policy Sciences*, *30*(3), 345–362.

McKenzie, P. (2022). 'Abroad, Jacinda Ardern Is a Star. At Home, She's Losing Her Shine', Available at https://www.nytimes.com/2022/06/27/world/asia/new-zealand-jacinda-ardern-popularity.html

Megget, K. (2022). How New Zealand's covid-19 strategy failed Māori people. *BMJ*, 376.

Ministry of Health. (2020). Single case of COVID-19 confirmed in New Zealand. Media Release 2020, Available at https://www.health.govt.nz/news-media/media-releases/single-case-covid-19-confirmed-new-zealand

Morris, S., & Bannock, C. (2019). Salisbury ruled safe a year after Skripal poisoning as police make fresh appeal. *The Guardian*, 1 March.

National Emergency Management Agency. (2022). 'Coordinated Incident Management System (CIMS)', Available at https://www.civildefence.govt.nz/resources/coordinated-incident-management-system-cims-third-edition/

Nostlinger, N. (2021). 'Revisiting Merkel's Refugee Pledge: Has Germany "Managed It"?', Politico, 7 December.

OECD. (2020). 'Job retention schemes during the COVID-19 lockdown and beyond', Available at https://www.oecd.org/coronavirus/policy-responses/job-retention-schemes-during-the-covid-19-lockdown-and-beyond-0853ba1d/

Prime Minister's Office. (2018). *PM Commons Statement on Salisbury Incident: 12 March 2018*. Available at www.gov.uk/government/speeches/pm-commons-statement-on-salisbury-incident-12-march-2018

Qvortrup, M. (2021). *Angela Merkel. Europe's most influential leader*, Duckworth, Richmond.

Rothstein, H., Demeritt, D., Paul, R., & Wang, L. (2022). True to type? How governance traditions shaped responses to Covid-19 in China, Germany, UK, and USA. In *Covid-19 and the Sociology of Risk and Uncertainty* (pp. 115–143). Palgrave Macmillan, Cham.

Stark, A. (2019). *Public Inquiries, Policy Learning, and the Threat of Future Crises*. Oxford University Press, USA.

Stark, A., & Head, B. (2019). Institutional amnesia and public policy. *Journal of European Public Policy*, 26(10), 1521–1539.

Stewart, H. (2019). "Despicable act": May Confronts Putin over Salisbury Poisoning. *The Guardian*, 28 June.

Stockman, J. (2021). 'How New Zealand eliminated COVID-19', *LSE Blog*, Available at https://blogs.lse.ac.uk/covid19/2021/01/04/how-new-zealand-eliminated-covid-19/

Summers, J., Cheng, H. Y., Lin, H. H., Barnard, L. T., Kvalsvig, A., Wilson, N., & Baker, M. G. (2020). Potential lessons from the Taiwan and New Zealand health responses to the COVID-19 pandemic. *The Lancet Regional Health-Western Pacific*, 4, 100044.

Unite against Covid-19. (2022). 'About our COVID-19 response', Available at https://covid19.govt.nz/about-our-covid-19-response/

Walker, P. (2018). Theresa may calls her response to Grenfell Fire "Not good enough". *The Guardian*, 11 June.

Walker, P., & Roth, A. (2018). UK, US, Germany and France unite to condemn spy attack. *The Guardian*, 15 March.

13

MANAGING THE "UNKNOWN UNKNOWNS"

Organizational Processes, Market Intelligence, and Leaders' Management of Grassroots Political Protest

André Turcotte and Vincent Raynauld

Introduction

One of the traditional aspects of political management is control. Leaders of political organizations often leverage wide-ranging management tools to oversee organizational processes and help ensure that all activities run smoothly and remain under relative control so they can appear competent and professional. However, maintaining control – even if a politician is in a position of leadership such as President or Prime Minister – can prove to be challenging in governance and politics. In particular, it can be especially arduous when dealing with unplanned political phenomena. As then U.S. Defense Secretary Donald Rumsfeld famously – and cryptically – said during a press conference in 2002, "there are known knowns. These are things we know that we know. There are known unknowns. That is to say, there are things that we know we don't know. But there are also unknown unknowns. There are things we don't know we don't know" (Shermer 2005).

Over the last two decades, one significant challenge that government leaders in Canada and internationally have faced and handled with varying levels of success is pop-up, grassroots-driven political protest with a strong social media component – referred to as "unknown unknowns" in this book chapter. These phenomena – which can be defined spontaneous, reactive, emotional, and largely unpredictable as they are often rooted in crisis, instability, and uncertainty (Gerbaudo 2022; Ramaciotti Morales et al. 2022) – have garnered significant journalistic attention and have been studied from a wide range of disciplinary angles. Among them include sociology, communication, and political science (e.g., Boulianne and Theocharis 2020; Raynauld et al. 2018). However, few scholars have taken a look at their manifestation and

DOI: 10.4324/9781003260677-13

their effects through the lenses of political management at the local, regional, and national level. This chapter addresses and fills part of this gap in the academic and professional literature. It does so by exploring how the management of market intelligence can play a role in feeding data into and informing leaders' decision-making processes in response to decentralized grassroots-driven political protest with a strong social media component.

Using a case study approach, this chapter examines Canadian leaders' reaction to the events surrounding the 2022 Freedom Convoy in Canada, with a focus on the organization and role of market intelligence in government. This protest initiative is of particular interest as it forced local, provincial, and federal governments into a "state of emergency" – which amounted to a failure of political management – due to the severe and, in many cases, long-lasting disruptions it caused to the daily social, political, and economic life throughout Canada (DeClerq 2022; Hagberg and Ljunggren 2022; Rozdilsky 2022). In particular, this chapter takes interest in the ways in which and to what degree the Canadian federal government perceived, understood, reacted to, and dealt with different facets of the Freedom Convoy in terms of leveraging market intelligence to design, evaluate, and deploy its response to the Freedom Convoy.

Key literature

The analysis presented in this chapter combines two streams in academic literature. The first one involves the current understanding of protest politics and grassroots leadership in the age of social media. As dynamics of social media-infused public political contention have gained traction over the last fifteen years, they have received growing scholarly attention internationally. Of note are works examining the U.S.-based Tea Party movement (e.g., Agarwal et al. 2014; Turcotte and Raynauld 2014), the international "School Strike 4 Climate" protest effort (e.g., Boulianne et al. 2020; Hee et al. 2022), and the France-based Yellow Vest movement (*Gilets Jaunes* in French) (e.g., Bergem 2022; Della Sudda and Gaborit 2022). This form of protest can be defined as connective in nature. It is characterized by the fact that "the communication process itself provides key organizational resources, allowing large crowds to act together with little need for prominent leaders, formal social movement organizations, and collective action frames, which require individuals to share common identities and political claims" (Poell and van Dijck 2018: 147). In this context, leadership is largely "organizationless" as it is decentralized, horizontal, and performed by fluid networks of individuals, "instead of being considered as holding power positions as in traditional movement leadership" (Cao 2022: 3). In some ways, the presence of more conventional organizational and power structures – oftentimes inspired by traditional institutional leadership – can be viewed as detrimental and discrediting by some segments of activists (Cao 2022).

Many scholars have zeroed in on the "power and consequences" of these protest efforts in Western-style democracies, namely how they have affected the unfolding and outcome of political and governance processes (e.g., policy debates, governmental decision-making, budgeting) (Freelon et al. 2018: 990; Richez et al. 2020). Also of interest is Lalancette and Raynauld's (2020: 224) work exploring grassroots-intensive contentious politics in Canada (e.g., Quebec student strike, Indigenous-led Idle No More movement). They note that recent trends in on and off-line politicking coupled with shifting norms of citizenship and political engagement have helped reshape "political and civic engagement outside the realm of established political structures" (see also: Oser 2022; Schnaudt et al. 2021).

Dalton (2022) echoes and expands on this argument from a governance perspective. He argues that recent decades have been marked by the progressive weakening of the public confidence and, to some degree, relatability in political institutions and processes (e.g., elected officials, civil servants, government agencies) and the loss of traction of more conventional – or brick-and-mortar – approaches to political and democratic engagement (see also: Memmott et al. 2021). He also observes that "protest and other forms of contentious action have increased, becoming an extension of conventional politics by other means" (Dalton: 2022: 354). Dalton (2022: 534) notes that they have provided the public with more entrepreneurial and individualized channels to be active politically, outside the purview of political institutions. These forms of political action can make political processes more reactive, short-term, equitable, and inclusive. They can also provide members of minority and marginalized socio-demographic and political communities with channels of engagement adapted to and/or aligned with their often-narrow needs, preferences, and objectives (Dalton 2022; Gerbaudo 2022). Taken together, these dynamics point to an extension, diversification, and fragmentation of the political engagement – and to some degree management – landscape as well as "a diffusion in the forms of participation" (Dalton 2022: 534).

Several recent phenomena – including the January 6, 2021 protest in the United States and the 2022 occupation of the vicinity of New Zealand Parliament House in Wellington – have caused important disruptions to social, economic, and political life, have upended members of the public's daily routine, and have challenged established norms of governance and democratic institutions internationally. Political actors and governments have struggled – and in some cases failed – to anticipate, fully understand, and deal with the manifestation and effects of these "unknown unknowns" on the public (e.g., Bond and Neville-Shepard 2021; Kananovich 2022; O'Brien and Huntington 2022). The protest *modus operandi* described in the previous paragraphs as well as the expansion of the political environment pose significant challenges to how political management is conceptualized and operationalized as well as to broader established political and governmental authority (Lees-Marshment 2021). As this chapter will show, the Freedom Convoy constitutes a stark case study with pertinent insights into how some facets of political management need to be rethought and retooled, especially in the Canadian context.

The second stream of literature of interest for this chapter concerns political leaders once elected to government. To explain and unpack the inadequate response of the Canadian federal government to the Freedom Convoy, this chapter zeroes in on complementary dimensions and themes of the political management toolbox: political leadership, control, and organizational processes in relation to market intelligence. On the one hand, political leadership can be defined as "that enacted by the holders of formal positions of authority who are elected (rather than appointed), act like representatives, and control the functioning of, as well as have an effect upon, constitutional and legal frameworks" (Spyridonidis et al. 2022: 681). It can also be characterized as political leaders' ability to leverage tools and strategies to generate and strengthen their power to respond to "the demands from politicians in their own party as well as the opposition to get anything passed in the legislature to achieve actual action in government" (Lees-Marshment 2021: 160–161). In recent years, leaders' ability to adjust their approach to unpredictable events – oftentimes with a short turnaround time and in ways giving limited ability for extensive political analysis and strategizing – has been a defining feature of their leadership capabilities. As Lees-Marshment suggests (2021: 161), "political management is about leaders getting multiple individuals and groups to support your plan" in a timely manner through the use of "both internal and external sources of power which are indirect and informal as well as official." A key pressure point for leaders transitioning from campaigning to governing is the need to persuade, collaborate with, as well as delegate and adapt to larger publics with competing interests (Lees-Marshment 2021). Also of importance is the evolution of the perception and understanding of leadership among a growing segment of the population. Indeed, the conceptualization and operationalization of leadership within the grassroots poses significant challenges to political elites as it does not align entirely with their perception, understanding, and performance of leadership (Cao 2022; Poell and van van Dijck 2018).

One important tool available to political leaders to reconcile diverse perceptions, demands, and involvement of different publics is market intelligence. Market intelligence can guide governmental response to unpredictable events and crises – especially in the case of pop-up, connective grassroots political protest with an important social media component. Opinion research is used in campaigns to win power, informing decisions about electoral strategy, targeting, and messaging (Turcotte 2021). Campaign operatives leverage opinion research findings to shape media coverage to their advantage – or to the detriment of their opponents – as well as a fundraising tool. However, the transition from campaigning to governing remains ill-defined. But once in power, elected officials must make decisions for the greater good, while keeping an eye on their re-election prospects (Turcotte 2021). In most situations, juggling the two dimensions may not be difficult but in times of politically divisive crisis – such as during Freedom Convoy protests – it can prove to be a challenging endeavor. The design and exercise of political leadership requires an understanding of the context that can be provided by market intelligence.

However, as discussed in the following, the manner in which Canadian leaders handled the Freedom Convoy demonstrates that this important tool needs to be further refined and adapted to the realities of leadership and governing as well as the broader state of politics, especially in a context where rapid response to political events and political agility are becoming of particular importance. As previous literature suggests, there has been a shift from traditional polling to what has been called "market intelligence" (Turcotte 2021). Once in power, politicians leverage the tool to promote and implement a political and policy agenda that will have some appeal among different factions of constituents. Most significantly, pollsters use their craft not to merely measure opinion but opinion formation (Turcotte 2021) – offering governing leaders an important tool to exercise more control over their government and agenda.

Methodology

As mentioned previously, this chapter takes a case study approach to analyze the government response to the 2022 Freedom Convoy movement in Canada from a political management perspective. As discussed later in this chapter, the Freedom Convoy paralyzed Canada's capital – Ottawa – and several other localities in the country. The unusual events captured media and public attention and not surprisingly, media polling firms kept busy measuring and quantifying the public response. As a result, details about the events and opinion data are readily available. The main polling firms – IPSOS, Angus Reid, Nanos, and Abacus Data – kept close tap on Canadians' views of the Convoy. This analysis relies on publicly available data to contextualize the government response.

Aside from the contextual data, the analysis presented in this chapter goes further into studying these events through public opinion data made available to the authors by Public Square, an Ontario-based public opinion research firm. The authors were given access to two specific opinion studies. The first study consists of 1,520 online interviews with Canadians over the age of 18 that was conducted between February 4 and 6, 2022. The second study used in the context of this research project was completed with 1,518 adult Canadians. It was conducted a week later, between February 11 and 14, 2022. Through the consideration of media reporting, public opinion data, and the studies conducted by Public Square, this chapter isolates lessons for political management to guide the handling of subsequent social media-fueled grassroots political protests.

Research findings

The 2022 Freedom Convoy began inauspiciously. On January 22, 2022, a convoy comprised of long-haul rigs and other vehicles left Prince Rupert, British Columbia, Canada and headed east. Over the following seven-day period, its members crossed several western provinces and were joined by allies who shared their concerns relating to some of the mitigation measures implemented by Justin Trudeau's Liberal federal government to combat the COVID-19 global pandemic as well as the scope and depth of the powers of the federal government. Many truckers were concerned by the federal vaccine mandates on cross-border travel between Canada and the United States that were instituted on January 15, 2022, which affected long-haul truck drivers' ability to travel across the border in context of their professional activities and limited their ability to earn a living (Parkhill 2022). At the same time, Freedom Convoy supporters based in Eastern provinces – including Quebec, New Brunswick, and Newfoundland and Labrador – also hit the road in direction of the capital city of Canada, Ottawa for a demonstration planned on January 29, 2022. The federal authorities slowly became aware that large – much larger than previously expected – groups of truckers and their supporters, which would become known as the Freedom Convoy (*Convoi de la liberté* in French), were converging towards the National Capital (Rouleau 2023).

The speed and velocity of the right-leaning Freedom Convoy were quite atypical in the Canadian context. It represented the type of grassroots-driven populist movements that have manifested themselves in the United States and in Europe (Della Sudda and Gaborit 2022; Gillies et al. 2023). It was led by a very small group of activists with, in some cases, large and energized social media followings. The Convoy expanded, intensified, and diversified organically and was either ignored or dismissed by conventional media until it became obvious that it could become the source of significant disruptions. As with many such phenomena, it began with a singular focus – the COVID-19 health emergency – and morphed into a vehicle for a disparate set of social grievances and perceived personal, economic, and ideological slights. As Gillies et al. (2023: 2) note:

> Some factions called for the end of vaccine mandates, vaccine passports and contact tracing programs [...]. Some denounced what they defined as the authoritarian, treasonous, and corrupt governing practices of prime minister Justin Trudeau and requested the dissolution of the government.

Specifically, the 2022 Freedom Convoy was initiated by *Canada Unity* and – at first – comprised a small number of core people in its leadership, including James Bauder and Tamara Lich (Parkhill 2022). According to Gillies et al. (2023):

> [...] the Freedom Convoy leaders identified and seized social and political opportunities linked to the COVID-19 health emergency. In turn, it allowed them to shape the emergence of the protest movement, as well as frame its grievances, demands, and objectives—or more broadly a protest narrative—to garner public support.

On January 28, 2022, the first group of heavy vehicles arrived in Ottawa for the planned demonstration. By January 29, 2022, the day of the demonstration, approximately 15,000 people and 3,000 trucks had amassed in the downtown core of the city of Ottawa (Huang et al. 2022; see also Sabin 2022). The next days were marked by protesters progressively surrounding Canadian Parliament complex, occupying different sections of the city of Ottawa, and initiating an organized political blockage that would last approximately three weeks. Freedom Convoy activists also took part in protest initiatives across Canada, such as by causing delays and other disruptions at Canada-United States border crossings in several provinces. The city of Ottawa would not be cleared until February 20, 2022 following the intervention of law enforcement agencies from across Canada (Huang et al. 2022; Rouleau 2023).

One development of particular interest of this social-media-infused protest was the ability of seemingly its organizers to gain the support of a few yet recognized politicians. Early on, Ontario elected official Randy Hillier as well as the former Leader of the Official Opposition in Ottawa – Andrew Scheer – supported publicly the Convoy. People's Party leader Maxime Bernier – who was known for leveraging COVID-19 vaccine-related issues to gain national attention and distinguish the political offer of his party from his opponents' priorities (Turcotte et al. 2023) – was also an early supporter. While not surprising but nevertheless noteworthy, those three politicians leveraged social media for political gains before many of their colleagues and likely understood the significance of this political protest movement and its level of support among some segments of the Canadian public (for more context: McKelvey et al. 2022).

Freedom Convoy activists and supporters were also very active online, leveraging mainstream and more niche social media outlets – including Twitter, GoFundMe, Facebook, GiveSendGo, Telegram, and Twitch.tv – to circulate information of interest as well as coordinate their fundraising, mobilization, and protest initiatives (Broderick 2022). In many ways, the ability of the Freedom Convoy to raise money and circumvent traditional media quickly could have played a key role in allowing them to catch government officials off guard in context of their political management response.

Many factors have been put forth to explain the inertia of all levels of governments. Among them include a lack of preparedness and political will, jurisdictional confusion, mismanagement, and incompetence. According to Sabin (2022: 748), the "inability of Ottawa's municipal police" and other local, provincial, and federal governmental agencies "to end the protest was not only a spectacular failure of local policing but also a failure of national security policy." This chapter takes a particular interest in the response of the federal government to the Freedom Convoy phenomenon from a different angle. One potential reason not often cited is that the Canadian public, while appalled by the actions of the truckers and their sympathizers, expressed a level of understanding – and in some cases support – for their frustration, which likely caught government officials off guard and potentially inhibited their political management response.

A series of media polls pointed to a surprisingly ambivalent citizenry electorate considering the brazen actions of the members of the Freedom Convoy and their sympathizers. A poll conducted by IPSOS (2022) between February 8 and 9, 2022 indicated that more than 40% of Canadians agreed "with a lot of what trucker protests are fighting for, even if they might not say it publicly" (Huang et al. 2022). Abacus Data found that 32% of Canadians felt "they had a lot in common" with the protesters (Mundie 2022). The protesters succeeded in turning Canadians against Prime Minister Trudeau. A poll conducted by Maru showed that almost half of Canadians (48%) said that the prime minister showed that he was not up for the job and an Angus Reid poll found that two-thirds of Canadians (65%) felt Trudeau had made the protest situation worse (Dale 2022).

Turning to the Public Square dataset (2022), we can go beyond the media coverage and use the tools of political management for in-depth analysis. Amidst the strong online presence and traffic which were monitored by government agencies and law enforcement authorities, market intelligence was projecting a picture of a confused and divided public. As Table 13.1 shows,

TABLE 13.1 Attitudes towards the trucker convoy

Statements	% Agree
The truckers protest went too far and has gone on for too long	69%
I am very concerned about the protest becoming violent and out of control	64%
I am afraid of right-wing extremists getting more power because of the protest	59%
I am afraid of the country becoming divided because of the trucker's protest	52%
We should do whatever it takes to shut down the truckers protest even if that means calling in the national guard	51%
The Pandemic restrictions went too far and have gone too long	58%
I don't agree with the truckers' protest behavior, but I understand their frustration with how government has handled Covid-19	48%

Canadians were aghast by the actions of Freedom Convoy activists and sympathizers. Specifically, 69% of Canadians agreed that the truckers were going too far and 64% were concerned that the protest was becoming too violent and out of control. Moreover, 59% were afraid of right-wing extremist influence and more than half of Canadians (52%) were disparaging the fact that the protest would divide the country. If this was the whole story, the authorities would have had a clear path for action and leadership could have fulfilled its usual functions. However, this was only one chapter of the story.

The Public Square study (2022) conducted between February 4 and 6, 2022 showed that 48% of Canadians sympathized with truckers' frustrations, while 47% held the opposite view (Public Square 2022). And when Public Square asked what should be done about the protest, only a very slim majority of respondents (51%) agreed that the government should do all it can to shut the trucker protest down.

The impact of the Freedom Convoy began to extend to other policy areas. In particular, the Freedom Convoy limited the Trudeau government's ability to lift some COVID-19 restrictions because doing so would no longer be seen as good political management, but as caving in to the pressure of protesters. Specifically, 68% of Canadians agree with the following statement: "I don't want to re-open just because some truckers got mad." In the same vein, 60% of Canadians agreed with the following: "I am worried that reopening sends the message that the far right can bully the government and dictate policy" (Public Square 2022). Additionally, a large proportion of Canadians (41%) noted that "the truckers' protests was Trudeau's fault." The protest tied the hands of the government and limited its ability to respond to the demands of the truckers, and this for political reasons instead of in the execution of political management practice.

At a time when political parties win or lose elections based on their reliance on market intelligence, the Freedom Convoy represents a case study showing that politicians, once elected, can experience difficulties leveraging those same market intelligence tools to inform and guide their actions when faced with digital-intensive, highly connective forms of grassroots protest. In many ways, it represents a failure of permanent campaigning, which has become a core feature of contemporary politics. It refers to an "approach to governance whereas the partisan elites who control the government apply strategies and techniques usually found in a campaign setting to the process of governing itself" (Marland et al. 2017: 5).

The market intelligence data discussed in this chapter would have been a boon for electoral politics. A divided electorate means that a political party can capitalize on the divisions and turn political segmentation into wedge issues and leverage it into electoral gains. Indeed, wedge politics can help politician sow division within the electorate for political gain by fostering the "emergence and/or strengthening of factions within the electorate and, by extension, heighten[ing] levels of polarization and mobilization among them" (Turcotte and Raynauld 2020: 129) But once in power, wedge issues are anathema and governments turn to market intelligence data for unity and, by extension, greater good rather than for fostering divisions. The authorities were further hampered by the fact that 58% of Canadians agreed that "the pandemic restrictions went too far and have gone too long" (Public Square 2022). While an electoral path was clear and the Conservative Party of Canada took advantage of this by aligning itself with the cause of the protesters, there was no easy way out for the government in power.

Following weeks of disruptions that affected different facets of Canadian society, Prime Minister Trudeau invoked the Emergencies Act on February 14, 2022. The following ten days were marked by local, provincial, and federal law enforcement agencies conducting operations to remove protesters who were blocking streets and disrupting daily life in the region of Ottawa as well as impeding the flow of traffic border crossings across Canada. Trudeau ended the Emergencies Actions on February 23, 2022 after most major protest events were quelled by police forces (Rozdilsky 2022). Evoking the Emergencies-related legislation for the first time in over 50 years turned out to be the only exit strategy for the Trudeau government. In many ways, the invocation of the Emergencies Act in February 2022 was an acknowledgment by Prime Minister Trudeau and the Canadian federal government that all more conventional political management tools at their disposal were not sufficient to tackle and quell the disturbances caused by the Freedom Convoy. Whether it was justified to evoke the Act and suspend civil liberties remains a complicated question beyond the scope of this book chapter. However, a better understanding of the climate of public opinion and a better use of market intelligence principles and tools could have prevented the need for the Act in the first place.

Recommendations for academic research

Political parties and individual politicians have been able to adapt their management of these new dynamics within the contemporary political market and harness them for electoral gain. Weisskircher et al. (2022) point out "developments in the protest arena and the electoral arena may strongly affect each other above and beyond the organizational level, most importantly, through shifts in public attention to the issues and demands at stake." In some cases, the aforementioned patterns of protest have represented an opportunity for members of social and political minority or marginalized communities to enter and shake up the traditional political landscape (e.g., running for office), often in collaboration with other established political actors (e.g., Yellow Vest movement in France) (Della Sudda and Gaborit 2022).

However, managing such developments in government while leading the country has been more challenging. Governments have been faced with needing to manage more spontaneous, reactive, self-confident, emotional, and elite-challenging publics – often including younger segments of civil society – expressing themself and being active politically in manners not necessarily aligned and/or compatible with their perception and understanding of politics as well as their political management style (Dalton 2022: 536; see also: Boulianne and Ohme 2022; Margetts 2018). In other words, more traditional principles guiding the practice – or, in many ways, performance - of citizenship, which includes "social order, allegiance to the state, and participation through traditional democratic channels as desirable traits of the 'good citizen'," are less influential in shaping public politicking (Schnaudt et al. 2021; see also: Bennett et al. 2011). Governments' political management style, which for the most part is tailored to engage with citizens' political action through more institutionalized channels, has been challenged by new and emerging dynamics, especially over the last ten years. More research work is needed to better understand how leaders can better address all facets of this type of behavior.

Recommendations for practice

While the Freedom Convoy was unparalleled in the Canadian context, the mishandling of the situation – as characterized in some sections of the Public Order Emergency Commission/Commission sur l'état d'urgence (Rouleau 2022) – offers several lessons for practitioners as well as a cautionary tale for those involved in political management. As discussed in this chapter, the Canadian government – and other local and provincial governments – were unprepared to observe, understand, react to, and manage these protest initiatives. During an October 18, 2022 hearing of the Public Order Emergency Commission/Commission sur l'état d'urgence, which investigated the "circumstances that led to the declaration of emergency that was in place from February 14-23, 2022," Jim Watson – who served as mayor of the city of Ottawa during the occupation of its downtown core by Freedom Convoy activists and sympathizers – noted that:

> There's no question that you know, when you look at – look back, you know, hindsight on what happened, there were many failure points along the way, and you know, whether it's the City or the provincial or the federal governments, we all have to take responsibility for the fact that we did not act fast enough and that the people of Ottawa suffered the most as a result of the fact that we did not clean up that occupation for three weeks. It should have been done sooner.
>
> *(Rouleau 2022: 91)*

Grassroots political and social uprisings much like the Freedom Convoy remain rare and drawing lessons from isolated events can be tricky. However, looking at the global context, many countries have experienced similar connective, digital grassroots protests in recent years, and such protests may no longer be such rarities. In many ways, government and elected officials' political management needs to be rethought and adapted to this trend in public political engagement. As a general starting point, the practice of political management needs to borrow and adapt what political parties and party strategists have understood for many years. It must borrow the speed, coordination, and adaptability of campaigns. At the same time, political management operates in a different context than campaigns; it aims to be more inclusive, obviously non or less partisan, and aim to protect the greater public good.

With this in mind, elected officials and political staff can ready themselves to manage these protest initiatives by taking into account the following elements:

- First, market intelligence tools need to adapt to the new data realities. The abundance of available data from social media and data management platforms is the most important shift. **The market intelligence field needs to do better at combining digital data with traditional opinion information to track behavior almost in real time.** The main obstacle to addressing this shift is that such an approach is costly and labor intensive. Governments are in a very favorable position to meet this challenge with their access to human and financial resources. If anything, this is an area where political management can be the most proactive and useful.
- Second, there was no shortage of information during the peak moments of the Freedom Convoy occupation but there was little sharing of that information. This is never conducive to success but the need to react quickly to digital grassroots protests makes this lack of sharing a recipe for disaster. **Officials need to behave more like businesspeople and collapse information silos.** During the Convoy protests, some officials were monitoring social media traffic and accumulating digital data about the truckers and their sympathizers, while others were relying on public opinion polling. **Unfortunately, the lack of coordination among the different political actors involved meant that a full picture of public sentiment remained elusive.** Recent elections campaigns in the United States and in Canada have successfully managed to combine disparate data sources into a coherent picture and if the past is an indication of what the future holds, government officials will shortly follow suit. However, the government apparatus is inherently compartmentalized, and this will represent an ongoing challenge for political management.
- Third, **data paralysis needs to be avoided**. Many people acknowledge the overabundance of data, but few know what to do with it. The first step to address this problem is to understand that the goal of gathering data is not to accumulate knowledge but to get actionable information to guide decision-making. Too often, data is gathered for the sake of gathering data rather than for its real goal; supporting decision-making. Once again,

we suggest that government officials tend to risk-averse and hesitant to respond making this another ongoing challenge for the field of political management.

- Fourth, **one way to overcome data paralysis is to adopt the mindset guiding data scientists**. Their approach is to approach situations as "problems" and ask five key questions:

  - Why is this problem important?
  - Who does this problem affect?
  - What if we don't have the right data?
  - When is this project over or how is this problem be resolved?
  - What if we don't like the results? (adapted from Gutman and Goldmeier 2021)

Finally, as market intelligence becomes more sophisticated, the broader field of political management needs to adapt in order to better communicate the complexities of data findings. The gap between the sophistication of the data analyses and the capacity of decision-makers to grasp the meaning of such analyses has never been greater. The field of political management – with its emphasis on communication – is uniquely positioned to close that gap and ensure that events like the occupation of Ottawa by a motley crew of truckers never happen again.

Recommended reading

Gerbaudo, P. (2022). Theorizing reactive democracy: The social media public sphere, online crowds, and the plebiscitary logic of online reactions. *Democratic Theory*, 9(2), 120–138.

Lees-Marshment, J. (2021). *Political Management: The Dance of Government and Politics*. Routledge, New York.

Spyridonidis, D., Côté, N., Currie, G., & Denis, J. L. (2022). Leadership configuration in crises: Lessons from the English response to COVID-19. *Leadership*, 18(5), 680–694.

Turcotte, A. (2021). *Political Marketing Alchemy*. Palgrave Pivot, Cham.

References

Agarwal, S. D., Barthel, M. L., Rost, C., Borning, A., Bennett, W. L., & Johnson, C. N. (2014). Grassroots organizing in the digital age: Considering values and technology in Tea Party and Occupy Wall Street. *Information, Communication & Society*, 17(3), 326–341.

Bennett, W. L., Wells, C., & Freelon, D. (2011). Communicating civic engagement: Contrasting models of citizenship in the youth web sphere. *Journal of Communication*, 61(5), 835–856.

Bergem, I. M. (2022). Leaving the discursive definition of populist social movements: The case of the Yellow Vest movement. *Political Studies*, https://doi.org/10.1177/00323217211063727

Bond, B. E., & Neville-Shepard, R. (2021). The rise of presidential eschatology: Conspiracy theories, religion, and the January 6th insurrection. *American Behavioral Scientist*. https://doi.org/10.1177/00027642211046557

Boulianne, S., & Theocharis, Y. (2020). Young people, digital media, and engagement: A meta-analysis of research. *Social Science Computer Review*, 38(2), 111–127.

Boulianne, S., Lalancette, M., & Ilkiw, D. (2020). "School strike 4 climate": Social media and the international youth protest on climate change. *Media and Communication*, 8(2), 208–218.

Boulianne, S., & Ohme, J. (2022). Pathways to environmental activism in four countries: Social media, environmental concern, and political efficacy. *Journal of Youth Studies*, 25(6), 771–792.

Broderick, R. (2022). How Facebook twisted Canada's trucker Convoy into an International Movement. *The Verge*. https://www.theverge.com/2022/2/19/22941291/facebook-canada-trucker-convoy-gofundme-groups-viral-sharing

Dalton, R. J. (2022). Political action, protest, and the functioning of femocratic governance. *American Behavioral Scientist*, 66(4), 533–550.

Della Sudda, M., & Gaborit, N. (2022). From Yellow Vests street protest to city council: When social movements run for office. *French Politics*, 20(3–4), 420–443.

Cao, H. (2022). Organizing an "organizationless" protest campaign in the WeChatsphere. *Big Data & Society*, 9(1), https://doi.org/10.1177/20539517221078823

Dale, D. (2022). Fact check: Strong majority of Canadians oppose convoy protests, poll after poll finds. *CNN Politics*. https://www.cnn.com/2022/02/15/politics/fact-check-canadian-protests-polls-trudeau-support-oppose-truckers-mandates/index.html

DeClerq, K. (2022). Ontario declares a state of emergency to end 'siege' in Ottawa and Windsor. *CTV News*. https://toronto.ctvnews.ca/ontario-declares-a-state-of-emergency-to-end-siege-in-ottawa-and-windsor-1.5777336

Freelon, D., McIlwain, C., & Clark, M. (2018). Quantifying the power and consequences of social media protest. *New Media & Society*, 20(3), 990–1011.

Gillies, J., Raynauld, V., & Wisniewski, A. (2023). Canada is no exception: The 2022 Freedom Convoy, political entanglement, and identity-driven protest. *American Behavioral Scientist*. https://doi.org/10.1177/00027642231166885

Gutman, A. J., & Goldmeier, J. (2021). *Becoming a Data Head: How to Think, Speak, and Understand Data Science, Statistics, and Machine Learning*. John Wiley & Sons, Indianapolis, IN.

Hagberg, L., & Ljunggren, D. (2022). Ottawa mayor declares state of emergency to deal with trucking blockade. *Reuters*. https://www.reuters.com/world/americas/protest-against-vaccine-mandates-paralyzing-canada-capital-mayor-says-2022-02-06/

Hee, M., Jürgens, A. S., Fiadotava, A., Judd, K., & Feldman, H. R. (2022). Communicating urgency through humor: School Strike 4 Climate protest placards. *Journal of Science Communication*, 21(5), A02.

Huang, S. H., Tsao, S. F., Chen, H., Bin Noon, G., Li, L., Yang, Y., & Butt, Z. A. (2022). Topic modelling and sentiment analysis of tweets related to freedom convoy 2022 in Canada. *International Journal of Public Health*, 67, 1605241.

Ipsos. (2022). Nearly half (46%) of Canadians say they "may not agree with everything" Trucker Convoy says or does, but...". *Ipsos*. https://www.ipsos.com/en-ca/news-polls/nearly-half-say-they-may-not-agree-with-trucker-convoy

Kananovich, V. (2022). From "angry mobs" to "citizens in anguish": The malleability of the protest paradigm in the international news coverage of the 2021 US Capitol attack. *American Behavioral Scientist*, https://doi.org/10.1177/00027642221118265

Lalancette, M., & Raynauld, V. (2020). Online mobilization: Tweeting truth to power in an era of revised patterns of mobilization in Canada. In T. Small & H. Jansen (Eds.). *Digital Politics in Canada: Promises & Realities*. University of Toronto Press., ON.

Margetts, H. (2018). Rethinking democracy with social media. *Political Quarterly*, *90*(S1).

Marland, A., Lewis, J. P., & Flanagan, T. (2017). Governance in the age of digital media and branding. *Governance*, *30*(1), 125–141.

McKelvey, F., DeJong, S., Kowalchuck, S., & Donovan, E. (2022). Is the alt-right popular in Canada? Image sharing, popular culture, and social media. *Canadian Journal of Communication*, 47(4), 702–729.

Memmott, T., Carley, S., & Konisky, D. (2021). Who participates in energy activism? Profiling political engagement in the United States. *Energy Research & Social Science*, 77, 102095.

Mundie, J. (2022). One third of Canadians say they have a lot in common with Freedom Convoy protesters. *National Post*. https://nationalpost.com/news/canada/one-third-of-canadians-say-they-have-a-lot-in-common-with-freedom-convoy-protesters

O'Brien, T., & Huntington, N. (2022). 'Vaccine passports equal Apartheid': Covid-19 and parliamentary occupation in Aotearoa New Zealand. *Social Movement Studies*, 1–7.

Oser, J. (2022). How citizenship norms and digital media use affect political participation: A two-wave panel analysis. *Media and Communication*, 10(3), 206–218.

Parkhill, M. (2022). Who is who? A guide to the major players in the trucker convoy protest. *CTV News*, https://www.ctvnews.ca/canada/who-is-who-a-guide-to-the-major-players-in-the-trucker-convoy-protest-1.5776441

Poell, T., & van Dijck, J. (2018). Social media and new protest movements. In Burgess, J., Marwick, A. & Poell. T. (2018). *The SAGE Handbook of Social Media*, 546–561. London: Sage.

Public Square (2022). Data connected between February 4 and 6, 2022. http://www.publicsquareresearch.ca/.

Ramaciotti Morales, P., Cointet, J. P., & Froio, C. (2022). Posters and protesters: The networked interplay between onsite participation and Facebook activity in the Yellow Vests movement in France. *Journal of Computational Social Science*, 5(2), 1129–1157.

Raynauld, V., Richez, E., & Boudreau Morris, K. (2018). Canada is# IdleNoMore: Exploring dynamics of Indigenous political and civic protest in the Twitter verse. *Information, Communication & Society*, 21(4), 626–642.

Richez, E., Raynauld, V., Agi, A., & Kartolo, A. B. (2020). Unpacking the political effects of social movements with a strong digital component: The case of# IdleNoMore in Canada. *Social Media + Society*, 6(2), https://doi.org/10.1177/2056305120915588

Rouleau, P. S. (2022). Public Hearing/Audience Public Volume 4. Public Order Emergency Commission/Commission sur l'état d'urgence. 278 pages. https://publicorderemergencycommission.ca/files/documents/Transcripts/POEC-Public-Hearings-Volume-4-October-18-2022.pdf

Rouleau, P. S. (2023). Report of the Public Inquiry into the 2022 Public Order Emergency Volume 1: Overview. 272 pages. https://publicorderemergencycommission.ca/files/documents/Final-Report/Vol-1-Report-of-the-Public-Inquiry-into-the-2022-Public-Order-Emergency.pdf

Rozdilsky, J. L. (2022). Emergencies Act revoked after 10 days of police clampdowns helped end blockades. *The Conversation*, https://theconversation.com/emergencies-act-revoked-after-10-days-of-police-clampdownshelped-end-blockades-177616

Sabin, J. (2022). Canadian federalism, multilevel politics and the occupation of Ottawa. *Canadian Journal of Political Science/Revue canadienne de science politique*, 55(3), 747–753.

Schnaudt, C., van Deth, J. W., Zorell, C., & Theocharis, Y. (2021). Revisiting norms of citizenship in times of democratic change. *Politics*, https://doi.org/10.1177/02633957211031799

Shermer, M. (2005). Rumsfeld's Wisdom: Where the known meets the unknown is where science begins. *Scientific American*. https://www.scientificamerican.com/article/rumsfelds-wisdom/

Turcotte, A., Coletto, D., & Vodry, S. (2023). The People's Party of Canada and the appeal of anger politics. In J. Gillies, V. Raynauld, & A. Turcotte (Eds.). *Political Marketing in the 2021 Canadian Federal Election*. Springer, Palgrave Macmillan, Camden, UK.

Turcotte, A., & Raynauld, V. (2014). Boutique populism: The emergence of the Tea Party movement in the age of digital politics. In J. Lees-Marshment, B. Conley, & K. Cosgrove (Eds.). *Political Marketing in the U.S.* USA: Routledge.

Turcotte, A., & Raynauld, V. (2020). *Divide Et Impera*: Wedge politics in the 2019 Canadian federal election. In J. Gillies, V. Raynauld, & A. Turcotte (Eds.). *Political Marketing in the 2019 Canadian Election*. Palgrave MacMillan, Cham.

Weisskircher, M., Hutter, S., & Borbáth, E. (2022). Protest and electoral breakthrough: Challenger party-movement interactions in Germany. *German Politics*, 1–25.

14

PRACTITIONER REFLECTIONS ON MANAGING POLITICAL PARTIES IN THE CZECH REPUBLIC

Anna Shavit, Marcela Konrádová, and Petra Koudelková

Introduction

This chapter focuses on how parties are 'managed' and goes within party organizations to explore how those practitioners involved in party management see political leadership and develop strategic visions and goals. It also explores political parties' approaches to diversifying power and exerting influence. An additional aim was to apply and compare established practice with management theory in the business.

The focus is on four political parties in the Czech Republic: Civic Democratic Party (ODS), TOP 09 party, Christian Democratic Union-Czechoslovak People's Party (KDU-ČSL), and ANO 2011. The first three are part of the current governing body (Government of the Czech Republic, 2023) and ANO 2011 is in the opposition. TOP 09's leadership style straddles the border between a personal and a personalized party (see Bobba & Seddone, 2011). This leadership style has garnered much interest from the media, political scientists, and voters. ODS and KDU-ČSL are traditional, well-established political parties with a sophisticated structure and a long history (Smolík, 2018). Traditional political parties founded in the 19th century were often put together using a complex structure, even at the regional level. Recently, they have adapted to personalization and the changing demands of a leader. They represent personalized parties (Calise, 2010). This is a reaction to increasingly personalized election campaigns in which the focus is on a single leader. It is, therefore, illogical to divert attention to other party representatives who are often equal partners but sometimes rivals to the party's leader (Hloušek, 2015) – transforming them into party personalities.

DOI: 10.4324/9781003260677-14

This change is a part of the electoral strategy, reflecting changes in party-political management and leadership. However, the structure is a better reflection of the representation of political interests rather than functioning as a practical tool to organize party activities such as elections effectively and efficiently. Additionally, while it may be advantageous when the party needs to mobilize political support, the structure often slows down management decisions and may be a disadvantage during time critical activities such as election campaigns.

The ANO 2011 political movement, representing an exemplary business-firm party, is often regarded as an example of a savvy, goal-focused formation trying to succeed in elections (Kopeček, 2016). The ANO movement is the youngest of all the parties, with an evolving business-like party structure. ANO represents a purely personal party with a strong, charismatic leader.

To understand how the parties function and operate we've combined a theoretical approach with interviews with the party's top management officials – managers and general secretaries. It should be noted that this text is the very first mapping of political management in the Czech Republic.

Key literature

The foundations of political management can be found in business management, which defines the basic managerial activities and describes the concepts and differences between leader and manager (Donelly et al., 1997). Although many experts perceive differences between a leader and a manager (Plamínek & Fišer, 2004; Bush, 2020), they agree that a good leader should be a good manager (Zehnder, 2016) and control all managerial activities. This is because 'leadership is the process by which one influences others to achieve goals and manages the organization in a way that makes it more cohesive and coherent' (Northouse, 2007, p. 3). Peter Drucker then defines a leader as one who sets goals and priorities and sets and maintains standards (Pilařová, 2016). Of course, there may be a situation where there is a strong leader in a particular organization/party, but their management skills might need improvement. In this case, the leader is not the party's 'manager,' which may translate into different organizational structures of political parties. An essential activity of the leader, as well as the central part of management, is organizing. Part of organizing is, among other things, setting priorities and identifying activities that it cannot provide for itself and therefore outsources (Blažek, 2011). That also helps to clarify the role of the leader, who can function well provided that the party finds the proper balance (or degree of organization) between the pre-set rules and what is dealt with immediately concerning an activity, striving for a sense of organizational harmony. Leaders also have many other responsibilities, such as decision-making, controlling, etc.

Considering leadership and leadership structure, we can start from traditional structures that offer linear, functional, and line-staff structures or from goal-project structures such as project coordination/structure and matrix structure. Alternatively, we can use agile management theory, which does not have fixed structures. Instead, they are variable, but we can generally talk about Holacracy or obliquity. In any case, the organizational structure serves to divide powers. This brings us to the so-called management styles, which often evolve together with the organizational structure, but are also often based on the values and character of the manager. The following management styles can be distinguished: participative, autocratic, and democratic.

The participative management style actively involves employees in tasks and problem-solving. In this case, the increased active participation of employees in the various activities of the companies/organization significantly increases their commitment and productivity, thereby improving their overall performance.

The autocratic style is based on imitation (Kalogiannidis et al., 2021). In his study, Al Kajeh (2018) states that in this management style, the most critical decision remains with the manager, and he expects employees to accept his choices. The manager serves as an example for the employees. He shows them how the task should be performed (Cai et al., 2020). However, employees are not immersed in the process. This management style is well suited to those companies where employees do not actively show interest in more meaningful and responsible tasks, do not want full responsibility, or where there is a young and inexperienced team.

The democratic management style is based on leaders or managers demonstrating their knowledge, power, and skills to the employees. In this case, managers interact with employees and then apply various policies and regulations without discrimination or favoritism to affect all employees equally (Khajeh, 2018). Research also suggests that when it comes to a democratic management style, leaders tend to encourage constant interactions between groups of employees and then focus on strengthening relationships between top management and other lower levels of management and the entire team of employees (Jamal & Soomro, 2011).

Methodology

The primary goal of political management is to utilize resources to achieve organizational goals effectively. This is influenced by the type of party and the position of the leader (personal/personalized). Identifying technical and political talents and political style preferences is imperative (Omoijiade, 2016, p. 17). It is pure political management to achieve (re)election. In this sense, we state that managerial activities inside the party are not visible but are more critical.

We focus on the most critical principles of political management – political parties' approaches to diversifying power and exerting influence. Therefore, we seek answers to these research questions:

RQ1: How much is the party development influenced by the election cycle, or do the parties have more strategic goals?

RQ2: What is the party managerial style?

RQ3: How does the party define their leadership style?

The RQs relate to how the candidates, or the party, achieve these political goals, focusing on the contribution of those responsible for the practical day-to-day functioning of the political party. The questions were answered using qualitative research. Interviews were conducted with party management representatives (Czech political parties have different managerial structures) and the responses were compared to official party information (the party statutes) and various theoretical approaches.

The semi-structured interviews were conducted with the party's general secretary, in the cases of TOP 09 and KDU-ČSL, and with the general manager, in the cases of ANO and ODS, in February and March 2023, which corresponds with the midpoint of the government's term. While the job descriptions of a party secretary and a manager differ in some respects, the workload is very similar. In both cases they are in charge of managing the party and dealing with practical issues. Their role is not to push ideological and substantive issues, but to focus on day-to-day or long-term operations.

Although the results of qualitative research are not easily generalizable (Hendl, 2005; Reichel, 2009), they can be used to understand the motivations and internal processes of political management. In this case, the semi-structured interview was the optimal tool, allowing the interviewer and respondents to communicate freely and naturally. At the same time, the collected data can be compared with each other (Reichel, 2009). Given that this is the first research on Czech political management, it is a precious foundation of data upon which to develop further findings.

Research findings

How much is the party development influenced by the election cycles, or do the parties have more strategic goals?

The interviews clearly showed that the regularly recurring elections for the parties are the alpha and omega that influence planning. During these elections, the party offices focus on organizing the campaign allowing everything else to go by the wayside. All parties also agree that because of this, they need more time to work with the membership, staff training, or work to develop the party further.

Interestingly, they can clearly describe this but do not see it as a significant problem for their continued existence; for example, comments included:

> There are no elections this year (2023), although the European elections are about to start, so we have time now to develop and focus on membership and internal party matters. We can now take a little breather before the next elections. Now there is room to improve things, to concentrate on the organization's management, our think tank, and things we need more time to do.
> *(TOP 09, 2023)*

In the case of the organization of election campaigns, the parties have different practices in the matter of hiring consultants. ANO and ODS regularly expand their teams at election time. Specifically, ANO exclusively hires external professionals for elections (ANO, 2023). TOP 09 has, in its own words, 'trained' consultants and regularly cooperates with them during campaigns. '*They know us; they know what we need*' (TOP 09, 2023).

On the other hand, KDU-ČSL, which had previously hired consultants to organize election campaigns, especially for strategy, decided to employ a strategist to work with them long-term (KDU-ČSL, 2023). None of the parties cooperates with experts on organization management outside the election period. Christian democrats ensure continuity by setting the primary communication and graphic campaign line for each election from the central office, using it to communicate the unified values of its brand (see Needham, 2006).

An important consideration for the electoral cycle in personal and personalized parties is the selection of candidates. The legal system outlines the nomination processes, however, each party's internal rules and norms, most of which are not publicly available, guide the majority of the processes (Spáč, 2013, p. 27). Of the freely available party statutes, very few, if any, are focused on candidate selection, creating an information barrier regarding the process of selecting and vetting the nominations, as well as their conduct. An even more significant problem is the existence of informal processes and the candidate selection process by political parties. The role of informal rules may or may not be central to the nomination process. In our case, respondents reported that they generally follow nomination rules that are regulated by statute. For example, ODS (2023) '*does not recognize any informal process in which the party chair or management interferes.*' The nomination process is described similarly by ANO (2023) – at the political level through local, regional, and provincial organizations based on nominations. '*The nominations are then submitted to the Party Committee for final approval as the highest political body of ANO between the national congresses.*' TOP 09 (2023), on the other hand, said that '*the political decision is up to the highest governing bodies,*' while the KDU-ČSL (2023) noted that *'sometimes someone is put on the list because it is convenient,'* although they all have to go through the primaries. However, management does not interfere in selecting candidates for any of the selected parties.

This is entirely outside the role of the manager in the company, who is, more or less, passively involved in the selection of team members according to the requirements of the manager or the department (see Griffin, 2013). We may find very little connection in that even the manager sometimes enters this process too reluctantly and only formulates the requirements for the position, which are disseminated to the candidates in the form of advertisements that may or may not interest them. In the same way, the party chairman formulates his program, which may lure potential candidates into the party.

In this case, the chairman and founder of the ANO movement, Andrej Babiš, plays a significant role. In this strongly staffed party, even the management is subordinate mainly to him. As it emerged from the interviews, a situation can also arise when the chairperson interrupts a relatively clearly defined process of selecting candidates (Statutes of the ANO political movement, 2013) in the form of a veto. While most decision-making takes place in a collegial manner in the relevant bodies according to the statutes, in some cases, for example, candidate lists, the statutes provide a specific veto right for the chair of the movement, which is highly unusual (ANO, 2023). One could assume that in traditional, personalized parties, the management is relatively unchanging.

Interestingly, then, the principal office of ODS assembles the team according to political objectives (*'the HC fulfils political objectives and for this purpose is formed by an appropriate team of staff'*). For others, it depends on the situation, especially the current elections' outcome. TOP 09 states that *'the staff composition of the management does not change even if there is a defeat'*; only if the defeat is significant and there is a reduction in the state contribution may the team be reduced (or, on the contrary, in case of success, expanded). However, the party tries to maintain the continuous stability of the party management, as it considers it an area that 'still few people can do.'

What is the party managerial style?

The party's managerial style is, in general, a pyramid structure. The party is headed by a general secretary (KDU-ČSL, 2023; TOP 09, 2023) who manages the other sections (press, social media management, analytical, economic, etc.). A director manages each section, leading another team of people, the size of which varies according to the focus of the section. An example of this would be ODS reporting an average team size of around five employees, which would be a maximum size for other parties who are more likely to report two- or three-person teams. The press team is usually the largest (ODS, 2023;

Statutes of the Civic Democratic Party, 2015). Given that the only position of 'superior' is usually that of the secretary general, respondents do not think '*it makes sense to define a superior-subordinate relationship in small teams of two people*' (KDU-ČSL, 2023). This type of structure is very similar to Holacracy, which is based on specific 'inward' self-organizing teams called circles (Van De Kamp, 2014) that communicate with each other.

On the other hand, from this description we can deduce that this respondent may only need help understanding managerial theories. Therefore, their description may be made more accurate. We may infer a classical linear structure (not because of the authoritarian approach but because it is a small organization) with elements of agile management.

However, it is about more than just the management of the central office but also the management of the lower organizational units (regional, district, and local) or at least some of the levels. For example, KDU-ČSL, the minor party in the SPOLU electoral coalition, states that '*the central office budget is currently around 3.2 million euros. At the same time, the regional organizations manage in the thousands and hundreds of thousands*' (KDU-ČSL, 2023). In this case, we are talking about a party with a line-staff structure, the most commonly used approach, which has one person designated as the main managing figure but may have several departments and other staff under them. This group is also likely to include ANO, although it is impossible to determine whether it is a line or line-staff structure. The transition here is fragile because there is much authoritarian power.

Interestingly, ODS is again an outlier, whose organizational structure is '*more horizontal, with an emphasis on working in micro-teams that share their experience and agenda*' (ODS, 2023). According to this description and the description below, the type of organization more closely resembles a project coordination, albeit not in a pure business form where these structures are more likely to be short-term in nature. However, there is also a turnover of teams after the elections. The similarity is now easy to see.

The management of the individual political parties fulfils political tasks (not only of the leader but also of other members of the party bureau; KDU-ČSL, 2023; ODS, 2023; TOP 09, 2023). They are involved in developing strategies, but these are subject to approval by the bureau (e.g., Executive Committee). '*The teams can also recommend to the party's political leadership or be in direct opposition*' (TOP 09, 2023). Still, the final say is with the party's political apparatus, to which the management is subordinate, especially regarding executive tasks. Again, this description corresponds to the line-staff structure, with the caveat that here we get a clear picture of a management style, specifically, a participative one. Specifically, in ODS, the central manager and the head of the media and analytical section are mainly responsible for the performance of tasks (ODS, 2023). Only ANO (2023) reported '*a strong position of political units at individual levels (from regional organizations to national bodies), which is subsequently reflected in the party's management.*' The different political levels set strategies and programs and make individual decisions. The central office then only implements the above and carries out the necessary support (ANO, 2023).

Management ideally works continuously according to long-term (e.g., the KDU-ČSL has an annual plan in which regional organizations participate) and short-term goals. Individual tasks are determined by management based on regular meetings with the political leadership of the party. Each party decides the frequency of those meetings, for example, in TOP 09 (2023), it is 2–3 weekly meetings according to the current political situation and the election cycle, while in ODS (2023), it is weekly meetings, and in KDU-ČSL (2023) it is monthly meetings. ANO does not specify the exact frequency of the meetings; it only speaks of 'regularity' (ANO, 2023). A particular category would be crisis communication – this is handled by a much narrower team than the usual agenda. The movement ANO may, if necessary, call on an outsider for an opinion (ANO, 2023). None of the other political parties surveyed reported hiring external consultants for crisis coaching. In TOP 09, for example, only the chairperson, secretary general, and spokesperson would handle any developing crises. They would also be the only members permitted to bring in external consultants (TOP 09, 2023). Without exception, work, tasks, and assignments are distributed by the Secretary-General, who is responsible for the results of the work of the teams (sections, departments). ODS deviates from this model, whose way of life is, in their words, *'rather agile'* (ODS, 2023).

Some of the abovementioned positions are fixed within the rules or statutes, particularly the general secretary (KDU-ČSL, 2023; TOP 09, 2023). An internal party decree defines others. This again applies especially to the post of spokesperson (TOP 09, 2023). For other positions, their definition is *'quite flexible and varies according to the current situation'* (e.g., TOP 09 recently created the positions of administrators of the new social networks Instagram and TikTok, TOP 09, 2023; in ANO, overlapping of individual positions is possible by prior agreement; ANO, 2023). Before the elections, election teams and staff are set up (national, regional, etc., depending on the type of elections; KDU-ČSL, 2023). Therefore, in KDU-ČSL, a management model with a permanently filled position of election manager was introduced in 2019. For specific elections, his team is created or renewed (KDU-ČSL, 2023).

The parties use modern technologies for internal communication – various Microsoft tools such as Outlook, Teams, and others such as SharePoint, Trello, etc. It is also worth mentioning specific party applications – the so-called Evlivd (register of the People's Party; KDU-ČSL, 2023) and 'My ODS' (ODS, 2023). Three parties (ODS, TOP 09, and KDU-ČSL) do not distinguish between employee-members and employee-non-members. The same rules apply to all of them, and the same communication principles. In the case of

ANO, the statutes do not preclude an employee from being a party member, but there are some restrictions on the performance of specific functions and possible incompatibility issues (ANO, 2023). The differences between the ratio of staff members to non-members are interesting, however, as they vary from party to party. For ODS (2023), TOP 09 (2023), and KDU-ČSL (2023), more or less, all employees are also members of the party. There is even a membership requirement for some managerial (CEO, regional manager) positions. These ratios were not available for ANO. The parties use different methods to motivate their employees, for example, TOP 09 awards annual bonuses, teambuilding, or courses however, these awards are based on the outcome of the elections (TOP 09, 2023). In KDU-ČSL, even a financial reward is expected for regional managers after successful elections (KDU-ČSL, 2023). However, work is also evaluated by the promotion of topics in the media or the reach of posts on social networks, etc. In ANO, employees are evaluated according to established internal rules, and for some positions, incentive factors are introduced as part of the remuneration (ANO, 2023).

How does the party define leadership style?

In a business environment, we consider a leader to be a person setting goals and persuading the rest of the organization to follow them. It is someone who is charismatic and is followed by those around him (see text above). However, the results of the interviews show that political parties may not have a clearly defined notion of what a leader is as they have often used it with multiple meanings. Second, except for ANO, they only have natural leaders. However, there is a block identifying this person as the leader. Namely, ANO explicitly identified the party committee as the figurehead of the movement. They then state that the party chairman is the natural leader. There needs to be clarity or understanding of the meaning of the word leader (ANO, 2023). ODS (2023), on the other hand, has clearly defined the meaning of leadership as '*Clear values anchorage, the modern concept of politics, inspiration, and vision for other party members, supporters, and citizens*' and refers to its chairman (who is certainly not as popular in any sense of the word as Babiš) as the leader. However, they use a phrase suitable for an election poster to explain that it is the chairman they see as the leader: He leads the party to long-term success with a clear and inspiring vision for the party and the whole country.

TOP 09 envisions leadership as managing and taking responsibility for everything that happens. Professional studies state that a leader is often a manager; that is not always true in politics. They also consider the chairman to be the leader of the party. This can undoubtedly be the case, but the statement '*Now we have, for example, solved the practical matter that if I want to buy a car, which we have now acquired as if it were the property of the party, the chairman has to give the full power of attorney to the person who buys or takes over the car on behalf of the party*' (TOP 09, 2023) leads us to believe that the party has not fully understood the meaning of a leader and confuses him with the person we would describe in business as a manager or executive. Like other parties, the KDU-ČSL agrees that the chairperson should be the leader and the leader the chairperson. However, they did not answer whether this is the case now. Regarding the understanding of leadership, they referred to the political scene of the 1990s and '*...figures like Lux, Klaus, and Zeman*'[1] (KDU-ČSL, 2023).

This study considers the chair to be the leader and, as such, should meet certain criteria such as coming up with innovative ideas, setting the agenda (at least in part), and being actively involved in the co-decision of funding. When we apply this to the parties considered in this study, we see that all of the parties agree that the appropriate body makes funding decisions. It is similar in business, where the finance department or finance coordinator is involved. Still, the leader (especially if he is also the manager) participates in or approves the process.

Regarding the new ideas, the KDU-ČSL says: '*It is certainly not just the chairman, although it is expected of him*' (KDU-ČSL, 2023). In ODS, it is mainly the presidency, while TOP 09 and ANO try to give space to all individuals. In the last case, we can see elements of correspondingly decentralized management and bottom-up lifting of demands. Even observing the distribution that this happens in half of the cases mentioned corresponds to the business environment.

Who is responsible for setting the agenda for the party may vary. For example, ANO (2023) stated that this is done in cooperation with the program committee, while TOP 09 states, '*The leader sets the political agenda, as far as the management of the party is concerned, it depends on who is the chairman, who is responsible, or who manages the party*' (TOP 09, 2023). Here we can see the contradiction in that they have already stated above that the party's leader is their chairman, and they see leadership as managing and taking responsibility for everything that happens. However, they contradict this statement by saying that the leader only manages the political agenda while the management of the party may be the responsibility of the chairman. The KDU-ČSL cites the Programme Council and ODS, the Bureau headed by the chairman.

Comparison of findings

The interviews with representatives of these parliamentary parties in the Czech Republic provided rare and unique information about their structure, functioning, and leadership. They also confirmed that the top priority for party management is to achieve electoral success. The highest priority in the Czech context is the elections to the Chamber of Deputies (the lower chamber of Parliament), followed by the Senate elections (the upper chamber of

Parliament), elections to the regional councils, elections to the European Parliament and, last but not least, the local elections (ANO, 2023; KDU-ČSL 2023; ODS, 2023; TOP 09, 2023). However, this would not be enough for the survival of a political party, which is why respondents also emphasized the political dimension – the elections to the Chamber of Deputies still play a primary role, as they are the primary elections.

'*However, the emphasis is, for example, on local rather than European elections*' (KDU-ČSL, 2023). They are a base for the political party, where new faces are sought, and the necessary organization is built for any further party activities. That is why central offices are involved in all types of elections. However, the degree of their involvement varies. Local and regional organizations with central assignments have more freedom in TOP 09 (2023), ODS (2023), and ANO (2023), while the Christian Democrats '*divide the central office share between Parliament 100%, the region 50%, and the municipality 30%*' (KDU-ČSL, 2023). However, whatever the level of involvement, it is always the case that the individual teams must follow the official, that is, centrally approved (electoral) line.

At this point, it can be noted that the most open were the respondents of the Christian Democrats and TOP 09. The respondent for the Civic Democrats answered very briefly and generally, sometimes not saying anything at all. It was evident that the party protects its environment regarding management and cannot be classified among more modern currents with a more agile mindset (although in interviews, they claim the opposite). A particular case is that of ANO, the most strongly staffed party in the Czech environment, in which the willingness to participate in the survey was very high.

Nevertheless, the answers were submitted to the Bureau members for approval. Thus, the authors were provided with the answers only after several urgings and, consequently, wondered to what extent the political leaders corrected them. In the case of the ANO movement, it should also be noted that we consider the answers given for this research somewhat official. However, the internal workings are subject to informal processes that this research could not reveal. On the other hand, it is interesting to compare this movement, which can be classified as a so-called party firm (Panebianco, 1988), with traditional political entities, given that its chairman, Andrej Babiš, is an entrepreneur – elements of management (and authoritarian management style) can thus be observed more than in other parties.

To summarize, Czech political parties are functioning very conservatively. Their political content and political activities focus almost exclusively on organizing elections above all else. Only the daily party functioning appears to be looked at with more importance. From a management standpoint, the parties could improve their management, leading to better performance in politics. The exception to this would be the ANO movement, which, especially when organizing election campaigns, used the position of its chairman, where he and his closest team approved all decisions regarding the content, form, and financing of campaigns.

Recommendations for academic research

Political science has stated that political parties' goals generally fall into three categories – policy-seeking, office-seeking, and vote-seeking (Strøm, 1990). However, this research makes clear that party managers engage in ongoing management activities to maintain organizational long-term health rather than just focusing on winning individual elections. Further research into the impact of the day-to-day operations on the electoral results and the party's position in the electoral market could bring significant findings. Political parties face many challenges and have undergone substantial changes in recent eras. Understanding how the parties operate and adapt to a constantly changing political environment is crucial. Likewise, it is essential to understand that the tasks of political management, whether setting goals, controlling them, or using resources effectively, have become integral to party success. While the classical view of the role of political parties plays up winning elections through effective campaigning, we have found that 'invisible' party management involves a complex range of activities in addition to the sub-tasks that have hitherto been the center of interest in prior research.

This approach could also bring a new understanding of the impact of elections and the electoral cycle on the functioning of a political party. This is primarily related to how the party's functioning is subordinated to the party management and tries to implement political-marketing strategies. Some political parties have begun to behave like election offices, with management subliminally influencing political outcomes.

Recommendations for practice

The management of political parties would benefit from setting long-term goals related to the party's development and, necessarily, to the elections. It would also bring a great deal of professionalism if the political leadership of the party and its values were to be separated to some extent from the practicalities of day-to-day operations and the organization of elections. There is also a significant gap in the Czech parties' work on developing the membership base, creating analytical teams, and supporting politicians in public relations, analytical background, etc. Working for a political party is highly compartmentalized; in many ways, a more significant investment in a team would pay off. It is also interesting that parties use only a few applications and various campaign software.

Recommended reading

Carothers, T., & O'Donohue, A. (Eds.). (2019). *Democracies divided: The global challenge of political polarization*. Brookings Institution Press.
Daft, R. L. (2021). *Management* (14th ed.). Boston: Cengage Learning.
Lees-Marshment, J. (2020). *Political management: The dance of government and politics*. Routledge.
Prange, C., & Heracleous, L. (2018). *Agility. X: How organizations thrive in unpredictable times*. Cambridge: Cambridge University Press, 2018.
Ungureanu, E. C., & Moga, L. M. (2019). "Performance and evaluation in political parties management." *Annals of the University Dunarea De Jos of Galati: Fascicle: I, Economics & Applied Informatics*, Vol. 25, No. 3, pp. 120–128.

Note

1 Key political figures in the 1990s and both Zeman and Klaus are former presidents of the Czech Republic. They both served two terms.

References

Interviews

KDU-ČSL. (2023). Interview with general secretary Pavel Hořava, February 24, Prague (recorded).
TOP 09. (2023). Interview with general secretary Miriam Faltová, February 27, Prague (recorded).
ODS. (2023). Interview organized by party spokesperson Václav Smolka, March 8, Prague (written form, not recorded).
ANO. (2023). Interview organized by the office manager and assistant to the party manager Klára Dubovská, March 17, Prague (written form, not recorded).
Al Kajeh, Ebrahim Hasan. (2018). "Impact of Leadership Styles on Organizational Performance." *Journal of Human Resources Management Research*, Vol. 2018, pp. 1–10.

Academic literature

Blažek, L. (2011). *Management-Organizování, rozhodování, ovlivňování*. Praha: Grada Publishing.
Bobba, G., & Seddone, A. (2011). *Personal and personalized party: Notes on a theoretical Framework*. 61st Political Studies Association Annual Conference.
Bush, T. (2020). *Theories of educational leadership and management*. London: SAGE Publications Ltd.
Cai, W., Khapova, S., Bossink, B., Lysova, E., & Yuan, J. (2020). "Optimizing employee creativity in the digital era: Uncovering the interactional effects of abilities, motivations, and opportunities." *International Journal of Environmental Research and Public Health*, Vol. 17, No. 3, pp. 1–19.
Calise, M. (2010). *Il partito personale: i due corpi del leader. Nuova ed. ampliata*. Řím: Laterza.
Donelly, J. H., Gibson, J. L., & Ivancevich, J. M. (1997). *Management*. Praha: Grada.

Government of the Czech Republic. (2023). (cit. 2023-03-19). (https://www.vlada. cz/en/).

Griffin, R. W. (2013). *Management.* Boston: Houghton Mifflin.

Hendl, J. (2005). *Kvalitativní výzkum: základní metody a aplikace.* Praha: Portál.

Hloušek, V. (2015). "Two types of presidentialization in the party politics of Central Eastern Europe." *Italian Political Science Review,* Vol. 2015, No., Special Issue 3, pp. 277–299.

Jamal, S. & Soomro, M. A. (2011). "Management styles and employee performance: A study of a public sector company." *South Asian Journal of Management Sciences,* Vol. 5, No. 2, pp. 65–71.

Kalogiannidis, S., Kontsas, S. & Chatzitheodoridis, F. (2021). "Managerial styles and employee performance. An empirical study from bank sector employees in Greece." *WSEAS Transactions on Environment and Development,* Vol. 17, pp. 1234–1244.

Khajeh, E. H. A. (2018). "Leadership styles on organizational performance." *Journal of Human Reseource Management Research,* Vol. 2018, pp. 1–10.

Kopeček, L. (2016). "I'm paying, so I decide Czech ANO as an extreme form of a business-firm party." *East European Politics and Societies,* Vol. 30, No. 4, pp. 725–749.

Needham, C. (2006). "Brands and political loyalty." *Brand Management,* Vol. 3, No. 13, pp. 178–187.

Northouse, G. (2007). *Leadership theory and practice.* (3rd ed.) Thousand Oak, London, New Delhi: Sage Publications, Inc.

Omoijiade, P. O. (2016). "The management of political actors in Institutions." *International Journal of Research in Business and Social Science,* Vol. 5, No. 4, pp. 17–30.

Panebianco, A. (1988). *Political parties: Organizations and powers.* Cambridge: Cambridge University Press.

Pilařová, I. (2016). *Leadership & management development: Role, úlohy a kompetence managerů a lídrů.* Praha: Grada Publishing.

Plamínek, J. & Fišer, R. (2004). *Řízení podle kompetencí.* Praha: Grada Publishing.

Reichel, J. (2009). *Kapitoly metodologie sociálních výzkumů.* Praha: Grada.

Smolík, J. (2018). "Party System in the Czech Republic." In: Kancik-Kołtun, Ewelina (Ed.). *Contemporary political parties and party systems in the Visegrad Group countries.* Lublin: Maria Curie-Skłodowska University Press.

Spáč, P. (2013). *České strany a jejich kandidáti. Případ voleb do Poslanecké sněmovny v roce 2010.* Brno: Masarykova univerzita, Fakulta sociálních studií, Mezinárodní politologický ústav.

Statutes of the ANO political movement. (2013). (cit. 2023-03-20). (https://www. anobudelip.cz/file/edee/ke-stazeni/vnitrni-predpisy/ano-stanovy-2013.pdf).

Statutes of the Civic Democratic Party. (2015). (cit. 2023-03-20). (https://www.ods. cz/docs/stanovy-ods-2015.pdf).

Strøm, K. (1990). "A behavioral theory of competitive political parties." *American Journal of Political Science,* Vol. 34, No. 2, pp. 565–598.

Van De Kamp, P. (2014). "Holacracy–A Radical Approach to Organizational Design. Elements of the software development process-influences on project success and failure. " In: Hans Dekkers, Wil Leeuwis, Ivan Plantevin (Eds.) *Elements of the software development process - Influences on Project Success and Failure.* Amsterdam: University of Amsterdam.

Zehnder, T. P. (2016). *Principles of leadership: Secular and theological principles that define success and growth.* Bloomington, IN: WestBow Press.

15

POLITICAL ORGANIZING ECOSYSTEM

The Brotherhood of People and Power

Hamid Reza Tafaghodi and Soroush Sayari

Introduction

The main objective of this chapter is to investigate how an ecosystem view-point toward political organizing can bring about a transformation in Iran's political organizations. Regarding the political perspective of Iran, the difficulties that the political organizations have to deal with are only one of the main political and managerial problems, on their way to achieve their goals. It is emphasized thoroughly in the political management definitions and principles. On one hand, such conditions not only have been criticized by academia but also by high-level political managers for years. On the other hand, it has been frequently indicated in the majority of strategic general policies of Iran. This chapter highlights that political organizing is the missing link for filling this academic and empirical gap. In this reference frame, the relationship between people and power would be reviewed and qualified wisely.

Key literature

Especially in developing countries like Iran, there is an undeniable need to necessarily implement the political management in functional areas as an integrated and holistic process. In political management, political organizing is one of the prominent areas. It is important to deal with the political and managerial problems that all developing countries have in common since its particular focus is on people and power relationship. The scope of political organizing includes creating and utilizing the power (to understand the diverse power sources and to decide how to gain and distribute it), organizing and connecting people (to organize people and their interactions

DOI: 10.4324/9781003260677-15

within an organization), identifying the requirements of improvement and development (to recognize the necessities and challenges in terms of change and innovation), enacting and managing improvements (to promote desired changes and to manage the resistances), and facilitating the effective internal communication (to establish an effective internal and interpersonal communication) (Lees-Marshment, 2021). The accomplished situation is synergetic and entirely affects a wide spectrum of political and managerial fields, ranging from campaigns' functions in elections to governments' political outputs.

The necessity of administrative system modification has been frequently emphasized by Iran's general policies and the regulations, which have been passed by legal authorities. To achieve the most desirable results in terms of effectiveness and efficiency within the governmental organizations, the highly advantageous approaches have been demonstrated, which are including the re-arrangement of organizational structures, the regulation of organizational communications regarding different managerial levels, the re-design and re-distribution of power sources (The Islamic Consultative Assembly of IRI, 2017), the value-based institutionalization of organizational culture, the implementation of a justice- and knowledge-based approach within organizational processes, the improvement of development measurement criteria, the introduction of an administrative system qualification, the application of nation capabilities, the enhancement of an efficient internal cooperation (The Expediency Discernment Council of the System, 2019, pp. 115–118), the deployment of electronic and information technology within administrative system (The Islamic Consultative Assembly of IRI, 2007), the management of challenges within a competitive environment, the re-formation of the role and government organizational structure, and etc. (Supreme Council of Administration, 2014).

In addition to these strategic plans, there are so many domestic researches, which have been conducted to recognize the gap existing between the current and the desired state of Iran's administrative system, presenting critical approaches. In this stream of Iranian researches, the main suggested requirements are as follows: the imbalance condition in distributing the power among organizational units and their authorities, the inefficiency of legal processes and procedures, the difficulties in changing organizational culture, the lack of interactive communications throughout organizations, the uncontrollable sources of bureaucracy, the old-fashioned technology systems, the inflexibility in organizations' adaption against changes, the lack of appropriate educational programs for managers and staff, the lack of an appropriate segregation regarding organizational duties, the imperfect identification of internal capacities and challenges, and the weak measurement criteria (Babaei et al., 2022). These researches have proposed multiple solutions, however, we believe that the political organizing would be the most useful solution to address the challenging conditions. As given in this chapter, the implementation of political organizing coupled with an ecosystem viewpoint will effectively and efficiently transform the Iran's governmental organizations to promptly fulfill their promises.

Methodology

Considering the purpose of this study, which is to provide a model for the design of political organizations to achieve their goals and deepen the connection between members and power, it is necessary to examine and analyze the experience of political experts who play a significant role in political organizations, through an exploratory process. Therefore, the qualitative research method should be used which is a subset of the interpretive paradigm. Considering the nature of this research, the method of qualitative content analysis (QCA) is a suitable choice due to the purposeful and systematic extensive review of research data and the extraction of concepts that directly include the objectives of the research.

We conducted 35 in-depth interviews with Iranian high-level political practitioners and officials such as former presidents, ministers, senior political consultants to supreme leader, parliament members, top political managers, in Iran. The interview data were analyzed using the QCA method. Data analysis identified 154 codes, 12 categories, and 2 themes. To prevent any bias in consequences, a triangulation approach and judgmental sampling was implemented. Among the interviews, our main question was: "based on your lived experience in Iranian political organizations, how can a political organization maximize its performance to fulfill its goals in Iran?"

Research findings

To achieve the goals of government and political organizations and create a strong relationship between employees and members, it is necessary to create an effective relationship between the two extracted themes, which are as follows: the form layer of an ecosystem and the content layer of an ecosystem

To design a desirable organization based on the goals and values, these two layers must be implemented simultaneously so that the synergy between them leads to the achievement of the macro goals of political organizations and their sub-groups. In the following, these two layers and their related categories are described in the following.

First theme: the form layer of an ecosystem

The form layer considers the functional and productive areas in political organizations and tries to guarantee the functional characteristics of the organization.

This layer consists of seven main categories as follows.

Organizational improvisation

Based on the conducted interviews, Mahmoud Ahmadinejad (the former President of Iran) believed: "Due to the complex and ever-changing political environment of Iran, political managers must be able to make quick and reliable decisions in a short period of time against unforeseen political events; therefore, there is a vital need for political organizations to train political managers in this way."

In today's world in which we live, sudden changes and unforeseen and unexpected events have become a part of normal life. In such a situation, if organizations are not able to respond appropriately to environmental changes and fluctuations, their decline and degradation will be inevitable.

For this reason, it seems necessary that according to the extremely complex environment that surrounded the political organizations and also the deliberate changes that are planned to harm their nature, these organizations should plan measures for an agile and appropriate response to these fluctuations. Therefore, the organizations that are designed and established under the set of political organizations should prepare their employees to face undefined situations as well as make sudden decisions based on wisdom, thought, and rationality. The process of making and implementing such decisions in unforeseen circumstances and in a short time is called organizational improvisation.

To deepen organizational improvisation in political organizations, continuous workshops should be defined for different units, in which, people are placed in "undefined" positions and gain different experiences. These experiences would embed in their subconscious and different situations, they can make effective decisions based on these experiences.

Knowledge sedimentation

Ali Larijani (the former Speaker of the Parliament of Iran) stated in an interview: "One of the problems of our managers in political organizations is that they use less of the past experience in Iran and the world. Many events that political managers face happened in the past or in different regions of the world, so if they have acceptable access to those experiences, the possibility of making correct political decisions will apparently increase."

One of the vital elements of any organization is knowledge and its related concepts. Knowledge means all information obtained from scientific-applied research or all experiences from understanding different situations. Political organizations should consider knowledge flow as one of the main axes of their organization's design and management.

To be more precious, all members of the political organization in any institution should have access to the latest and most up-to-date content and concepts of knowledge related to their work in the form of an operational dashboard. This dashboard should be continuously updated and provide the users with the organizational experiences of the members of the organization as well as the scientific experiences at the national and international levels. On the other hand, the educational needs of different units must be continuously reviewed and met.

Of course, the spirit of learning and research should be created in the members. It is only in this way that the nature of knowledge is deposited and institutionalized in the heart of the organization. For example, in no way should the continuing education of the employees of political organizations be prevented and all the restrictions and obstacles must be removed. Also, by using incentives and creative processes, employees should be informed that they will be noticed and accepted in the organization if, in addition to having access to current knowledge, they have an exploratory spirit and continuously develop their scientific level, even seek to fulfill their educational needs outside the organization.

Strategy translation

One of the main problems of organizations, especially political organizations, is the lack of practical attention to strategies and their implementation. Therefore, unfortunately, instead of the designed strategies being considered valuable intangible assets of the organization, they are considered tangible but low-value assets in the form of archival documents.

In this regard, Masoumeh Ebtekar (the former Vice President of Iran) also stated in her interview: "My experience in working with many political managers was that most of them do not have a comprehensive understanding of their organizations' strategies; therefore, they cannot correctly analyze them in their organizations. This issue ceases the process of achieving the objectives of their political organizations."

One of the reasons for this lack of attention to strategies is the lack of proper understanding of the macro strategies of the political organization and, as a result, the inability to transform them into the specialized strategies of each political institution. On the other hand, the lack of knowledge of the members of the political organizations about the macro strategies of the organization and the subgroup in which they operate makes them unable to act appropriately and effectively even if they have the desire to pay attention to the strategies. Based on this, it is necessary to pay special attention to the training of managers in understanding, interpreting, transforming, and transferring the macro strategies of political organizations to the main strategies of their organizations and subordinates, in the design and management of the organization. In other words, if the organization's design and management do not pay attention to its strategic direction, its final output will not have any value in practice, because it will not be in the direction of the goals of the political organizations.

Environmental monitoring

All political organizations that are designed have different environments that are resulted from the relativity of organizational boundaries. In other words, every political organization has an internal environment and two external environments, the first of which is related to the political organization itself, and the next two include other political organizations and the environment outside these political organizations. Each political organization, according to the type of its goal setting and strategies, must continuously monitor these three environments and, in addition to removing environmental restrictions and obstacles, take advantage of elements that can act as a lever to increase the efficiency of the political organization.

Hossein Dehghan (the former Vice President of Iran) believed during the interviews: "In Iranian political organizations, the importance of the environment is much greater than in other organizations. Considering that the continued survival of complete political organizations depends on the events in their external environment; hence, a special focus should be placed on this external environment. Of course, the internal environment should be modified and adjusted according to the external environment in order to achieve the aims of political organizations."

One of the important points to keep in mind while studying the organization's environment is exploring the environment based on the goals of the political organization. In other words, if this environmental study and monitoring are not purposeful, it can lead to the acquisition of misleading information that diverts the organization's progress.

Another thing to keep in mind is to study the environment without any preconceptions or judgments. Such an approach to monitoring the environment brings attention to points that were not paid attention to before, due to the assumption of certain concepts or elements, and as a result, they were not used in analytical interactions.

Organizational gap analysis

One of the methods of applying rationality in designing and reforming an organization is to study and analyze its documents and missions. This means that we should first analyze that political organization in the present time frame and its environment, and then examine the past and the history of the concepts of that organization. In these studies, the process that determines the necessity of the formation of the political organization in the present and the past should be investigated. The necessity of the formation of that political organization and the extent of its success in achieving its goals, the ups and downs that the organization faced during its life, the interaction of that organization with its environment, the stakeholders and decision-makers of the organization, and the goals they pursued, the proportion and quality of the organization with the main set of political organizations should be evaluated. The answers provide a suitable basis for understanding the existential and functional nature of the organization.

During an interview with Mohammad Reza Bahonar (the former Member of the Parliament of Iran), he stated: "If our political leaders know exactly why their political organizations were formed, what their main missions are, and what have happened during their life-cycle, then a clear picture of the path ahead will be created for them which shed light on their future condition."

In the next step, organizational chat analysis is needed. For this purpose, at first, two desirable futures and possible futures for the political organization should be considered. Then the gaps between the current situation of the political organization and these two futures are analyzed. The purpose of this analysis is to achieve the desired future of the political organization. By analyzing the distance between these two situations, it is possible to determine the tools, infrastructure, inputs, and processes necessary to guide the political organization toward the desired future.

Technology strategic leadership

Political organizations have no way to improve the speed and quality of their performance except to pay attention to technology. The concept of technology deals with the process of transforming science into practice. Based on this, it is necessary to redefine the conventional concept of technology in the organization. According to this concept, even a scientific and creative method that can correctly diagnose or solve the problems of the organization is also considered technology. Therefore, political organizations should give as much importance to theoretical methods and solutions that have practical applicability as to technology.

Mohammad Javad Zarif (the former Minister of Foreign Affairs of Iran) emphasized in his interview: "We should consider technology as a tool to solve various problems in political organizations. In this case, we can see political science as a technology and our approach towards solving problems will change. Naturally, changing the problem solving tool can create more appropriate answers to problems."

Information technology is considered one of the important areas in political organizations, which enables communication and integration between the elements of the political organization, as well as between different organizations, and increases the speed and quality of data transmission. This concept can greatly reduce time delays caused by administrative bureaucracies and bring agility to the political organization. For better performance of information technology, it is better to design the roles of the internal and external communication of the political organization in question and meet the technological needs to reduce the gaps as much as possible.

In all political organizations, the technological needs assessment of each unit in each political organization should be done so that the technologies that can guarantee great benefits are injected into the political organization. This needs assessment process should be done continuously in the political organization. Moreover, technological needs assessment should be done in all units of political organizations, and technologies that are capable of guaranteeing large benefits should be used in the organization. This needs assessment process should be done continuously in the political organization.

Human capital strategic leadership

One of the most important topics in human capital is the concept of talent. In the first step, the concept of talent must be defined and then, talents can be divided into human and non-human categories. Talent means "potential ability to do something." This potential ability can be related to humans or caused by environmental elements, equipment, or any other non-human element in the political organization. Based on this, the processes of identifying, attracting, and cultivating talent, which is based on the goals and needs of the political organization, should give equal importance to human and non-human factors. The talent indicators should also be defined based on the needs of the organization and avoid dealing with non-purposive indicators that are not necessarily related to the needs of the organization. On the other hand, the issue of succession should be given special attention. Unfortunately, this issue has been neglected for a long time. This issue makes the current political organization to be person-oriented, not process-oriented.

Mohammad Javad Azari Jahromi (the former Minister of the Information and Communications Technology of Iran) said in his interview: "Unfortunately, the variety of human resources used in our political organizations is very limited, and regardless of expertise, most people who are ideologically closer to that political organization are hired. This problem underestimates talents and slows down the speed of reaching the objectives of political organizations."

Second theme: the content layer of an ecosystem

The content layer deals with the value and spiritualistic areas of political organizations and tries to implement them to keep the organization at a high level from a value-oriented perspective and convert values into beliefs instead of habits. Paying attention to emotional relationships and spiritualism, strengthening the revolutionary fervor, and inclusion of religious and revolutionary values are among the characteristics of the content layer of the organization and its designed principles.

Structural promotion of values

It is clear that to transfer value to a group of people, it cannot be expected to accept it by simply emphasizing that value. This is a human process that requires appropriate structural and individual basis and infrastructures.

Crystallization of values in the essence and the structure of the political organization is one of the most important principles in transferring those values. For example, if we want to convey a high value such as justice to people, they must feel the existence of such a value in the structure of the political organization; otherwise, not only will they not accept that value, but they may also react negatively to it. The impact of structure on human behavior has been proven both in religious and contemporary scientific literature. Therefore, to train and cultivate value-oriented employees in political organizations, the structure of that organization must be treated first. Accordingly, the three elements of justice, expertise, and rationality are very important factors that shape a value-oriented structure and provide a suitable platform for their acceptance. Therefore, a plan should be thought out so that these three elements of justice, expertise, and rationality crystallize in the structure.

Individual promotion of values

As mentioned in the previous section, the transfer of values requires providing a suitable basis for employees and members of the political organization to accept them. This setup has two structural and individual dimensions. The structural dimension is described in the previous part.

As proven by various studies, the environment that people interact with has a great impact on shaping their behavior. In other words, companions, friends, and managers can play an important role in an individual's behavioral output. Managers and officials are among the people who have a high impact. If the managers of a political organization have a caring and interactive spirit and can communicate well with their employees, and on the other hand, have the necessary qualifications for that managerial position, then their spiritual influence on their subordinates would increase. Therefore, it is necessary to plan for the appointment of interactive and committed managers, increasing the communication between managers and employees and benefitting from moral and religious discourses and literature in the political organization. On the other pole, a basis should be provided where employees can freely think and share their thoughts. Based on this, their doubts, concerns, and expectations are heard and adjusted, and by responding to them, a basis for accepting the values of the organization is provided.

Daily promotion of values

Based on this category, the values of Islam, revolution, political organizations, and the considered organization should be continuously established in the organization life of the organization through symbols, culture, speeches, value-based ceremonies, attractive visual elements, creative ideological marketing, etc. Of course, the transfer of values should not lead to coercion and discouragement in accepting the value.

Political organizing ecosystem model (POE)

Based on the two layers introduced in the previous section, which seek to improve the effectiveness of political organizations and realize their goals both from a functional and value point of view, a model of the political organizing ecosystem was created – see Figure 15.1.

Based on the political organizing ecosystem, two form and content layers of political organizations should be in continuous and dynamic interaction with each other. Deficiency in any of these layers will diminish the effectiveness of the other one. Focusing on the form layer (functional application) and not paying enough attention to the content layer (value-based application) cannot fully realize the goals of political organizations that are based on values and ideology and vice versa.

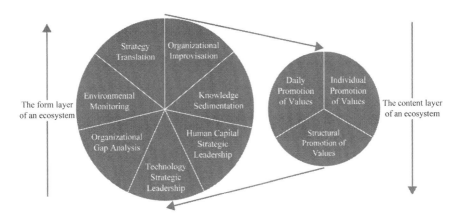

FIGURE 15.1 Political organizing ecosystem model (POE)

Operational plan for the implementation of the political organizing ecosystem

In the following, an operational plan for the implementation of form and content layers of the political organizing ecosystem is presented – see Table 15.1.

Recommendations for academic research

In this research, two layers of form and content were extracted through in-depth interviews with high political practitioners. These layers can have a direct impact on the effectiveness of the organization and the realization of its goals.

Of course, the elements of these two layers are not equally important, and each one must be analyzed to be implemented. It is suggested that in future studies, the causality relationships of 7 categories of the form layer (functional application) and 3 categories of the content layer (value-based application) of political organizations should be investigated. The sensitivity analysis of these categories will help to identify the most effective and the most sensitive categories. On this basis, operational planning can be done for the effectiveness of the layers.

Recommendations for practitioners

1 The goal of implementing the formal layer of political organizations is to increase their effectiveness and function in line with their missions. Focusing on seven categories of organizational improvisation, knowledge deposition, strategy translation, environmental monitoring, organizational gap analysis, strategic technology management, and strategic human capital management provides organizations with tools and capabilities that will lead to a better realization of their goals.

2 The goal of implementing the content layer of political organizations is to place the macro values of government in political organizations. Practitioners should know that if the macro values of political organizations are not well aligned with the macro values of government, even if they perform well, they will not be able to fully realize political goals. Therefore, the content layer of the organization considers the transfer of government values to political organizations through three categories individual, structural, and daily promotion of values.

3 It is very important to pay attention to the form (functional application) and content (value-based application) layers of political organizations at the same time. For the effective design and management of the political organization, both layers should be considered simultaneously. Neglecting each of these layers will create obstacles in the way. It creates the full realization of the organization's goals.

TABLE 15.1 Implantation elements of political organizing ecosystem

No.	Category	Requirements	Description
		The form layer of an ecosystem	
1	Organizational improvisation	Holding continuous and interconnected workshops on decision-making in conditions of uncertainty and unforeseen situations in political organizations.	At least every three months, an 8-hour workshop should be held (for senior political managers).
2		Holding continuous and interconnected workshops on improving risk tolerance and risk management in decision-making in political organizations.	At least every three months, an 8-hour workshop should be held (for senior political managers).
3		Using management labs to strengthen awareness and decision-making skills among people in political organizations.	—
4		Holding continuous and interconnected workshops on improving creative decision-making in political organizations.	At least every three months, an 8-hour workshop should be held (for people).
5	Knowledge management	Creating a political organizational task, to explore the continuous training needs (software and hardware) of different departments based on defined missions and tasks, and documenting them.	At least once every two months.
6		Providing training needs assessment reports to the senior political management and trustees of each organization.	At least once every two months.
7		Holding workshops on the identified educational needs and presenting the report to the senior political management and trustees of each organization.	At least once every four months.
8		Report writing training for people and political managers.	At least every three months, a 4-hour workshop should be held.
9		Providing the technical and technological infrastructure of the panel of political organizational experiences and publishing it.	The report on the provision and continuous development of this infrastructure should be submitted to the senior political management and trustees of each organization every two months.

(Continued)

TABLE 15.1 (Continued)

No.	Category	Requirements	Description
		The form layer of an ecosystem	
10		Creating a personalized panel for everyone in the political organization to access the organizational experiences.	The report on the provision and continuous development of this infrastructure should be submitted to the senior political management and trustees of each organization every two months.
11		Continuous planning is designed to create material and spiritual motivations in employees to develop and improve their own or others' organizational experiences and publish them in the designed system.	The report on the provision and continuous development of this infrastructure should be submitted to the senior management and trustees of each organization every year.
12		Design and implementation of a scientific dashboard for all members and publishing the latest global findings related to their duties and missions.	The report on the provision and continuous development of this infrastructure should be sent to the senior management and trustees of each organization every two months.
13		Continuous quantitative and qualitative review and evaluation of people's knowledge level, based on the latest global findings published in the scientific dashboard.	This evaluation should be done at least once every three months.
14		Designing incentive programs to motivate people to use extra-organizational training courses related to their duties and missions, including university studies, training workshops, etc.	The report on the design, implementation, and evaluation of these programs on the educational motivation of employees must be submitted to the senior political management and trustee of each organization once every three months.

(Continued)

TABLE 15.1 (*Continued*)

No.	Category	Requirements	Description
		The form layer of an ecosystem	
15	Strategy translation	Designing a political strategic puzzle and defining the position of all the organizations on that puzzle.	This puzzle must be updated once every six months.
16		Holding meetings of the heads of excusive, legislative and judicial forces with the officials of related organizations, in order to explain the different strategies of governance and to explain the position of each of the organizations in these strategies.	These meetings should be held at least once every six months.
17		Designing and compiling the strategic axes of each political organization (including the statement of mission, vision, values and policies) by its trustees, and evaluating it based on alignment with the goals and macro strategies.	These strategies must be updated and reported to the considered center, once every year.
18		Designing the strategy of each political organization by its trustees, and evaluating it based on alignment with the goals and macro strategies.	These strategies must be updated and reported to the considered center, once every year.
19		Holding meetings by the trustees of each political organization with managers and people of that organization, in order to explain the strategies of the organization, and its position in advancing the goals and macro strategies.	These meetings should be held at least once every six months.
20		The operational translation of the strategies of each political organization for its different departments and units (including the design of the processes of specialized units and the description of the duties of the units) and continuous monitoring to ensure its executive alignment with the goals and strategies of the organization.	The report on operational translation of the strategies and its continuous monitoring must be submitted to the defined unit every six months.

(Continued)

TABLE 15.1 (*Continued*)

No.	Category	Requirements	Description
		The form layer of an ecosystem	
21	Environmental monitoring	Managing the political organization based on each of three mentioned environments (based on the needs, characteristics, goals and missions of each organization) and identifying environmental elements that affect the effectiveness of each organization.	These political organizations must be updated every six months and the report should be submitted to the senior political manager and trustee of the organization.
22		Continuous monitoring of the organization's internal environment, based on environmental monitoring, as well as the goals, characteristics, and strategies of the political organization to identify obstacles and leverage points.	The results of these monitoring should be submitted to the senior political manager and trustee of the organization every three months.
23		Continuous monitoring of other political organizations, based on the environmental ecosystem, as well as the goals, characteristics, and strategies of the organization to identify obstacles and leverage points.	The results of these monitoring should be submitted to the senior political manager and trustee of the organization every three months.
24		Continuous monitoring of the government's external environment, based on the environmental ecosystem as well as the goals, characteristics and strategies of the organization in order to identify obstacles and leverage points.	The results of these monitoring should be submitted to the senior political manager and trustee of the organization every three months.
25	Study and analysis of the documents and missions	Designing an Identity certificate for the political organization, including the history of formation, goals, features, and missions and loading it in the organizational experience panel. It must be available to all members of the organization.	Should be reviewed and updated every year.

(*Continued*)

TABLE 15.1 (*Continued*)

No.	Category	Requirements	Description
		The form layer of an ecosystem	
26		Continuous monitoring of the extent of deviation from the effective implementation of the goals, missions, and fundamental and pre-defined characteristics of the organization. Based on this continuous monitoring, an analysis of the reasons for success or failure in reducing this deviation should be reported.	The results of these monitoring should be submitted to the senior political manager and trustee of the organization every six months.
27		Drawing the desired future of the political organization based on its goals, as well as the possible future of the organization based on the current trend, and analyzing and explaining the factors affecting the existing gap.	The results of these monitoring should be submitted to the senior political manager and trustee of the organization every six months.
28	Technology management	Continuous monitoring of current methods in all departments and areas of the political organization and checking the feasibility of replacing them with more effective and cost-effective methods.	The results of these monitoring should be submitted to the senior political manager and trustee of the organization every six months.
29		Continuous monitoring of the political organization's current and future needs, with existing technologies, based on the goals, missions and characteristics of the organization.	The results of these monitoring should be submitted to the senior political manager and trustee of the organization every six months.
30		Strengthening and continuous development of information technology infrastructures in communicating between different units of the political organization as well as with other organizations and different departments of government through the use of organizational architecture and process management appropriate to the characteristics of the organization.	The report on the provision and continuous development of this infrastructure should be submitted to the senior political management and trustees of each organization every six months.

(*Continued*)

TABLE 15.1 (*Continued*)

No.	Category	Requirements	Description
		The form layer of an ecosystem	
31	Human capital management	Continuous assessment of the organization's needs for human and non-human talents, directly based on the goals, characteristics and mission of the political organization and away from extravagances. The requirement of an academic degree to obtain job positions, without the actual need for that degree, is considered one of the extras. People's expertise should be prioritized, not their educational qualifications.	This needs assessment report should be submitted to the senior political management and trustees of each organization every six months.
32		Continuous planning to discover talents within the organization, based on the goals, characteristics and missions of each organization.	This needs assessment report should be submitted to the senior political management and trustees of each organization every six months.
33		Continuous planning to cultivate talents within the political organization, based on the goals, characteristics and missions of each organization.	This needs assessment report should be submitted to the senior political management and trustees of each organization every six months.
		The content layer of an ecosystem	
34	Structural promotion of values	Continuous monitoring of people and their job positions in terms of specialization compliance. Planning to ensure the injection of expertise in the structure of the political organization, according to the characteristics and performance of people (it should be noted that accurate qualitative and quantitative indicators should be set in accordance with job position of the people).	This monitoring must be continuous and its report should be submitted to the senior political management and trustees of each organization every six months.

(*Continued*)

TABLE 15.1 (*Continued*)

No.	Category	Requirements	Description
		The content layer of an ecosystem	
35		Redefining the types of organizational justice and its dimensions (for example, distributive, procedures, and relations justice) in the form of a charter and planning to localize and implement it in the political organization.	The report on the design and redesign of the justice charter and its planning and implementation must be submitted to the senior political management and trustee of the organization once a year.
36		Continuous monitoring of the process of justice in the organization, based on the charter of justice.	The results of these monitoring should be submitted to the senior manager and trustee of the organization every three months.
37	Individual promotion of values	Planning for maximum organizational coexistence of managers with employees and subordinates which can be determined according to the characteristics of each organization. For instance, in some organizations the distance between the managers' room and ordinary employees can be minimized so that the difference is not noticeable.	The report on this planning and implementation must be submitted to the senior political management and trustee of the organization once a year.
38		Holding interactive and transformational leadership workshops for political managers.	These workshops should be held once a year and their results and the employee feedback should be evaluated at the end of each year through a questionnaire. So, employees measure the leadership style of their managers through standard questionnaires.
39		Continuous planning for organizational and unit socialization of people. Of course, this process should consider the mood of the people.	The report on this planning and implementation must be submitted to the senior political management and trustee of the organization once a year.

(*Continued*)

TABLE 15.1 (*Continued*)

No.	Category	Requirements	Description
		The content layer of an ecosystem	
40		Holding free-thinking meetings to resolve ideological and political doubts of people and managers, without restrictions or censorship.	These meetings must be held once every six months.
41	Daily promotion of values	Planning to hold religious lectures by people who have verbal appeal and attract the audience. Senior managers and trustees of the organization should choose the appropriate times to hold these lectures.	These lectures must be held at least once every two months, and the report of their planning and implementation, as well as the outstanding and significant features and attractions of the speakers, must be submitted to the senior management and the trustee of the organization every six months.
42		Continuous planning to use religious and political symbols in physical and non-physical places related to the organization. The use of these symbols should be based on semiotic knowledge and be consistent with aesthetic elements. Also, these symbols should change continuously to attract attention.	The report on this planning and implementation must be submitted to the senior political management and trustee of the organization once a year.

Recommended reading

Abdulhosseinzadeh, M., & Ghoreishi, M. (2018). *Analysis of the history of reforming the administrative system in Iran.* Tehran: The Research Center of The Islamic Consultative Assembly of IRI. Retrieved from Child Care & Early Education Research Connections: https://doi.org/10.1080/01900699908525410

Abolhasani, A., Daneshfard, K., & Faghihi, A. (2018). An Agenda Setting for the Reformation Policies of Administrative System in Iran. *Journal of Public Administration, 9*(4), 615–640. https://doi.org/10.22059/jipa.2018.248615.2154

Abedi Ardakani, M., & Soltani, L. (2020). The Relationship between the Administrative System and Political Development in the Islamic Republic of Iran Iran (Using the Joghurib Theoretical Model). *Politics, 50*(2), 629–649. https://doi.org/10.22059/jpq.2020.247064.1007185

Mohammadi, H., Alvani, S., Memarzadehtehran, G., & Hamidi, N. (2017). Designing and Developing Iran Administrative system Effectiveness Model. *Journal of Public Administration, 8*(4), 591–616. https://doi.org/10.22059/jipa.2017.62178

References

Abdulhosseinzadeh, M., & Ghoreishi, M. (2018). *Analysis of the history of reforming the administrative system in Iran.* Tehran: The Research Center of The Islamic Consultative Assembly of IRI. Retrieved from Child Care & Early Education Research Connections: https://doi.org/10.1080/01900699908525410

Babaei, S., Vaezi, R., Pourezzat, A., & Hosseinpour, D. (2022). A Meta-Synthesis of Internal and External Factors and Facilitators of The Administrative System Reform. *Public Administration Perspective, 13*(3), 35–71. https://doi.org/10.52547/jpap.2022.226151.1168

Lees-Marshment, J. (2021). *Political Management: The Dance of Government and Politics.* New York: Routledge.

Supreme Council of Administration. (2014, 4 19). *the Road Map for Reforming the Administrative System.* Retrieved from Ministry of Culture and Islamic Guidance: https://nosazi.farhang.gov.ir/fa/filepool/1369

The Expediency Discernment Council of the System. (2019). *The set of general policies announced by the Supreme Leader until 2019.* Tehran: The Secretariat of the Expediency Discernment Council Publication.

The Islamic Consultative Assembly of IRI. (2007, 10 16). *the Civil Service Management Law.* Retrieved from The Research Center of The Islamic Consultative Assembly of IRI: https://rc.majlis.ir/fa/law/show/130021

The Islamic Consultative Assembly of IRI. (2017, 4 15). *the Sixth Five-Year Economic, Social and Cultural Development Plan of the Islamic Republic of Iran (6NPD).* Retrieved from Law and Regulations Portal of Iran: https://dotic.ir/news/364

16

EFFECTIVE LEADERSHIP STYLES IN POLITICS

An Application of Goleman's Typology

Wojciech Cwalina, Maria Naureen Shahid, and Milena Drzewiecka

Introduction

One of the core areas of political management is political leadership and the development of leadership skills (Lees-Marshment, 2021). Political leaders cannot function in democratic political systems until their power gets legitimated, that is, until they gain citizens' support. Political leaders distribute responsibility, empower people and aid deliberations, they also have to know how to construct or reconstruct situations that require public attention. Leadership is perceived not only in terms of personality (*Great Man History theories*), nor in terms of time of action (*Zeitgeist theories*), but also in terms of interaction between leaders and followers. As Tucker (1977, p. 384) states: "A central function of leadership is the defining of situations for the group and the devising of policy responses designed to resolve the problem in accordance with the group's interests as perceived by the leaders and others." The main condition of political leadership then is an ability to influence others to follow a leader willfully.

Unfortunately, politicians have ruined more than they have built, brought suffering and disasters, exacerbated inequality, and made life difficult for those whose livelihoods they want to improve. Political leadership is challenging and hard to understand or manage, which is one of the main reasons this concept has been explained with a wide range of terms. Political analysis of today and global public discourse frequently criticize political leaders and leadership. In addition to other factors, this criticism demonstrates just how essential leaders and leadership are for the functioning of political regimes as a whole and their interactions with one another. This conviction appears to

DOI: 10.4324/9781003260677-16

be broadly supported. In fact, leadership is crucial in terms of setting direction and providing guidance, as well as coming up with answers to shared challenges, due to the ever-increasing complexity of politics in a world that is becoming more interdependent (Helms, 2012).

The goal of this chapter is to identify a profile of ideal political leadership style, as well as to relate it to actual political leaders in nations with varying levels of democratic maturity (Switzerland, Poland, Georgia and Pakistan). The chapter focuses on the development of effective leadership skills, competencies and personal characteristics within a political environment based on Goleman's leadership theory.

Key literature

The success of a politician in a democracy depends on the support he gets from voters during elections. All citizens want their country to be ruled by the best or an almost ideal political leader. However, the following questions arise: What is this "ideal"? What features should the ideal leader have?

Studies on social perception demonstrate that in citizens' minds, an "ideal politician" is a prototype, an example of the category of people professionally dealing with politics (Cwalina et al., 2011). Such a cognitive schema is a reference point for people when passing judgments on candidates running for a certain office or when making voting decisions. For example, Wattenberg (1991) analyzed the evaluations of the personality features of all the candidates running for the U.S. presidency between 1952 and 1988. He found that a candidate's personal attributes can be divided into five general categories: (1) integrity – associated with the candidate's trustworthiness and incorporates comments concerning honesty, sincerity, and any reference to corruption in government; (2) reliability – a candidate being dependable, strong, decisive, aggressive, stable, or the converse of these; (3) competence – refers to a candidate's experience, ability as a statesman, comprehension of political issues, realism, and intelligence: (4) charisma – a candidate's leadership abilities, dignity, humbleness, patriotism, and ability to get along and communicate with people; and (5) personal aspects of the candidate – appearance, age, religion, wealth, former occupation, family, and so on. The results of analyses performed by Wattenberg (1991) showed that in seven cases out of ten, the candidate who got higher ratings in public opinion polls regarding the previously mentioned personality categories won.

The prototype of the "ideal leader" is a reference point for citizens to assess the actual politicians seeking their support. However, this requires forming an impression of what features a given politician has and what features he does not have. The basic source of information that allows for such conclusions is the behavior of politicians. This behavior is, to a large extent, a manifestation of a personal leadership style.

A leader's repetitive practice in building bonds, gathering information, re-acting and making decisions could be described as a leadership style. Lewin, Lippitt and White (1939) in their pioneering work, proposed three styles of leadership: autocratic (strongly focused on command and control), demo-cratic (more participative, offer guidance to their followers) and laissez-fair (leave decisions and goals to group members). The other theories of leader-ship styles built their categorization upon a polarization, for instance, task vs. people orientation, enhancing the role of leader's focus. Task-oriented leaders concentrate on reaching goals as fast as possible, while people-oriented lead-ers set group climate and people's personal development before. Concern for people vs. concern for production built also two main axes of the managerial grid proposed by Blake and Mouton (1964). Among 81 styles derived from combination of leader's behavior, five are most important: (1) country club style (the most concern for people and the least concern for production), (2) impoverished style (the least concern for production and people), (3) team style (high concern on production and people), (4) authority-obedience style (the most concern for production, the least concern for people) and (5) middle-road style (balanced concern for people and production). One of the most common theories of leadership styles was proposed by Burns (1978), who distinguished transactional and transformational leadership. While a trans-formational leader is sensitive to the motives of followers, tries to meet their needs and engage them in achieving common goals, a transactional leader fo-cuses on bargaining with followers, persuading them and getting them to re-ciprocate her favors. According to Burns (1978) Franklin Roosevelt, Lyndon B. Johnson or Charles de Gaulle represented transactional leadership, while Fidel Castro, Mao Zedong, or John F. Kennedy exemplify transformational leadership.

There is a wide variety of leadership style theories as well as studies ex-amining their effectiveness. To answer the question of what constitutes the good/ideal leadership, researchers explore, for example, social skills (Argyle, 1978), self-presentational tactics (Leary, 1996) or competencies and motives (McClelland, 1953). Based upon McClelland's (1953) work on the need for power, affiliation, and achievement, Goleman (2011) proposed six styles of leadership.

Goleman (2011) is well known for his research on emotional intelligence (EI), however, his theories and studies widely presented in business books are not that explored in a political marketing context. Even if political market-ers or scholars deal with Goleman's concept of EI, his leadership style theory based upon EI abilities remains rather silent.

It is still arguing, to which extent EI influences effective leadership, how-ever, there is no doubt that there is a relation between EI and effective leader-ship, at least its transformational style (Barling et al., 2000). Furthermore, EI correlates with achievement in these occupations, which require recognition and response to emotions (Joseph & Newman, 2010). If we agree that dealing with voters' emotions is important if not crucial for political leaders, candidates must be ready not only to control their own emotions but to arouse positive ones. The strong link between affection and voting behavior (Cwalina et al., 2011) makes candidates and their experts responsible for building bonds with the electorate.

Goleman (2011) argues emotional intelligence is "must have" for successful leaders. His leadership style typology includes six styles: coercive ("Do what I tell you"), authoritative ("Come with me"), affiliative ("People come first"), democratic ("What do you think"), pacesetting ("Do it as I do, now") and coaching ("Try this"). The phrases mentioned in brackets are mottos or commands, which characterize leaders of certain leadership style. Each style derives from a certain combination of EI abilities. A brief explanation of each style collates Table 16.1.

TABLE 16.1 Six styles of leadership proposed by Goleman

Leadership style	Leadership Style Characteristics	
	Main characteristics	Underlying EI abilities
Coercive (commanding)	demands immediate compliance, does not let others to work on their own initiative, has an overall negative impact on climate in organization, works well in times of crisis or in the case of problems with workers	drive to achieve, initiative and self-control
Authoritative (visionary)	mobilizes people toward a vision; works exceptionally well, whenever new vision or clear direction is required	self-confidence, empathy, change catalyst
Affiliative	concentrates on harmony and builds emotional bonds; works well, when people face stressful circumstances	empathy, communication, building relationships
Democratic	forges consensus through participation; works successfully, if there is a need to build consensus, or to obtain input from valuable team members	team leadership, communication skills, collaboration
Pacesetting	sets high standards for performance and quickly replace these employees, who do not rise to the occasion; destroys climate, but works effectively with motivated and competent people	conscientiousness, drive to achieve, initiative
Coaching	develops people for the future: works especially well, if there is a need to help others improve their performance or develop long-term strengths	developing others, self-awareness, empathy

Source: Based on Goleman (2011, p. 60; Goleman et al., 2013, pp. 53–88).

According to Goleman (2011), successful leaders are masters of more than one style. The most effective styles are those that have a positive impact on group climate. Coercive and pacesetting leaders score lowest on likeability and support while authoritative, democratic, coaching and affiliative leaders have an overall positive impact on the organization's climate; however, the impact of authoritative leaders is found to be the most positive. Coercive and pacesetting leadership appear to correspond to autocratic, transactional or task-oriented style, whereas authoritative, democratic, coaching and affiliative are related to people-oriented and transformational leadership.

According to Goleman (2011), what makes the biggest distinction between the two groups of styles is their impact on group climate (positive vs. negative). Then, the styles might be considered in terms of two more global and fundamental dimensions of people evaluation: agency (competence) and communion (integrity) (Cwalina & Drzewiecka, 2015, 2019).

Psychological research indicates that primary, universal dimensions of social cognition do include social intent for good or ill (morality or communion) and capability to enact those intentions (competence or agency) (Fiske et al., 2006). Intentions are seen to follow from dispositions. Moral content dominates a person perception because it typically has a direct and unconditional bearing on the well-being of other people surrounding the person who is described by the trait (including the perceiver). Competence (agency) dominates self-perception because it has a direct bearing on the well-being of the perceiver. When forming global evaluations of others, the perceiver is more interested in their moral qualities (communion) than competence (agency); construes their behavior in moral terms, and his or her impressions and emotional responses are more strongly based on morality than competence considerations.

Morality and competence are also the core features of a politician's images that positively and strongly influence voters' behavior toward them (Cwalina et al., 2011). Moreover, there are central qualities of an ideal presidential prototype (Cwalina & Falkowski, 2006).

Methodology

To check whether and if so, how leadership styles proposed by Goleman (2011) are perceived in politics, we conducted a research program consisting of four studies (Cwalina & Drzewiecka, 2015, 2019; Drzewiecka & Cwalina, 2014; Shahid & Cwalina, 2023). The research was conducted in the years 2009–2020 in four countries with different levels of democratic maturity: Switzerland, Poland, Georgia and Pakistan.

Cross-cultural perspective

Poland (European Union member), Switzerland (non-European Union member), Georgia (candidate for future membership in European Union) and

Pakistan are four countries of different political history and at different stage of democracy consolidation (different level of democracy maturity). Switzerland is a federal republic with a unique political system that favors agreement, and with strong direct democracy. Both Poland (now a parliamentary republic) and Georgia (now a representative democratic semi-presidential republic) used to have experience of Soviet dependence, however, Poland – contrary to Georgia – was never a part of the Soviet Union. The collapse of communism in Poland is matched by The Round Table Agreement in 1989 and with first free parliamentary elections in 1991. Although Georgia became independent in 1991, some authors argue, Georgian first serious steps towards modern mature democracy had been taken with parliamentary elections in 2012.

Concerning Democracy Index published by The Economist Intelligence Unit (EIU) (2014), Switzerland displays full democracy, Poland – flawed democracy, Georgia – hybrid regime and Pakistan – a hybrid regime. EIU's Democracy Index, on a 0 to 10 scale, is based on the ratings of 60 indicators grouped in five categories: electoral process and pluralism; civil liberties; the functioning of government; political participation; and political culture. Full democracies (scores of 8 to 10) are these, in which there are only limited problems in the functioning of democracy; political freedoms and liberties are respected, the government is satisfactory, media are independent and diverse, and the system of checks and balances works effectively. Flawed democracies (scores of 6 to 7.9) have also free and fair elections; however, they experience significant weaknesses such as undeveloped political culture or low levels of political participation. In hybrid regimes (scores of 4 to 5.9), elections have substantial irregularities, civil society is weak and government pressure on the opposition as well as on journalists or judiciary is not that rare. The lowest maturity of democracy shows authoritarian regimes (scores below 4) with the absence of political pluralism, state-owned media and no independent judiciary. In authoritarian regimes – often called dictatorships – some formal institutions of democracy may exist but have little substance and elections, if they do occur, are neither free, not fair.

Georgia is gaining on its democracy maturity as its score raised from 4.62 in 2008 to 5.95 in 2013 (the year of the Study 2 conduction). Although, there was no EIU's Democracy Index published in 2009 (the year of the Study 1 conduction), analysis of scores across a few years shows that positions of Poland and Switzerland remain quite stable in the index. Polish score was 7.30 in 2008, 7.05 in 2010 and 7.12 in 2013 while Swiss: 9.15 in 2008, 9.09 in 2010 and 9.09 in 2013.

Pakistan's analysis of democracy maturity since 2008 (when the score was 4.46) reveals a slight improvement up till 2013–2014. Then the score began to decline. Democracy maturity score decreased from 4.64 in 2013 to 4.31 in 2020–2021 (the year of the study conduction). According to its constitution, Pakistan is a democratic parliamentary republic with an elected form of government. Since its independence, Pakistan's political system has alternated between civilian and military regimes at various times. Democracy has endured to varying degrees all this time, despite its flaws.

Methods

The research program consists of four studies: one experiment (Poland vs. Switzerland) and three surveys (in Poland, Georgia and Pakistan).

The experimental study in Poland and Switzerland was conducted online in 2009. The sample comprised 136 Swiss participants (64 females and 72 males; mean age: 27.5 years) and 178 Polish participants (84 females, 94 males; mean age: 32.6). The questionnaire with the stimulus material was available at a website specially designed for this purpose. After entering the website, the subjects were randomly assigned to the experimental conditions. Information about the study was disseminated using social media (including students.ch, 123people.ch, and Facebook). Moreover, in Switzerland the request to participate in the study was addressed to students associated with the Swiss branch of ESN - an organization that takes care of students of the Erasmus program, and in Poland – to participants of a training project carried out by a professional company.

In each country, participants were randomly divided into six groups based on the typology of six leadership styles proposed by Goleman (2011), so that each participant got a description of political leader written along with one of the leadership style characteristics (traits and behaviors), and applied to political leaders activity. No political name or party affiliation was mentioned. Each description started with a sentence "X is a leader of one of the Polish/Swiss parties."

After reading the political leader description, subjects were, among other things, asked to evaluate leader's image with 14 semantic differential scales (e.g., professional-amateurish, trustworthy-untrustworthy, efficient-inefficient, honest-dishonest). The objective of this question was to obtain voters' perceptions of certain leadership styles. Participants were also asked to express the intention to vote for a candidate from the party led by the leader whose description they have read (where 1 – *definitely not*, and 5 – *definitely yes*).

The online surveys carried out in Poland, Georgia and Pakistan had the same structure, differing only in the specific politicians and parties to which participants responded. The link to the questionnaires was shared with responses on Twitter, Facebook groups, and customized emails. The questionnaire comprised three main parts: (1) demographics and political involvement, (2) leadership style perception, and (3) leadership style preferences. To obtain voters' perceptions we asked participants to evaluate ideal president's leadership styles and these displayed by real political leaders in reference to each style from Goleman's typology (coercive, authoritative, democratic, affiliative, pacesetting, coaching). Short characteristics (traits and behaviors applied to political activity) of six styles were given and with regard to each of the styles, the respondents were asked to determine to what extent (7-point scale, where 1 – *definitely not*, and 7 – *definitely yes*) a given style characterizes each of the listed political leaders. The list of leaders was country specific and consisted of presidents, prime ministers and party leaders represented within parliament.

The studies in Poland (103 females and 90 males, aged between 19 and 70) and Georgia (58 females and 40 males, aged between 18 and 67) were conducted at the end of 2013 and in 2014. In turn, the survey in Pakistan was carried out between July and November 2020 (139 females and 214 males, aged between 18 and 60).

Research findings

The purpose of the analysis of data collected in four studies was to identify a profile of ideal political leadership style, as well as to relate it to actual political leaders in nations with varying levels of democratic maturity (Switzerland, Poland, Georgia and Pakistan).

Leadership style perception and preferences: Poland vs. Switzerland

In a cross-cultural comparative experimental study conducted in Poland (European Union member/flawed democracy) and Switzerland (non-European Union member/full democracy), it was found that voters recognize Goleman's leadership styles in the political area. Voters were able to match coercive, pacesetting, authoritative, democratic, coaching and affiliative styles of leadership with party leaders; however, their perception varied between countries (Drzewiecka & Cwalina, 2014).

Perceptual maps (separately for Polish and Swiss samples) computed with exploratory principal component analyses yielded two-factor solutions, explaining 56.76% of the total variance in the Polish sample, and 53.45% in the Swiss sample. These two factors are consistent with two fundamental dimensions underlying social judgments: communion/morality (warmth, cooperation) and agency/competence (experience, ambition). These two dimensions indicate a coordinate system, which serves as a perceptual map of six leadership styles. The perceptual maps of leadership styles are presented in Figure 16.1 for Poland and Figure 16.2 for Switzerland.

Concerning location of six leadership styles on perceptual maps we see, that Polish as well as Swiss voters perceive leaders of democratic and coaching styles similarly. Coaching leaders are perceived as highly competent and cooperative (especially by Polish voters) while democratic leaders are perceived as highly cooperative and quite competent. Location of democratic

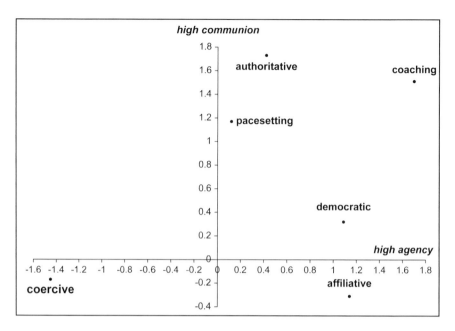

FIGURE 16.1   Perceptual maps of leadership styles (Poland)

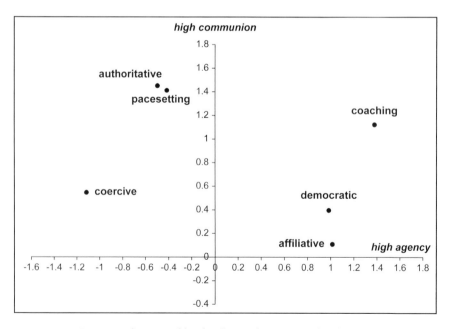

FIGURE 16.2   Perceptual maps of leadership styles (Switzerland)

leadership is nearly 100% the same for both samples, which enables us to assume, that the image of a democratic style of leadership might be constant cross-culturally. Other styles of leadership, however, are perceived differently, at least in one dimension. Affiliative leaders are perceived by both groups as high in the agency, however, Swiss voters perceive this style of leadership as slightly cooperative while Polish – as slightly uncooperative. Similarly, authoritative leaders are perceived by both groups as highly focused on others and their well-being (high level of the community); however, in the eyes of Polis voters, these leaders are also quite competent, while in the eyes of Swiss- they are rather incompetent. Coercive leaders are perceived to have a low level of competence; however, Polish voters do not see any communion qualities in this kind of leadership contrary to Swiss voters. Pacesetting leaders although relatively similar and cooperative in the eyes of voters of both countries, are diversely perceived in terms of agency (Swiss voters perceive pacesetting leaders as not competent, while Polish as at least a little bit competent).

Concerning voting intention, results of analysis of covariance showed that in Poland as well as in Switzerland voting intention for a political party depends on the leadership style displayed by the party leader. No matter what parties offered in their programs, voters in Poland preferred parties led by coaching, authoritative and democratic leaders. In Switzerland, voters preferred parties led by affiliative and democratic leaders. Moreover, the results correspond in general to what Goleman (2011) found in the business area, where coercive and pacesetting leadership styles do not gain such positive ratings as democratic, coaching, affiliative and authoritative leaders do.

It might sound strange to argue this, especially after the victory of right-oriented party Law and Justice (Prawo i Sprawiedliwość) in presidential and parliamentary elections in Poland, in 2015, as the party is well known for its coercive leader Jarosław Kaczyński. However, it should be remembered that in the 2015 political campaigns, his figure and style were barely presented. Polish people voted for "Good change" (campaign parole) personified by Beata Szydło in parliamentary elections or Andrzej Duda in presidential elections. First became prime minister, and second won the presidency. Both were presented as cooperation and good climate builders. To check whether Polish voters found Szydlo's and Duda's leadership style as more democratic, affiliative, authoritative or coaching leaders, further research would be needed. However, there is no doubt, images of both were built upon communion (morality/integrity). Coercive or pacesetting elements were stressed neither in campaign videos nor in political debates. In this sense, marketers of the PiS campaign responded to voters' needs with such political leadership style image (president and prime minister, respectively) the electorate was dreaming of. This example shows again, how important it is to create a proper image of the candidate and what power candidate's image has. But do people want a different president's leadership style from that of the prime minister's?

Politicians' ideal leadership style: Poland vs. Georgia

One of the aims of the surveys carried out in two post-communist countries, Poland (European Union member/flawed democracy) and Georgia (non-European Union member/hybrid regime), was to try to find an answer to the question, what leadership style voters expect from an "ideal" president and prime minister (Cwalina & Drzewiecka, 2015, 2019).

Comparison of data analysis results from both countries shows sharp differences in voters' expectations of ideal president's and ideal prime minister's leadership style. Results of four analyses of variance with six styles (coercive vs. authoritative vs. affiliative vs. democratic vs. pacesetting vs. coaching) as repeated measures are presented in Figures 16.3 and 16.4 for Polish and Georgian samples, respectively.

In the Polish sample, the leadership style of the ideal president was identified as coaching, while in the case of ideal prime minister – authoritative. Moreover, expectations toward ideal president's leadership style were significantly different from expectations toward the ideal prime minister's leadership style. The ideal president should be more affiliative, democratic and – marginally – coaching in comparison with the ideal prime minister. On the other hand, the ideal prime minister should be more coercive, authoritative and less pacesetting than the ideal president.

In the Georgian sample, voters expected the ideal president to display affiliative and coaching leadership style, while the prime minister – coaching.

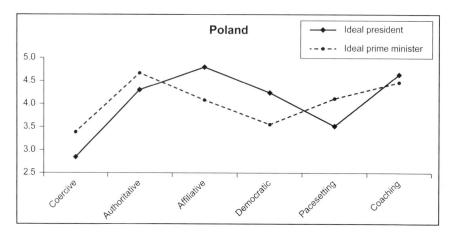

FIGURE 16.3 Expectations of ideal president's and ideal prime minister's leadership style in Poland

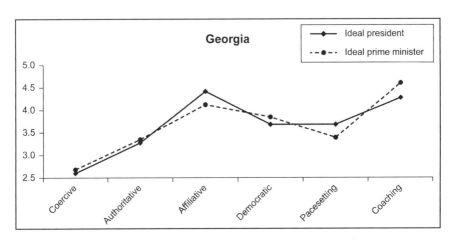

FIGURE 16.4 Expectations of ideal president's and ideal prime minister's leadership style in Georgia

Furthermore, the ideal president should be more affiliative and pacesetting, and marginally less coaching in comparison to the prime minister. Other differences occurred to be statistically insignificant. Moreover, Polish voters expected to a greater extent than Georgian voters for their ideal president to be authoritative, democratic, affiliative and coaching, and for the ideal prime minister- to display coercive, authoritative and pacesetting leadership style. All these differences were found statistically significant.

These differences in leadership style expectations show again, how much attention image makers and marketers should pay not only to what voters expect from a political leader in general but from a political leader for a certain post, in a certain political system and moreover, in certain political culture. Even a highly successful image campaign made in one country might fail in another one. Although voters' dream of a competent and moral leader seems to be universal, the proportions of abilities and traits displayed on these two dimensions do not have to be that universal. The mentioned study in Poland and Georgia showed, for instance, that Polish voters expect from their president more warmth and cohesiveness (communion) than competence and ambition (agency). Agency remains as important as communion in the case of the Polish ideal prime minister. In Georgia, however, voters' expectations from the ideal president and ideal prime minister seem to remain nearly the same: the agency is not as important as communion.

Political parties and managers got used to build campaigns upon leader's image. In most cases it seems to be right, however in some – exposing leaders and their styles might lower the appeal of the party and its program. The results show that a leader and his style are not always an asset for a party as long as voters do not have his party identification.

Politicians' ideal leadership style: Pakistan

Pakistan is a state with a lower level of democratic maturity than European nations. In the survey, the respondents were asked, among other things, to assess the leadership styles of ideal politicians and real ones (Shahid & Cwalina, 2023). The list of real political leaders contained country's most renowned political figures from the three mainstream parties namely Pakistan Muslim League Nawaz (PML-N), Pakistan People's Party (PPP) and Pakistan Tehreek e Insaf (PTI). Included in the list were Imran Khan (Chairman, PTI); Zulfiqar Ali Bhutto (former President of Pakistan and founder of PPP); Benazir Bhutto (former Prime Minister of Pakistan and chairman PPP); Asif Ali Zardari (former President of Pakistan and chairman PPP); Nawaz Sharif (former Prime Minister of Pakistan and founder PML-N); and, Shahbaz Sharif (current leader of the opposition in the National Assembly of Pakistan, former Chief Minister of Punjab province and current President PML-N). Two of them, Zulfiqar Ali Bhutto and Benazir Bhutto, have passed away but they are still very much alive in Pakistani politics.

Factor analysis yielded two-factor solutions explaining 79.67% of the total variance such that: factor 1 (*communion*) comprised affiliative, democratic, pacesetting, coaching and authoritative styles (68.16%), and factor 2 (*agency*) comprised coercive leadership style only (11.51%). These two factors correspond, then, with two fundamental dimensions underlying social judgments: communion (integrity, cooperation, support) and agency (competence, ambition, control).

The perceptual maps of politicians based on evaluations of their leadership styles are presented in Figure 16.5 (responses of all 353 respondents).

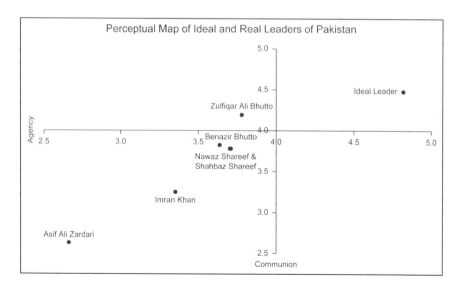

FIGURE 16.5 Perceptual map of ideal and real Pakistani political leaders

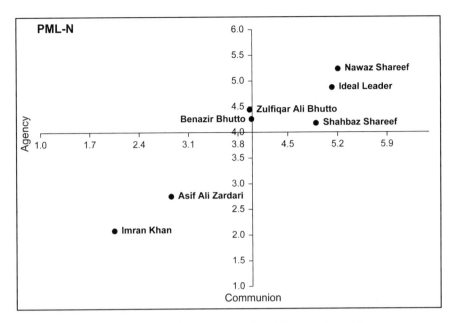

FIGURE 16.6 Perceptual map of ideal and political leaders from PML-N

It appears from the ideal leader position on the perceptual map that electorates expect both communion (integrity, reliability, trust) and agency (competence, ambition, and control) from an ideal leader. While all of the political leaders appear to lack communion abilities. Pakistani voters want a leader who has both communion (integrity, reliability, and trust) as well as agency (competence, ambition, and control).

To verify if the party leader has a significant influence on the electorates and influences the way electorates perceive the leaders, the data were divided into three groups (representing each of the three parties). And the tests were run on each of the groups. Results showed that the leadership of PML-N (Figure 16.6) and PTI (Figure 16.7) are perceived as close to the respondent's ideal leader. Outcomes for the PPP (Figure 16.8) leadership came out unexpectedly differently from what was anticipated, particularly because Zulfiqar Ali Bhutto and Benazir Bhutto (late) became the two most prominent political figures to date. The perception about the ideal leader, Zulfiqar Ali Bhutto and Benazir Bhutto depicts that electorates assess them on competence, mostly.

One striking discovery was that the second factor appeared to be built just using coercive tactics (i.e., agency). While pacesetting (which is the exhibition of the highest level of diligence) is associated with a negative influence on the group performance and is also considered as an agency factor, it has appeared to be a communion factor, in this study. This indicates that Pakistan's perspective of leadership style is different from that of Poland and Georgia.

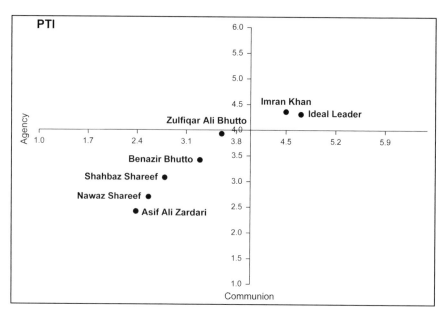

FIGURE 16.7   Perceptual map of ideal and political leaders from PTI

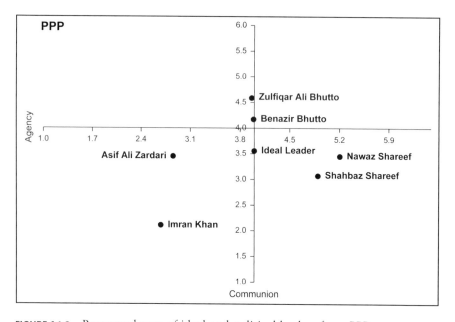

FIGURE 16.8   Perceptual map of ideal and political leaders from PPP

Coercive leaders are eager to take initiative, ready to act, and motivated to raise performance to satisfy high criteria of perfection and are good at managing their emotions and impulses. The difference in the results between this study and the studies carried out in Poland and Georgia could be because of the cultural, social, and emotional diversity among the general public.

Influence of leadership style displayed by the political leader on his/her evaluation, party evaluation and voting intention is a complex problem. Results of different studies confirm leadership style influences party and leader evaluation. Concerning Goleman's (2011) leadership style typology, voters – similarly to subordinates in a business area – prefer leaders with a style with a positive influence on group climate. The perception of certain styles, however, might vary cross-culturally.

The other factor managers should take into account is to what extent voters expect competence (agency) and morality (communion) from individual leaders. As it was shown, proportions could vary depending on whether people vote in presidential or parliamentary elections. The ideal image of president's leadership style might vary from expectations toward prime minister's leadership style, depending on the democratic maturity level and political system. It is worth mentioning that all studies described here were conducted in democratic countries in peace. Political campaigns in a time of crisis have their own dynamic and require candidates to display different traits and abilities than in peaceful time (e.g., Volodymyr Zelenskyy, president of Ukraine before and after the aggression by Russia). Changing political and economic conditions often change voters' preferences toward leadership. It is the role of political leaders as well as managers to recognize and react to these changes. As parties need to select a theme that is convergent with voters' wishes, so the political candidate needs to develop such leadership style (or at least its image), which makes connections with the voters and their "dreams" and sets a contrast between that leader and his opponents. The "shift from citizenship to spectatorship" (Harris, 2001, p. 35) and from a party to a leader, sets the question not which but how a candidate's leadership style should be accentuated? Studies results described in this chapter show that citizens in countries as diverse as Poland, Georgia, Pakistan and Switzerland favor authoritative, democratic, coaching and affiliative styles. This favor might be transferred to the leader's party support, no matter how the political program looks (Drzewiecka & Cwalina, 2014).

Recommendations for research

The chapter adds to the body of knowledge of leadership style preferences, and demonstrates the influence a leader's style may have on his success in elections and governance. It also opens a discussion on people preferred affiliative, democratic, authoritative and coaching style more than coercive and pacesetting. It is worth considering whether Goleman's (2011) typology of six styles cannot be reduced to two-three, as the preferences are usually based upon distinction: positive vs. negative influence on group climate. This, however, does not spoil Goleman's theory in total. The leadership abilities outlined here do matter. Emotional intelligence abilities of a leader do matter. On the one hand, it agrees with the assumption that people vote more with their hearts than with their minds and with the connection between affection and voting (Cwalina et al., 2011). On the other one, it might make managers concentrated on leader's style development, staying blind for other variables influencing party evaluation and voting intention. Are effective political leadership styles the same in times of peace and war? Does the ideological orientation of politicians and voters affect leadership style expectations? What "should" be a conservative and what "should" be a liberal leader? These questions indicate further areas, the empirical exploration of which can contribute to the development of both the theory of leadership and practical guidelines for conducting politics in a modern, democratic world.

Recommendations for practice

From a political management perspective, leadership will never be an exact science. But neither should it be a complete mystery to those who practice it. When developing the capabilities of politicians, consultants should take into account voters' expectations. What degree of competence (agency) and morality (communion) do voters expect from political leaders? What styles of political leadership are preferred by voters, and which of them (or their mix) increases the chances of electoral success and effective governance of the country?

The consultants should also remember that the ideal leadership style of the president might vary from expectations toward the prime minister's leadership style, depending on democracy maturity level and political system. Furthermore, governance and political campaigns in a time of crisis have their own dynamic and require candidates to display different traits and abilities than in peaceful time. It is the role of political managers to recognize and react to these changes by developing the candidate's leadership skills adapted to the circumstances and needs of citizens.

Leaders establish strategy, motivate people, establish missions, and develop cultures. The sole duty of the leader is to achieve outcomes. The question of what a leader can and should do to encourage the highest performance from their followers has long been a riddle. Goleman (2011) accentuated the significance of emotional intelligence in leadership. In his view, the key characteristic that unites the most effective leaders is that they all possess a high level of emotional intelligence. Not that intelligence and technical proficiency are unimportant. These are important, but they are also the prerequisites for executive roles.

Aligned with what Goleman professes and existing scholarship, the results of the research presented in this chapter have proven that individually, the six styles may have a distinct and direct influence on the politician's performance and perception. However, leaders who achieve the highest results don't rely just on one type of leadership. Depending on the political scenario, they use several styles or all of the styles efficiently and to varying degrees, in a given period. Our results have shown that the optimum performance and effective positioning is created by leaders who have mastered any or all four or more leadership styles, particularly the *authoritative*, *democratic*, *affiliative*, and *coaching* styles.

Therefore, the most effective leaders can quickly and easily change between many leadership philosophies. Instead of adjusting their style to fit a predetermined set of circumstances, leaders should move much more freely between the styles. They need to learn and train to effortlessly modify their manner of functioning to achieve political goals. Unfortunately, not every leader is knowledgeable on how to apply all six styles. In such situations, the leader can build a team/party with candidates/politicians who have styles that the leader does not possess. For instance, a party leader can assign the task of improving the political offering's performance standards to a member of his team or party who is skilled at using an authoritative tone, while a politician who is good at pacesetting (with the changing political environment/scenario) to always accompanied the leader on the implementation of significant tasks and policy formulation.

The other idea that Goleman has encouraged which could be applied to political leaders is to identify their weak areas and train themselves to diversify their arsenal of styles. To do this, we believe that political leaders must begin by identifying the emotional intelligence skills that underlie the leadership philosophies/styles/attitudes that they lack. Good affiliative political leaders appear as the masters of interpersonal interactions and social communications. This is especially true when it comes to speaking and doing the correct and appropriate thing, and/or making the appropriate political gestures at the proper time. Hence, if the political leadership style tends to be pacesetting and the situation requires the leader to be able to employ the affiliative style more frequently, the political leader should work on developing empathy as well as interpersonal and communication abilities.

The foundation of the most crucial political acumen, administrative, and strategic intelligence, is attention (Goleman et al., 2013). Therefore, paying attention is one of a political leader's main responsibilities. Political leaders need to practice self-focus to achieve this objective and to improve his/her arsenal of styles. When a leader is able to comprehend, regulate, and sympathize with the emotions of the party members, their followers as well as their own, they tend to be very good relationship managers.

Emotional intelligence has an influence on the emotional competence of a leader. Any leader's capacity to learn the skills that are built around emotional intelligence's five components (self-awareness, motivation, self-regulation, empathy, and relationship competence), is influenced by his/her emotional intelligence. His/her emotional competence demonstrates how much of that potential has been turned into practical skills. We believe that emotionally intelligent leaders are good listeners who are open to feedback/criticism, have a will to improve their arsenal of skills, understand their and party's core competencies and try to reach out to the people to solve their problems, satisfy their needs to win them over and know when to be tough and how to build a network of allies to collaborate with for the achievement of the larger objectives.

Recommended reading

Burns, J.M. (1978). *Leadership*. New York: Harper and Row Publishers.
Cwalina, W., Falkowski, A., Newman, B.I. (2011). *Political marketing: Theoretical and strategic foundations*. New York: M.E. Sharpe.
Goleman, D. (2011). *Leadership: The power of emotional intelligence. Selected writings*. Northampton: More Than Sound.
Helms, L. (ed.) (2012). *Comparative political leadership*. London: Palgrave Macmillan.
Lees-Marshment, J. (2021). *Political management: The dance of government and politics*. Abingdon: Routledge.

References

Argyle, M. (1978). *The psychology of interpersonal behaviour*. Harmondsworth: Penguin.
Barling, J., Salter, F., & Kelloway, E.K. (2000). Transformational leadership and EI: An exploratory study. *Leadership & Organizational Development Journal*, 21(3), 157–161.
Blake, R.R., & Mouton, J.S. (1964). *The managerial grid*. Houston: Gulf Publishing Company.
Burns, J.M. (1978). *Leadership*. New York: Harper and Row Publishers.
Cwalina, W., & Drzewiecka, M. (2015). Ideal president like ideal boss? Looking for preferences of political leadership style: Cross-cultural study in Goleman's typology. *Przedsiębiorczość i Zarządzanie*, 16(3), 99–115.
Cwalina, W., & Drzewiecka, M. (2019). Who are the political leaders we are looking for? Candidate positioning in terms of leadership style. A cross-cultural study in Goleman's typology. *Journal of Political Marketing*, 18(4), 344–359.
Cwalina, W., & Falkowski, A. (2006). Political communication and advertising in Poland. In L.L. Kaid and C. Holtz-Bacha (eds.), *The Sage handbook of political advertising* (pp. 325–342). Thousand Oaks: Sage Publications.
Cwalina, W., Falkowski, A., & Newman, B.I. (2011). *Political marketing: Theoretical and strategic foundations*. New York: M.E. Sharpe.
Drzewiecka, M., & Cwalina, W. (2014). What political leadership styles do we prefer? Cross-cultural study in Goleman's typology of leadership. In *SCIECONF – Proceedings in Scientific Conference*, 2(1), 161–166.

Fiske, S.T., Cuddy, A.J.C., & Glick, P. (2006). Universal dimensions of social cognition: Warmth and competence. *TRENDS in Cognitive Sciences*, 11(2), 77–83.

Goleman, D. (2011). *Leadership: The power of emotional intelligence. Selected writings.* Northampton: More Than Sound.

Goleman, D., Boyatzis, R., & McKee, A. (2013). *Primal leadership: Unleashing the power of emotional intelligence.* Boston: Harvard Business Review Press.

Harris, P. (2001). To spin or not to spin-that is the question: The emergence of modern political marketing. *Marketing Review*, 2(1), 35–53.

Helms, L. (2012). Introduction: The importance of studying political leadership comparatively. In L. Helms (ed.), *Comparative political leadership* (pp. 1–24). London: Palgrave Macmillan.

Joseph, D.L., & Newman, D.A. (2010). Emotional intelligence: An integrative meta-analysis and cascading model. *Journal of Applied Psychology*, 95(1), 54–78.

Leary, M. (1996). *Self-presentation: Impression management and interpersonal behavior.* Boulder, CO: Westview Press.

Lees-Marshment, J. (2021). *Political management: The dance of government and politics.* Abingdon: Routledge.

Lewin, K., Lippitt, R., & White, R.K. (1939). Patterns of aggressive behavior in experimentally created "social climates." *Journal of Social Psychology*, 10(2), 271–299.

McClelland, D.C. (1953). *The achieving society.* Princeton, NY: D. Van Nostrand Company.

Shahid, M.N., & Cwalina, W. (2023). Pakistani political leaders: A cross-sectional study in Goleman's typology. *Manuscript prepared for publication.*

The Economist Intelligence Unit (2014). *Democracy Index 2013. Democracy in limbo. A Report from The Economist Intelligence Unit.* http://www.eiu.com/public/topical_report.aspx?campaignid=Democracy0814.

Tucker, R.C. (1977). Personality and political leadership. *Political Science Quarterly*, 92(3), 383–393.

Wattenberg, M.P. (1991). *The rise of candidate-centered politics: Presidential elections of the 1980s.* Cambridge, MA: Harvard University Press.

17

MANAGING POLITICS AND GOVERNMENT

Recommendations for Research and Practice

Jennifer Lees-Marshment, Mark Bennister, Todd Belt, Caroline Fisher, André Turcotte, and Ashley Weinberg

Introduction

Political Management in practice has demonstrated that there is a strong need for political management – both more research and improved practice – but that standard HRM practices do not easily transfer to politics in practice. The book has provided insights from in-depth analysis of political management around the world including the UK, the US, Canada, Australia, Sweden, New Zealand, the Philippines, Germany, Czech Republic, Switzerland, Poland, Georgia, Pakistan and Iran. It draws on rich new empirical data, including interviews with practitioners, surveys, participant observation, public opinion data as well as analysis of politician and party policies and statements. This research shows that the core principles of managing people effectively remain crucial to both effectiveness and wellbeing whether it is a campaign, party, political office or government, but they have to be integrated into the political environment. However scholarship and the development of standards for the practice of political management needs to be geared to the specific political environment, rather than just transplanting or extending public service or business concepts to the political arena.

In this chapter, we summarise the key research findings, and synthesise the recommendations for practice and future research and reflect on the democratic need for better political management. With this we hope to provide a sense of direction for both the community of practitioners and field of research of political management.

DOI: 10.4324/9781003260677-17

Key research findings

The case for political management

The research in this book confirmed the strong need for effective political management.

Political workplaces are precarious, fast-paced, unpredictable, long hours and insecure jobs can be lost at any moment if a minister loses their position or an election campaign is lost. The extreme reality that political practitioners face is well below what supports optimal individual functioning, which also mitigates against effective government. Yet the increasingly rapid speed of communication within a highly digitised media environment means that there is also a need for greater management of overall political messaging from political parties, both for individual politicians to coordinate with their party and for the party to recognise and tailor messaging to the idiosyncrasies of each senator's constituency. And for those running governments, all around the world managing the media is a necessity, not an option. Pop-up grassroots-driven political protest movements propelled by social media have now added another source of unpredictability that disrupts conventional political decision-making and communication management. Additionally, voters in democracies are not only demanding but able to clearly identify differing leadership styles including more authoritarian approaches and may reject or kick a leader out if they don't adopt a desired style. Such a challenging environment makes the case for good management even stronger.

Party managers therefore engage in ongoing management activities to maintain organisational long-term health – rather than just focus on winning individual elections – as they have to adapt to a constantly changing environment. This involves "invisible" party management – and complex range of activities. Even more organic movements utilise traditional management elements such as personnel and skills training, communications support and good-old fashioned message discipline are valuable.

Once in power, political leaders set priorities and some smartly go make more effort to be strategic and plan effectively, such as by creating delivery and strategy units to create policy making and delivery processes to achieve strategic government aims. They also deploy a variety of leadership traits to be successful in differing political, cultural, and economic situations and in particular a crisis where they need to use specific tools to achieve success. The most effective leaders can quickly and easily change between many leadership philosophies the optimum performance and effective positioning is created by leaders who have mastered multiple leadership styles.

It is also vital to recruit people fit for purpose into those who work behind the politicians – political advisers or staffers – as they are an invaluable resource and crucial to sustaining political leaders in power. Better systems of support are needed for advisers to enhance the performance of political offices and create more welcoming and supportive workplaces.

The need for improvement in political management practice

The research also identified limitations in the standards of political management in practice and many areas where improvements are needed.

There is often a lack of strategic and coordinated thinking and behaviour in parties and government. For example, research found that there is sometimes a significant gap in the Czech parties' work on developing the membership base, creating analytical teams, and supporting politicians in public relations. US parties have struggled to implement a clear vision in political party organisations, not just because of the federated and decentralised nature of US parties but the limited influence the parties continue to have over the policy choices of their candidates, even when the party controls the presidency. There is an overall lack of clear coordination within political parties, and US Senatorial candidates resist central party message coordination, even when they are the out-party and need to align as a party. There is also a lack of strategic planning in government, which is then seen in policy failures such as the NHS IT programme in the UK. A lack of overall planning entrenches a silo mentality that hinders collaborative policy development and in turn responses to events such as war, economic shocks and a pandemic.

Additionally, the management of politicians and their staff and advisers needs more work to be up to standard. The methods used to recruit and select staff is problematic – whilst the temptation to reward loyalty in one situation is a touchstone of politics more widely, it does not confer suitability for the job and tends to entrench a lack of diversity. The absence of open recruitment processes makes for an appointment system that is often broken and at the very least sub-optimum. Poor selection processes are exacerbated by lack of training and preparation for the job, poor pay, little recognition and bad management and lack of leadership and HR support. The organisational culture within political offices is often problematic the work is both stimulating and difficult; hopeful and harrowing. Whilst the work of politician's staffers is rewarding it is also emotionally draining.

However the performance management for MPs is also very limited. Whilst there have been ad hoc efforts they not surprisingly have yielded ad hoc results. Without some kind of performance evaluation, promotions will be left in the hands of the leadership team and poor performance is often times overlooked. Perhaps not surprisingly then, those who ascend to the position of party leader or prime minister vary in their ability to deploy necessary skills. In particular, individual leaders' ability to have and use skills required in a crisis varies from one case to another. For example, New Zealand Prime Minister Ardern was able to achieve success in the fight against COVID-19, both from a policy perspective and a public perspective, by excelling along the different tasks of public management but German Chancellor Angela Merkel's handling of the Syrian refugee crisis her neglect at involving stakeholders limited her effectiveness.

Complications from over-management or too much control

At the same time, there are complications and downsides to trying to exert too much management – or at least too much control.

If political leaders exert too much control it can backfire. Overly centralised organisation and a hierarchy of roles in the organisation may severely unbalance the relative weight of different categories of staff and create tensions among staffers. Extended control also hinders information sharing, despite the need for close collaboration between different political practitioners in a time of crisis. In cases such as the Freedom Convoy protests in Canada, information silos and lack of information coordination prevented political leaders from having a full understanding of public sentiment. Whereas it can be better to decentralise, as seen in the ability of the Robredo campaign in the Philippines to create and manage "decentralised volunteers." They supported volunteers without imposing too much control, using social media to let the volunteer campaign grow organically.

Thus management concepts, whilst vital in political and government, do need to be adapted and applied with care. Effective democratic practice can only be enhanced through adopting and adapting key HR principles for bespoke frameworks and positive change. Academically, there is the need for agile cross-disciplinary conceptualisation to produce appropriate frameworks that will be positively meaningful to the practitioners carrying out these roles.

Recommendations for future practice

Think long term not short term

The most important advice for practitioners is to take a long-term perspective to political management and consider the impact of how political management is used beyond one campaign or parliamentary term.

We can see this in a range of areas. For example, the work involved in ensuring political parties can be successful is not limited to election campaigns. Party managers need to utilise ongoing management activities to maintain organisational long-term health instead of just focusing on winning individual elections. They also need to set long-term goals related to the party's development in the long term.

Moreover, there needs to be more thinking about the impact of management approaches beyond just one short leadership term or electoral term.

Actions to exert control may appear to have short-term benefits but eventually cause multiple negative consequences such as loss of organisational reputation and trust that not only leads to losing the next election but makes it harder for the party to rebuild its reputation under a new leader afterward. Similarly, any party leader who wants to ensure their vision will actually be implemented should involve the whole party in developing it and creating a unique vision statement outlining both the short and longer-term policy and political objectives, rather than just imposing their view. They also need to offer candidates incentives to get behind the new vision, such as informational and financial resources. This will help to synchronise both local and national party and candidate policy messaging.

Politicians and political staffers also need to be more strategic in government. Indeed, better preparation and planning for strategic policy management should start in opposition, and then increase once in government. Strategic thinking needs to be embedded throughout a range of areas, including policy development, delivery, crisis management and HRM for political staffers/advisers and politicians. This requires prioritising, creating and resourcing fit for purpose political management. In the UK, a House of Commons (2023) liaison sub-committee is currently undergoing an inquiry into scrutiny of strategic thinking across the Government in light of big cross-cutting challenges such as pandemics, artificial intelligence and climate change. As the Chair of the Liaison Committee, Sir Bernard Jenkin MP, said: "major events such as Brexit, covid-19 and Ukraine demonstrate the need for long-term planning and delivery across multiple departments and across the duration of several Parliaments…the Government needs to be more agile in its ambition – and it should also be coordinated across departments and sustainable over time."

Prioritise and advocate for bespoke HRM and improved working conditions in politics

Thinking more strategically and long-term also leads to the need to prioritise the creation and use of bespoke HR structures, processes and practices. Best practice is to create a dedicated and expert team composed of political staffers, public servants and HR experts to develop and deliver bespoke processes, policies, job descriptions, orientation and training to suit the political workplace.

Good management requires investment of time and politics is no different. Governments and parties need to adopt human resource management practices and principles as standard for all MPs' staff, to help ensure fair and reasonable practices and build sustainable teams. Using professional processes to recruit and select people will increase the chances of having staff in post who actually have the competencies the jobs require. And effective management once people get into their post will help them survive and thrive as individuals but in turn increase the functional effectiveness of political offices. Appropriate training is also necessary for politicians and political staff to work effectively is also important for building healthy and trusting employment relationships, that feed into career development, facilitates engagement and retention in an otherwise insecure employment relationship (with elections always a possibility). Even the performance evaluation of MPs should not be left to the voters; appropriate feedback and development is needed for everyone who works in politics and government.

There should also be greater recognition and reward. Political practitioners confront greater career instability than their corporate and public sector colleagues. Therefore efforts should be made by political management staff to increase their career security, even though this may be difficult to achieve given that political practitioners serve at the pleasure of the politician or party that they work for. Paying political staff a wage commensurate with the skills required will positively impact turnover, reduce loss of valuable co-workers and minimise the need for retraining costs.

Professionalisation of political practice actually saves time in the long run as it supports higher functioning staff, offices, politicians and ministers and reduces problems that can damage not just individuals but democracy as a whole. It reduces the potential for causes of grievance. And it goes some way to mitigate the challenges of the political workplace by developing appropriate support systems. Mental health training and developing physical and psychological safeguards both in person and online is paramount in what can be an increasingly volatile and potentially toxic social media-led environment.

Coordination and management of information

More effort should be made to cultivate and boost dissemination and preservation of institutional knowledge/memory in the political world. There is also a need for better and co-ordinated market intelligence to better reflect online sentiment and shape responses, especially when unpredictable events develop. Data needs to be gathered with a purpose in mind to avoid data paralysis and provide political leaders with actionable information to guide decision-making. Political organisations need to organise their different functions in line with their mission to increase their effectiveness and functioning.

Anyone involved in managing others needs to model and use good practices

In campaigns, professional political managers need to be built to strengthen campaign teams and party organisations. They need to be able to build an effective volunteer team before major campaigns start.

Senior staff such as Chiefs of Staff and politicians involved in line management need to be more aware of the role they need to play and reflect on their management style, and meet high standards or codes. They need to understand how people work and how to motivate them. They should also be aware that they set the tone for the workplace and thereby the culture of the political office.

The role of MPs as employers requires modelling of appropriate behaviour and leadership to ensure optimal team performance. MPs could also have behavioural and conduct issues built into performance appraisals.

Political leaders need to be adaptive rather than controlling

Political leaders need strong emotional intelligence to help them build a close connection with voters. However, they also need to be agile and be ready to deploy a range of management approaches to suit the requirements of events, variable voter demands and increasing online activism and media fragmentation. Being agile is better than being controlling. Political leaders who have tried to exert too much control over things have lost power. Instead, they should build and maintain relationships with the media and colleagues based on respect for professional autonomy, and avoid exerting too much control over messaging and access to information as this can build animosity and resentment. Similarly, there is the need to reflect on the power and authority of advisers given they are not the ones elected by voters. And in crisis situations like a protest information needs to be shared – using silos will only make things worse. Political practitioners need to behave more like business professionals and collapse information silos.

Recommendations for future research

Given the need for political management but also gaps in current standards in practice there is considerable scope for growth in research into political management.

Firstly, now that we have academic research that visualises how political management can and should work in the political workplace, future research can assess the most recent practices against these principles to both record the progress made towards higher standards and stimulate further reform and innovation.

Secondly, the researchers in this book suggested a range of topics that would benefit from further exploration such as:

- How to best coordinate and implement strategy across the complexity of government.
- How chiefs train and develop staff.

- How party leaders manage the performance management of MPs and the interplay between performance management practices (or the lack thereof) and political or electoral outcomes.
- Political and parliamentary misconduct could take into account HRM approaches.
- How to manage loss of institutional memory and professional expertise when one leader and their staff exits either due to leadership selection/deselection or an election which impacts on quality of practices in political management.
- How to mitigate the inescapable career instability that besets political practitioners.
- A comparative analysis of political management of volunteers in global south countries.
- The indigenous origins of volunteerism and how this can be used in managing political volunteers.
- The deployment of the skills by political managers in sub-national, local and regional settings, as well as within political parties and other political organisations.
- How to organise and process data informing decisions via market intelligence.
- How best to organise political organisations to inform operational planning and in particular how different aspects such as strategy translation, organisational improvisation, and human capital connect with each other most effectively.
- How leaders maintain control in face of protests whilst still being responsive.

There are also many nuances to explore further, such as:

- How to interject strategic thinking and behaviour into government.
- Why each political leader can't deploy the same skills successfully.
- How different skills are needed in different contexts and countries.
- Identify and understand the environmental factors that militate against the development of strategy.
- How roles differ depending on the individual carrying them out and the context.
- The impact of rules around post-political career employment especially for political staffers but also politicians.
- The pros and cons of the creation of trade unions or some other representative body to represent political practitioners.
- How to ensure enough control to enable government to function but avoid over-centralisation – further research is needed to better understand where the sweet spot lies between centralised and coordinated media operations and respectful, accountable government.

- The impact of media advisers in government given the power they hold and the implications of this for control and authority given advisers are not elected.
- How volunteer groups can be a force for political reforms in countries with weak democratic institutions.

Political management research also has a strong potential for research impact. For example, there are many chapters on political staffing strategic thinking, which have been the focus of parliamentary reviews and inquiries in multiple countries. Additionally, Weinberg's surveys of politician's staff were commissioned by the MPs' Staff Wellness Working Group, indicating the potential for researchers to collaborate with political practitioners on topics of mutual interest.

The democratic need for better political management

Lastly, the democratic implications of political management should be considered. On one hand, it is argued that good political management is needed to help democracy function better by making political offices and organisations – and thus government – more effective.

There is definitely a strong case for better HRM of political staffers and their well-being. Positive employee mental health relies on, among other things, experiences of appropriate levels of control, skill use, supportive supervision and manageable workloads. By embedding HR principles within vital roles that inform the actions of democratic institutions and their principal actors, helping to make sense of experiencing multiple and unremitting demands, democracy is strengthened. A political office should be considered as a cooperative type of workplace that sets the tone, enhancing the functioning and the reputation of democratic institutions.

Leaders also need good information to consider when making decisions. Whilst the pressured pace of decision-making at senior levels appears a given, due diligence is unlikely to follow from failure to develop knowledge and informed opinions due to lack of effectively managed staff or if the market intelligence information and data is siloed instead of shared effectively. Poor decisions clearly weaken the practice and experience of democracy. And the absence of systematic training compounds inefficacy, as staff are rushed into the process of policy making. Political management standards impact outcomes from government, so this is important not only for the reputation of a PM and their government but the delivery of democratically mandated policies.

Good recruitment practice involves a more professionalised selection process that advertises political work to the widest possible audience – indeed this is key to reflecting the clear principles of democracy. Moreover, diversity of thought is bound to follow from broadening the spectrum of people who can do political staffing, which in turn enhances political debate and decision-making

Nevertheless, whilst it is generally assumed that management practices will bring much-needed discipline to the practice of politics, there are potential negative repercussions. An emphasis on short-term reactive communication and focus is often at the expense of developing policy strategy, and over-control of communication can lead to too much dominance over other aspects of government which is problematic for democracy. As the research field of political management develops, more reflection on this is needed.

Therefore, when developing political management theories and policies, both scholars and practitioners need to ensure they are fit for purpose, and this means considering both the realities of the political workplace and the democratic principles surrounding it.

Reference

UK House of Commons. (2023). Liasion Sub Committee on Scrutiny of Strategic thinking in government. https://committees.parliament.uk/committee/677/liaison-subcommittee-on-scrutiny-of-strategic-thinking-in-government/news/195917/liaison-committee-new-inquiry-to-explore-select-committee-scrutiny-of-strategic-thinking-across-government/

INDEX

Note: Pages in *italics* represent figures and **bold** indicates tables in the text.

Manufactured by Amazon.ca
Bolton, ON

39332642R00160